Restoring God's Foundation

CATHOLIC MEN'S INTEGRITY PROGRAM

D1737662

Participant Handbook

PHASE 3 Weeks 17-35

Dann Aungst
Road to Purity

5/23

Nihil Obstat: **Tomas Fuerte, S.T.L.**
Censor Librorwn

Imprimatur: **+Most Reverend Samuel J. Aquila, S.T.L.**
Archbishop of Denver
Denver, Colorado, USA
May 22, 2020

Dann Aungst/Road to Purity
12650 W. 64th Ave, Unit E505
Arvada, Colorado 80004
www.roadtopurity.com

Book Layout ©2017 BookDesignTemplates.com

Ordering Information:
Quantity sales: Special discounts are available on quantity purchases by corporations, associations, and others. For details, contact the "Special Sales Department" at the address above.

Restoring God's Foundation – Participant Handbook/Dann Aungst —1st ed.
ISBN 9798620712427

Contents

Restoring God's Foundation was developed by Dann Aungst, president and founder of Road to Purity. Dann is a Certified Addiction Counselor, speaker, author and a recovering sex addict.

Dann's restored relationship with Jesus was so powerful that he felt personally called to devote his life to telling others that the profound emptiness, worthlessness, rejection, and abandonment felt by most addicts is not the truth of their identity in Christ and to help these men and women in this bondage of lies to find truth, healing and authentic love in God and in their personal relationships. Dann has answered God's call through the mission of Road to Purity, a non-profit organization he founded in 2015.

Road to Purity would like to recognize all those who contributed to, participated in, and inspired the development of this program.

Fr. John Lager, O.F.M. Cap.

Rev. Dan Barron, O.M.V.

Robert Peters

David Aungst

Jim Walsh

Steve Juhasz

Dedication

This program is dedicated to the Blessed Virgin Mary, under the approved title, "Our Lady of America" – as she represents the virtue of purity. May she be at the side of all who struggle with purity.

Quote

"The struggle is the sign of holiness. A Saint is a sinner that keeps trying."
-- St. Josemaria Escriva

Introduction

Welcome to Phase 3 of Restoring God's Foundation.

Before we begin, we need to have a brief introduction to Phase 3 of Restoring God's Foundation.

Phase 3 of the program is focused on healing. This involves understanding the roots of our behavior, searching for our brokenness, implementing techniques for healing, and seeking a deeper purpose of our relationship with God, self and others.

You will notice that the **Daily Recovery Inventory Tracker** has been replaced with the **Recovery Action Guide**, containing both **Daily** and **Weekly** versions. This Action Guide changes and evolves as the weeks progress. Also, your homework in many lessons involves taking notes and documenting the results of work done each week in **Appendix G.** The notes you put there will accumulate and be used in later lessons, including work done in healing recovery.

It is now more critical than ever to keep up with homework and do the exercises put before you. Effective healing and recovery will not happen if you do not do the work.

Reminder: Guide for Sharing

- Try to avoid giving lengthy explanations; be brief and to the point.

- Don't rationalize or intellectualize when sharing; share your feelings, your inner wounds, even if uncomfortable or painful. Be honest and transparent. This is a big part of healing.

- Accept responsibility for your actions, don't blame others for your behaviors.

- Support others by listening and offering constructive feedback, but not telling them how to solve their problems.

Phase 3 Lessons

Healing
Weeks 17-35

Week 17: Cleansing of Sin and the Fellowship with God

Meeting Protocol

Group Invocation of the Holy Spirit
> *"Come Holy Spirit, renew me, dwell in me and protect me."*

Facilitator Leads the Group in Prayer

Confidentiality Bond – Group Recites Together
> *"I _____ pledge to honor each person present or not present today in this group. I will do so by keeping all comments and discussions offered here today and at all future meetings confidential. I also pledge to keep the identity of all members confidential. I also pledge to make no statements of judgmental nature about anyone in this group, including myself."*

Welcome New Members

Check-in Round 1: Feelings/Mood
Check-in Round 2: Significant event since last meeting (30-60 seconds)
Check-in Round 3: Temptation Rating (On a scale of 1–10; 1 a low temptation, 10 a high temptation)
Check-in Round 4: Primary or Secondary Boundary Violations
  If a Primary Violation occurred, the following questions/factors need to be addressed:
  - ✓ **What do you think led to acting out?** – life events 24+ hours before
  - ✓ **What were your feelings before acting out?**
  - ✓ **Did you call anyone?**
  - ✓ **What Secondary Boundaries did you violate this week?** – include those that were prior to your Primary Boundary Violation, if you had one.
  - ✓ **Group affirmation and acceptance of sharing.**

Check-in Round 5: Victories

Scripture Verse

1 John 1:7 "But if we walk in the light as He is in the light, we have fellowship with one another, and the blood of Jesus Christ His Son cleanses us from all sin."

Group Discussion Question: How does this verse relate to your battle with sexual sin?

Week 17 Recovery Foundation Lesson

Thus far, you have been guided in practical steps to managing your pornography behaviors using worldly practices along with the direction of minimal prayer or mediation and the Sacraments of Confession and the Eucharist. At this stage in your recovery, it is time to begin to understand more deeply the spiritual practices required for true freedom from any sin.

As we continue our journey toward recovery from sexual sin, we must also grow in our fellowship with God. The two must be one journey. It is impossible to progress successfully in one without the other. As sinners, we will never be free from our sexual sin if we are not in fellowship with God. Conversely, it is impossible to be in fellowship with God if we are in the bondage of sexual sin. This seems like a "Catch 22" situation. God, however, will guide us through both simultaneously, but we need to invite Him to guide us in this journey. While you have engaged in fellowship with your brothers in Christ in this group, fellowship with God is infinitely more powerful and also critical in your journey. It is time to look beyond the basic goal of freedom from porn addiction. Your focus must be that of striving for holiness, of getting to heaven. While the depth of knowledge and personal transformation of this goal is a lifelong path, it is considerably beyond the scope of the Restoring God's Foundation program. Still, you need to understand the basic dynamics of the spiritual life.

In Phase 3 of this program, you will be guided in healing from your personal brokenness, you will discover false beliefs that fuel the addictive cravings and behaviors, and you will work towards an increased union with God.

First and foremost, we are ALL called to be saints. We are also ALL given the grace to achieve this, but we must accept the invitation of God to make it happen.

1 Corinthians 1:2 "To the church of God that is in Corinth, to those who are sanctified in Christ Jesus, called to be saints, together with all those who in every place call on the name of our Lord Jesus Christ, both their Lord and ours."

"None of us can make ourselves saints. None of us can even say the name of Jesus in faith without his grace. It is God who reaches out to us, not we who first choose God. God reaches out to us every day in a million ways, so grace is always there. It all starts with God and it ends with God, and in between there are nothing but God-laden moments, although we may not always recognize them as such." - Lucy Fuchs PhD; Franciscan Spirit

"It is by living with love and offering Christian witness in our daily tasks that we are called to become saints… Always and everywhere you can become a saint, that is, by being receptive to the grace that is working in us and leads us to holiness." - Pope Francis

The battle with sin, especially an addictive sin like pornography and other sexual sins, fosters a self-focused attitude. When exercising sin, the behavior is about us, about our pleasures, our wants, our needs. This creates an environment that impedes grace.

Fellowship with God starts with confessing our sins to Him. As we discussed in the past couple weeks, the Catholic Church gives us the Sacrament of Reconciliation to do this. When we are in fellowship with God, His love flows through us to others. The practice of being a "gift of self," which you record in your Daily Recovery Inventory Tracker, reveals precisely that. When you are in fellowship with God, giving of self is second nature. In fact, when fellowship is not being blocked or hindered by sin, the evidence of God flowing through you is nearly impossible to stop.

Until now, the "gift of self" that you have been expected to practice daily was a kind of preparatory exercise. At the beginning, practicing this behavior was likely a chore. It was something you had to think about and purposefully remember to practice. You may have found that you either struggled, or that the practice did not come naturally. If so, consider whether you were self-focused and possibly even in a sinful state; not necessarily a sexual sin, but perhaps in some other kind of sin. Could it be that you may even have believed and participated in false beliefs and lies about yourself? Lies or beliefs such as, "I am a bad person," "I am unlovable," or "I am unworthy." These false beliefs, and others similar in nature, as we will discuss in later weeks, are influential in your brokenness and are a part of your false identity that has developed over time. God created you as perfect and loveable, and believing in these lies is sinful from the perspective that you are denying the truth of God. Until you are able to reveal these false beliefs and identities, your fellowship with God will be hindered. This is the everlasting journey that we all experience. These particular sins, while not realized, are venial sins. They do not separate you from God in the same way as mortal sins, but they do inhibit your full relationship with Him and weaken you spiritually, increasing your risk of committing a mortal sin. These unrealized sins do serve to impact your behaviors, your personal freedom and to a degree, your fellowship with God. Confession does eliminate this inhibition of fellowship as it puts you in the complete state of Grace. Unfortunately, these unrealized beliefs very quickly, many times within minutes after confession, begin to interfere with your self-image and thus impact your outward relationships, including those with God. It is our concupiscence (tendency toward sin) that can cause those temptations to hit after confession. It is the practice of the opposite virtue of a sin, that strengthens us not to commit it again. So, against the sins of believing lies about who we are, the opposing virtue would be to discover the truth of how God actually sees us. Similarly, for lust, the opposing virtue is chastity. Practicing chastity can be manifested in modest thoughts, modest dress, averting our eyes from immodest sights and conversations (people, commercials, movies, ads, etc.). We can also fight these habitual thoughts and behaviors by offering a Hail Mary or other quick prayer for the person we just saw or heard in that group or TV ad, etc.

Know however, that there is hope. Several Saints did once battle with sexual sin only to later become saints. Some of these are St. Augustine, St. Mary of Egypt, and St. John the Long Suffering. (You can read more about these saints on the Road to Purity website under recovery resources) Another good one is St. Mary Magdalene…and talk about forgiveness – she was the FIRST PERSON Our Lord appeared to, upon His resurrection! Our God is a forgiving God to all those who repent and follow Him.

While the steps to becoming a saint are a lifelong pursuit and are also beyond the scope of this program, we can point out that the self-focused behaviors of sexual sin are paramount in blocking the grace and fellowship of God required for sanctification. A good first step is to become self-aware of this inward character and self-focus.

This perspective of living, while necessary for fellowship with God, is profoundly difficult in today's world. Living in a culture that promotes "self" interest rather than "other" interest makes the task of living in a selfless manner seem counter-intuitive with those around us.

Review the scripture:
Matthew 6:24 "No one can serve two masters. Either you will hate the one and love the other, or you will be devoted to the one and despise the other…"

Essentially, if we don't worship God, we worship ourselves. We put our own self-interest, our own pleasures, as our primary focus in life. Sin, especially grievous sin such as sexual sin, is a method of serving ourselves. We all desire, even crave, happiness and peace. True peace does not come from choosing self, rather it comes from choosing others and most of all, choosing God.

So long as you practice being "self-focused," you will have extreme difficulty being "other-focused."

Matthew 12:25 "Every kingdom divided against itself is laid waste, and no city or house divided against itself will stand."

Essentially, you cannot be self-focused and other-focused, simultaneously. You cannot give and take at the same time.

From this point forward, look at the times when you struggle to be a gift of self and use this time to trigger yourself to look inward. Ask yourself, "Am I in fellowship with God?" and if not, "What might be in the way?" also, "What beliefs do I have about myself that push God away?" Begin to be more self-aware of emotions or events in your life that trigger or cause you to be self-focused. Begin to note these in a personal journal (your homework will direct you to Appendix A for this). In later lessons in this Phase 3 of the Restoring God's Foundation, you will be asked to recall these, to do further work.

Fasting: Growing in Fellowship through Denial of Self

"Fasting gives birth to prophets and strengthens the powerful; fasting makes lawgivers wise. Fasting is a good safeguard for the soul, a steadfast companion for the body, a weapon for the valiant, and a gymnasium for athletes. Fasting repels temptations, anoints unto piety; it is the comrade of watchfulness and the artificer of chastity. In war it fights bravely, in peace it teaches stillness."

—*St. Basil the Great*

Fasting can be the ultimate weapon in your arsenal to combat sinful behaviors. This is especially true if your fast is performed as an act of surrender or an act of gift of self.

Most people think of fasting (or technically abstinence from meat) as when you give up meat on Fridays during Lent. But fasting is more than this. It could, and should, be a regular part of one's life. Fasting is an act of surrendering your will. This surrender is most powerful when the purpose is "for" someone or "to" someone, such as to Christ. The entire goal of changing unwanted behavior is to cleanse oneself and invite the Holy Spirit in. Especially with addictions or compulsions, the behavior is experienced to soothe something inside that we want to medicate and hide from ourselves.

Romans 8:13 speaks to this:

Romans 8:13 *"For if you live according to the flesh, you will die; but if by the Spirit you put to death the deeds of the body, you will live."*

The exercise of fasting is an act of abstaining, but for a purpose—a purpose that is greater than simply stopping your sinful behavior; it has a purpose of becoming closer to and uniting yourself with God.

Fasting Erodes the Resistance to God's Grace

This grace is what we truly crave. As we know by now, all our unhealthy and selfish behaviors are false and misguided attempts to fill the soul with God's presence and His grace. This is the ultimate search for inner peace. Think about it: If you felt completely content, completely peaceful, and completely filled with love, you would have no desire for porn, alcohol, or drugs. Even the desire to seek approval, success, and acceptance would be diminished because you would already have an inner peace that surpasses all those desires. Fasting helps cleanse the inner self so more of God's grace can enter and help you achieve this peace.

To be fair, most of us never get to the point where we are free from all worldly desires and pleasures. But if you trade the goal of seeking your next porn session for craving God's grace, then you have begun the difficult task of overcoming the addiction.

How to Fast

Outside of the Catholic Lenten fasting requirements, there is no one 'right' way to fast. It's up to you to make that decision and let your heart lead you in what is best. I will say that the more difficult the fast, the more spiritual power it brings. A priest once told me that "Fasting is the heavy artillery of praying." So the bigger the weapon, the better. With that said, it is expected that a person who has never even held a gun isn't given a missile launcher. They must be trained. Start small and work your way forward. Fasting can be simple. The intent is what's important. Each time you fast, have a purpose.

Say to yourself:

"Lord, I give up this dessert for the purpose of surrendering my will and desires to you. I ask you to fill my heart with your peace," or *"Lord I give up this _____ for the past victims or past partners in reparation of my actions"* or simply, *"Lord, I give you my will."*

Here are some examples of different ways to fast:

- ✓ Get the small fry instead of the large at McDonalds.

- ✓ Give up dessert on set days or for a period of time.

- ✓ Give up watching TV one day a week.

- ✓ Give your dessert to your significant other. (This can be an act of surrendering your desire for the benefit of another, a "gift of self.")

- ✓ Fast from salt on your food.

- ✓ Fast from soda—if you can't do it permanently, do it two days a week.

- ✓ Fast for an entire day! (Maybe even set one day a month to fast for the day.)

Don't grumble or complain; do it silently. Remember your fast isn't about punishing yourself—it's about surrendering your will to the will of God. Pray every time you fast.

Group Questions

✓ As required in your daily activities, have you been successfully doing an act that is a "gift of self"

✓ What has been difficult with this daily exercise?

✓ What kind of actions have you exercised?

✓ After this lesson, does the act of "gift of self" have new meaning for you? How?

Meeting Close
Check Out

What do you need? – 5 min

Is there anything the group can offer any member?

– *Prayers*
– *Phone calls/texts*
– *Private meeting*
– *Ride to meetings*
– *Etc.*

Closing Prayers

Week 17 Homework

Journaling

Do I have a genuine desire to give to others, to give my time and talent to others freely?

At least once during each week, take a minimum of 30 minutes and meditate on these questions: (preferably in front of the Blessed Sacrament). Directive to do this is later in the **Weekly Action Guide** of the homework.

Is it a chore, or does it seem like work to do the "gift of self" activity every day?
Do I have to step back and actually think of something to do?
Is it becoming more natural to give of myself, as time progresses in this program?

When I have difficulty giving of myself, why? (look deep and be honest)
- Do I fear that if I give to someone else that I may have to go without?
- Do I think, "Why should I give to someone else, what about me?"
- Do I fear that my own needs won't get met, if I am focused so much on others?
- Do I feel entitled, therefore, I focus on myself rather than on others?

Recommended Self-study
For further growth in the spiritual life, further study of the following topics is recommended:

- ✓ Lectio Divina
- ✓ Elements of Ignatian Spirituality
- ✓ Theology of the Body
- ✓ Study of the Theological Virtues and Gifts of the Holy Spirit

Week 17 Recovery Action Guide

Note: Starting this week, you will see that the **Recovery Inventory Tracker** has been replaced with the **Recovery Action Guide**. This **Action Guide** includes **Daily Actions** as well as **Weekly Actions**. You also will no longer keep score with your tracking. At this point, your recovery is more than just a daily tally of actions, it goes deeper into behaviors. You will notice, as well, that as the weeks progress, the Guide evolves with new activities. It is a little more work; however, this is where your recovery gets more serious and digs into long-lasting personal healing, rather than simply managing behaviors.

Daily Action Guide

(next page)

Day 1

1. Did you violate any Primary Boundaries in the last 24hrs?   Yes   No

      If No, go to **#2**, If Yes, then complete the following:

      What Boundary did you violate? _____

      What events led up to the behavior?

      _____

      _____

      What Secondary Boundaries did you violate leading up to the Primary?

      _____

      _____

2. Did you violate any Secondary Boundaries in the last 24hrs?   Yes   No

      If No, go to **#3**, If Yes, then complete the following:

      What Boundaries did you violate?

      _____

      _____

3. How much time did you spend in prayer/meditation in the last 24hrs? (30-minute goal) _____

4. How much time did you spend reading scripture in the last 24hrs? _____

5. What **Gift of Self** did you perform in the last 24hrs?

_____

_____

6. Did you recite the 7 Cornerstones of Commitment? *(Found in Appendix B)*   Yes   No

7. Did you recite the Surrender Prayer? *(Found in Appendix D)*   Yes   No

8. What was your mood/feeling over the last 24hrs? *(Feelings Wheel in Appendix A)*

Encouraged   Discouraged   Hopeful   Defeated   Depressed   Other: _____

9. Fasting

Did you fast (give up) anything in the last 24hrs?   Yes   No

      If yes, describe: _____

Day 2

1. Did you violate any Primary Boundaries in the last 24hrs?   Yes   No

    If No, go to **#2**, If Yes, then complete the following:

    What Boundary did you violate? _____

    What events led up to the behavior?

    _____

    _____

    What Secondary Boundaries did you violate leading up to the Primary?

    _____

    _____

2. Did you violate any Secondary Boundaries in the last 24hrs?   Yes   No

    If No, go to **#3**, If Yes, then complete the following:

    What Boundaries did you violate?

    _____

    _____

3. How much time did you spend in prayer/meditation in the last 24hrs? (30-minute goal) _____

4. How much time did you spend reading scripture in the last 24hrs? _____

5. What **Gift of Self** did you perform in the last 24hrs?

_____

_____

6. Did you recite the 7 Cornerstones of Commitment? *(Found in Appendix B)*   Yes   No

7. Did you recite the Surrender Prayer? *(Found in Appendix D)*   Yes   No

8. What was your mood/feeling over the last 24hrs? *(Feelings Wheel in Appendix A)*

Encouraged   Discouraged   Hopeful   Defeated   Depressed   Other: _____

9. Fasting

Did you fast (give up) anything in the last 24hrs?   Yes   No

    If yes, describe: _____

Day 3

1. Did you violate any Primary Boundaries in the last 24hrs?   Yes   No

If No, go to **#2**, If Yes, then complete the following:

What Boundary did you violate? _____

What events led up to the behavior?

_____

_____

What Secondary Boundaries did you violate leading up to the Primary?

_____

_____

2. Did you violate any Secondary Boundaries in the last 24hrs?   Yes   No

If No, go to **#3**, If Yes, then complete the following:

What Boundaries did you violate?

_____

_____

3. How much time did you spend in prayer/meditation in the last 24hrs? (30-minute goal) _____

4. How much time did you spend reading scripture in the last 24hrs? _____

5. What **Gift of Self** did you perform in the last 24hrs?

_____

_____

6. Did you recite the 7 Cornerstones of Commitment? *(Found in Appendix B)*   Yes   No

7. Did you recite the Surrender Prayer? *(Found in Appendix D)*   Yes   No

8. What was your mood/feeling over the last 24hrs? *(Feelings Wheel in Appendix A)*

Encouraged   Discouraged   Hopeful   Defeated   Depressed   Other: _____

9. Fasting

Did you fast (give up) anything in the last 24hrs?   Yes   No

If yes, describe: _____

Day 4

1. Did you violate any Primary Boundaries in the last 24hrs?   Yes   No

    If No, go to **#2**, If Yes, then complete the following:

    What Boundary did you violate? _____

    What events led up to the behavior?

    _____

    _____

    What Secondary Boundaries did you violate leading up to the Primary?

    _____

    _____

2. Did you violate any Secondary Boundaries in the last 24hrs?   Yes   No

    If No, go to **#3**, If Yes, then complete the following:

    What Boundaries did you violate?

    _____

    _____

3. How much time did you spend in prayer/meditation in the last 24hrs? (30-minute goal) _____

4. How much time did you spend reading scripture in the last 24hrs? _____

5. What **Gift of Self** did you perform in the last 24hrs?

_____

_____

6. Did you recite the 7 Cornerstones of Commitment? *(Found in Appendix B)*   Yes   No

7. Did you recite the Surrender Prayer? *(Found in Appendix D)*   Yes   No

8. What was your mood/feeling over the last 24hrs? *(Feelings Wheel in Appendix A)*

Encouraged   Discouraged   Hopeful   Defeated   Depressed   Other: _____

9. Fasting

Did you fast (give up) anything in the last 24hrs?   Yes   No

If yes, describe: _____

Day 5

1. Did you violate any Primary Boundaries in the last 24hrs?   Yes   No

    If No, go to **#2**, If Yes, then complete the following:

    What Boundary did you violate? _____

    What events led up to the behavior?

    _____

    _____

    What Secondary Boundaries did you violate leading up to the Primary?

    _____

    _____

2. Did you violate any Secondary Boundaries in the last 24hrs?   Yes   No

    If No, go to **#3**, If Yes, then complete the following:

    What Boundaries did you violate?

    _____

    _____

3. How much time did you spend in prayer/meditation in the last 24hrs? (30-minute goal) _____

4. How much time did you spend reading scripture in the last 24hrs? _____

5. What **Gift of Self** did you perform in the last 24hrs?

_____

_____

6. Did you recite the 7 Cornerstones of Commitment? *(Found in Appendix B)*   Yes   No

7. Did you recite the Surrender Prayer? *(Found in Appendix D)*   Yes   No

8. What was your mood/feeling over the last 24hrs? *(Feelings Wheel in Appendix A)*

Encouraged   Discouraged   Hopeful   Defeated   Depressed   Other: _____

9. Fasting

Did you fast (give up) anything in the last 24hrs?   Yes   No

If yes, describe: _____

Day 6

1. Did you violate any Primary Boundaries in the last 24hrs?   Yes   No

If No, go to **#2**, If Yes, then complete the following:

What Boundary did you violate? _____

What events led up to the behavior?

_____

_____

What Secondary Boundaries did you violate leading up to the Primary?

_____

_____

2. Did you violate any Secondary Boundaries in the last 24hrs?   Yes   No

If No, go to **#3**, If Yes, then complete the following:

What Boundaries did you violate?

_____

_____

3. How much time did you spend in prayer/meditation in the last 24hrs? (30-minute goal) _____

4. How much time did you spend reading scripture in the last 24hrs? _____

5. What **Gift of Self** did you perform in the last 24hrs?

_____

_____

6. Did you recite the 7 Cornerstones of Commitment? *(Found in Appendix B)*   Yes   No

7. Did you recite the Surrender Prayer? *(Found in Appendix D)*   Yes   No

8. What was your mood/feeling over the last 24hrs? *(Feelings Wheel in Appendix A)*

Encouraged   Discouraged   Hopeful   Defeated   Depressed   Other: _____

9. Fasting

Did you fast (give up) anything in the last 24hrs?   Yes   No

If yes, describe: _____

Day 7

1. Did you violate any Primary Boundaries in the last 24hrs?   Yes   No

    If No, go to **#2**, If Yes, then complete the following:

    What Boundary did you violate? _____

    What events led up to the behavior?

    _____

    _____

    What Secondary Boundaries did you violate leading up to the Primary?

    _____

    _____

2. Did you violate any Secondary Boundaries in the last 24hrs?   Yes   No

    If No, go to **#3**, If Yes, then complete the following:

    What Boundaries did you violate?

    _____

    _____

3. How much time did you spend in prayer/meditation in the last 24hrs? (30-minute goal) _____

4. How much time did you spend reading scripture in the last 24hrs? _____

5. What **Gift of Self** did you perform in the last 24hrs?

_____

_____

6. Did you recite the 7 Cornerstones of Commitment? *(Found in Appendix B)*   Yes   No

7. Did you recite the Surrender Prayer? *(Found in Appendix D)*   Yes   No

8. What was your mood/feeling over the last 24hrs? *(Feelings Wheel in Appendix A)*

Encouraged   Discouraged   Hopeful   Defeated   Depressed   Other: _____

9. Fasting

Did you fast (give up) anything in the last 24hrs?   Yes   No

If yes, describe: _____

Weekly Action Guide

Fellowship with God – Weekly Activity

What is in the way of me being in fellowship with God?

_____

_____

What events happened this week that caused or triggered me to be self-focused?

_____

_____

What feelings were triggered by these events that caused me to desire to be more self-focused?

_____

_____

Appendix G Work

What beliefs do I have about myself that cause me to be selfish?

Answer this question in **Appendix G,** in the section, **"Fellowship with God – Beliefs"**

Week 18 The River Under the River

Meeting Protocol

Group Invocation of the Holy Spirit
"Come Holy Spirit, renew me, dwell in me and protect me."

Facilitator Leads the Group in Prayer

Confidentiality Bond – Group Recites Together
"I _____ pledge to honor each person present or not present today in this group. I will do so by keeping all comments and discussions offered here today and at all future meetings confidential. I also pledge to keep the identity of all members confidential. I also pledge to make no statements of judgmental nature about anyone in this group, including myself."

Welcome New Members

Check-in Round 1: Feelings/Mood
Check-in Round 2: Significant event since last meeting (30-60 seconds)
Check-in Round 3: Temptation Rating (On a scale of 1–10; 1 a low temptation, 10 a high temptation)
Check-in Round 4: Primary or Secondary Boundary Violations
   If a Primary Violation occurred, the following questions/factors need to be addressed:
   ✓ **What do you think led to acting out?** – life events 24+ hours before
   ✓ **What were your feelings before acting out?**
   ✓ **Did you call anyone?**
   ✓ **What Secondary Boundaries did you violate this week?** – include those that were prior to your Primary Boundary Violation, if you had one.
   ✓ **Group affirmation and acceptance of sharing.**
Check-in Round 5: Victories

Scripture Verse

Romans 7:15 *"I do not understand my own actions. For I do not do what I want, but I do the very thing I hate*

Group Discussion Question: How does this verse relate to your battle with sexual sin?

Week 18 Recovery Foundation Lesson

Two key facts set the tone for this and future lessons:

✓ While prayer is paramount and critical in recovery, the process of recovery is not merely a "pray it away" methodology.
✓ The urge to act out never just "happens!"

Our behaviors, all of them, happen for a reason. They are a response to an outside stimulus and are chosen based on life experiences and our beliefs. We are all, to a large extent, formed by social interactions, childhood events, and basic life experiences. It's the nurture part behind 'nature versus nurture.' Our parents, siblings, other family members, teachers, and so many more people and happenings shape our ideas, our emotional reactions, our impressions, and our beliefs about ourselves. In certain circumstances, these events and people (basic life) can begin to slowly compromise our self-worth system. Virtually 100 percent of the time the people who cause these harms are not intending to inflict pain and turmoil in our lives. Frequently, it's simply people reacting out of their own flawed self-worth that influences someone else. These behaviors and their lasting effects are typically transparent to both parties at the time. Many of our behaviors are unconsciously designed to protect this fragile self-worth system. Feelings of insecurity, insignificance, incompetence, worthlessness, powerlessness, and so on are protected when we act out with anger, aggression, defiance, overachieving, underachieving, materialism, narcissism, withdrawal, self-mutilation, dishonesty, integrity issues, arrogance, fear, and anxiety, just to name a few self-destructive behaviors.

Every one of us (yes, including you) is a good person at the core. Our actions, beliefs, decisions, and responses to life around us may not be the perfect choices and can frequently hurt those around us, sometimes intensely. But at the core, we are created by God and are good people. We are created in His image and therefore are designed for perfection. Our choices and behaviors, and even our self-image, are what's flawed.

Our behaviors in everyday life make up what we call "the river". The reasons we behave the way we do (habits, poor self-image, flawed beliefs, insecurities, and so on) are what drives this behavior – thus the "river under the river." The key to success in your journey of recovery is revealing what is in your "river under the river."

Changing a behavior, particularly one that has become a compulsion or an addiction, requires a process of learning a new habit as well as revealing and healing the flawed internal beliefs and emotions that drive the behavior – the river under the river. Additionally, as you learned in, "**Lesson 14: Biology and Chemistry of Sex,**" there is a biological component to your addictive behavior. Over the next several weeks, we are going to work on all three components of changing behavior, to:

- ✓ Help develop new coping mechanisms or habits.
- ✓ Figure out why you do what you do.
- ✓ Move toward rewiring your brain so the addictive behavior isn't a simple "knee-jerk" reaction.

Transforming Pain

Another perspective on the river under the river concept is looking at your underlying pain. Every human, without exception, has internal emotional pain, or brokenness. This includes pain developed over the course of our lives as a result of what I spoke of a few paragraphs ago. The behavior, or way of reacting to this pain, is in fact transmitting this pain. If we don't transform this pain (in other words, heal it), we will transmit it to others.

Examples

Many of the concepts discussed in this lesson may be new to you. This is perfectly normal, and even expected, that this information has been difficult to follow. Because it is critical and a cornerstone in recovery, what follows are a few examples of how this "river under the river" theory reveals itself in real life.

Example 1

John grew up in a family where both parents worked. His parents provided everything John needed materially. He always had the best clothes, newest model of bikes, his own room, all the video games he wanted, and more. John's mother, however, was an insecure person who focused nearly all her attention on her career, as she needed to achieve to feel worthy. As a result, she was self-focused and didn't give John the loving affirmation he needed growing up. She was never mean or denied John his basic needs; she just wasn't there in an intimate motherly manner. Although John wasn't aware of it, this led him to feel rejected and unimportant or insignificant. He actually felt unworthy of being loved. John developed emotional walls to protect this inner pain of unworthiness and insignificance. As an adult, he experienced failed relationship after failed relationship, as he was unable to connect emotionally with women. John had an unconscious fear that they would ultimately reject him. Keep in mind that John had no awareness of this – he simply lived his life not understanding why he was unhappy. He longed for personal connection, personal intimacy, but he was also intensely afraid of true intimacy, for fear of it being taken away and being rejected. Again, he was completely blind to this internal fear.

At fourteen, one of John's friends introduced him to pornography. It was his first exposure to sex, as his father had never had the traditional "sex talk" with him, nor had he had the opportunity to learn what healthy sexuality was about. Porn was exciting to John, and something inside him said, "This is what getting love looks like." As his life progressed, John did not learn what authentic love and intimacy were, but porn became a regular experience for him. It fed him, though in an unhealthy and misguided way. It was all he knew.

This porn habit followed John into his relationships. He was unable to connect with his partners emotionally because of his childhood experience and woundedness. He turned to porn in an unconscious attempt to find connection – after all, relying on porn was safer because it would never reject him like a real woman likely would. However, viewing porn created an unrealistic idea of what sex should be like. In his mind's eye, sex was an act that was void of true intimacy: the giving of one's self, an authentic emotional connection. The result was horrible sex experiences for his partners who felt objectified and used rather than loved. The relationships ultimately failed.

This same pattern occurred in relationship after relationship. The rejection and insignificance John felt as a child was repeated as an adult, but now abandonment was added to the pain. John ultimately felt extreme despair and became suicidal.

Transmitting pain

John transmitted the pain of rejection and insignificance he felt in his childhood to the women in his relationships by not being able to be emotionally open to connect with them. His being emotionally unavailable to them caused them to feel rejected by him! In this way, he was transmitting his pain to his partners. This pain that allowed him to accept pornography as a representation of love also contributed to the pain of objectification he transmitted to his partners. John's feeling of rejection and insignificance were the river under the river of his behavior of being emotionally unavailable to women, as well as the behavior of reaching out to porn for intimacy (although this was false intimacy, it was a form of intimacy, nonetheless).

The lies of rejection and insignificance from John's childhood must be transformed before John can have any real success with authentic relationships.

If you don't transform your pain, you will transmit it!

Example 2

Bob was an angry person. His anger was his way of protecting himself, a pattern of behavior resulting from many poor experiences and abuse from his father, growing up. Bob frequently turned to pornography to experience a sense of connection, as well as a release of inner stress caused by the constant anger. (Note that the connection he achieved from viewing porn was a false connection – and thus for only a few minutes the stress was released due to the surge of serotonin after ejaculation, a process that induces the addiction cycle, as learned in earlier lessons.)

Here's how Bob transmitted his pain:

Bob was driving to work when another driver needed to make a quick lane change to exit. Bob perceived this action as a personal attack, as if the other driver had no regard for him. This triggered intense anger and feelings of revenge within Bob. The anger was disproportionate to the situation, but it was fueled by Bob's inner feelings of rejection and shame from his abusive father. As a youth, he felt disregarded, belittled, and dismissed as a person and now anytime someone ignored or rejected Bob, he felt intense anger. Anytime he experiences anger, it is compounded by the pain and woundedness he experienced from his father. Angry, Bob now sped off the next exit toward his usual stop at Starbucks. Bob was now in a foul mood. While placing his order, he snapped at Jennifer, the barista, making her feel incompetent. He was angry inside and was transmitting that anger to those around him. Barista Jennifer ultimately had a horrible day, experiencing feelings of rejection herself.

As you can see, Bob has woundedness from his youth. This unhealed woundedness causes Bob to overreact to events in life that trigger the same deep feelings of rejection, belittlement, and dismissal. His reaction is typically anger. These feelings are triggered by seemingly minor life experiences, like being disagreed with, a waitress making a mistake on his order, someone not listening to him, and, obviously, a driver cutting him off on the freeway. Bob has not transformed his pain (emotionally healed) and, therefore, transmits it frequently. This untransformed pain that causes Bob to behave the way he does is the river under the river. The reaction of feeling incompetent that Jennifer, the barista, experienced, is a ripple effect of Bob's untransformed pain. This untransformed pain spreads to those around us.

Example 3

Lisa grew up with a mother who was very critical. Lisa's mother was much like Bob in the previous story, as her mother (Lisa's grandmother) had belittled and rejected her daughter (Lisa's mother). The constant criticism of Lisa's mother made Lisa feel very insecure and unworthy. In Lisa's case, this caused her to be a person who was always reaching out to friends and neighbors to offer help, almost in a compulsive way. Lisa was the type of person who always jumped in to help at parties. While it may seem like the criticism of Lisa's mother led to a very admirable personality trait in Lisa, the deeper result was that Lisa was starving for acceptance, and to be liked. Unfortunately, Lisa was a very unhappy person and felt deeply unworthy of anyone's love. She had many medical problems stemming from intense anxiety and her constant seeking of approval. People who didn't know Lisa well simply thought that she was a wonderful, giving person. Yet it was transparent to most that she was starving for the love and acceptance that she never received from her mother. *Note: It is this lack of love and worthiness that causes women like Lisa to seek false intimacy with men through various forms of sexually promiscuous behaviors, in an attempt to fill that void of being unloved or invalidated.*

Lisa's story is much subtler that the previous two stories. It is an example of how untransformed pain can be transmitted to multiple generations. In fact, the pain that Lisa transmits is not visibly harmful to the outside world but is certainly damaging to herself.

Example 4

This last example is more subtle and is a personal behavior of the author of this program.

"This behavior developed later, after I had learned to manage and heal from my main addiction of sex and pornography. At that point, I began to see that there were other behaviors in my life that were not necessarily harmful to others or even unethical, but nonetheless were behaviors that had hidden, underlying causes – the river under the river.

I had a job that required me to spend a lot of time driving around scouting for products to sell on the internet. Typically, I would eat fast food for lunch. It was quick and cheap. However, I noticed that at times, I would go to more expensive or "nicer" places to eat – something like Chili's or Buffalo Wild Wings. These weren't high-end restaurants, but much nicer than McDonalds and a place to sit and chill for a bit. In my self-awareness search, I noticed that there was a pattern for this behavior. I chose a better place and allotted more time for lunch when I was having a bad day. Anything could trigger it – bad sales day for my business, argument with my wife that morning, car problems, and so on. I found that the days I wanted to splurge a bit were when I was experiencing feelings of incompetence, unworthiness, or insignificance or when I wasn't in control of the day's events. These feelings had once triggered a choice to act out in an unhealthy and destructive way, but now they were redirected so I made other choices. While, those feeling still came up, my unconscious reaction was to intentionally choose something that I was in control of, that brought me pleasure, and that made me feel deserving – sort of a reward to convince me that I wasn't that bad or unworthy.

The exercise made me see that this simple decision to eat lunch at a nicer place was actually driven by something deeper. Since realizing this motivation, now, every time I feel like I want something nice (food, things, etc.), I ask myself, "What's behind the desire?" I find out what's driving the urge, address it (using methods we will discuss in later weeks), and do my best to seek healing of the river under the river. I must note that even though I was working through this process, since the choice I was making was not harmful, destructive, or unethical, I may still choose the behavior. I may still eat at the nicer restaurant, but I do so while fully realizing that the decision was driven by something; it was not a mere whim. While this was no longer working towards recovery from sexual sin, it was however, an acknowledgement in working towards further healing and recognizing internal brokenness that still caused certain behavior choices – the river under the river.

Fear

There is an additional component you need to be aware of that will be critical in this journey, something that can sabotage your very efforts for change if it is not addressed.

Looking inside oneself is a very scary prospect. The reason you are struggling with this addiction to begin with, is that you are either unaware of the underlying causes or you are consciously or unconsciously choosing to avoid them. The exercises and discussions we will present in the coming weeks will likely unearth some very unpleasant memories, feelings, and experiences. The prospect of knowing this can, itself, trigger fear and can trigger the urge to act out. It is perfectly normal to have thoughts like, "This is going to be too hard – I can't do it," or, "I'll do this at a later time, when I feel more ready, when life slows down a bit." These thoughts are not yours! Yes, that's what I said: They are not yours! They are suggestions planted by the enemy, Satan. He does not want you to heal. Your woundedness that triggers your destructive behaviors are his playground, and he uses those suggestive thoughts to contaminate your soul. Simply be aware of this and use some of the exit strategies discussed in Week 7. Even make some of the "out loud" statements referenced in that lesson when you feel any apprehension or fear triggered by these thoughts. Prayer, while obvious, is also commonly overlooked. Make it a priority. Spend some time in adoration and ask Jesus to reveal the sources of your fear. After receiving Holy Communion at Mass, say to yourself, "Jesus, I receive you into my entire body and existence, please take all fear that exists within me and replace it with your peaceful presence."

Group Questions:

- ✓ Name a behavior you have, sinful or not, and tell about the life events or past relationships that have prompted or fueled your behavior.

- ✓ Describe the emotional woundedness or poor self-image that has developed from these life events or relationships.

- ✓ Do you believe that these events, relationships, and self-image partially define your identity?

Meeting Close
Check Out
What do you need? – 5 min
Is there anything the group can offer any member?
- – *Prayers*
- – *Phone calls/texts*
- – *Private meeting*
- – *Ride to meetings*
- – *Etc.*

Closing Prayers

Week 18 Homework

Journaling Questions

Concerning the emotions that you identified in the group as being under some of your behaviors, what effects have they had on your relationships?

_____

_____

_____

In your current or past troubled relationships, which has played a larger part in their difficulties: your underlying emotions/woundedness or the resulting behaviors?

_____

_____

Name the persons you have hurt in past relationships by the behaviors resulting from your woundedness?

_____

_____

What would the persons you hurt with your behaviors say about your actions?

_____

_____

Week 18 Recovery Action Guide

Daily Action Guide

(next page)

Day 1

1. Did you violate any Primary Boundaries in the last 24hrs?   Yes   No

> If No, go to **#2**, If Yes, then complete the following:

> What Boundary did you violate? _____

> What events led up to the behavior?

> _____

> _____

> What Secondary Boundaries did you violate leading up to the Primary?

> _____

> _____

2. Did you violate any Secondary Boundaries in the last 24hrs?   Yes   No

> If No, go to **#3**, If Yes, then complete the following:

> What Boundaries did you violate?

> _____

> _____

3. How much time did you spend in prayer/meditation in the last 24hrs? (30-minute goal) _____

4. How much time did you spend reading scripture in the last 24hrs? _____

5. What **Gift of Self** did you perform in the last 24hrs?

_____

_____

6. Did you recite the 7 Cornerstones of Commitment? *(Found in Appendix B)*   Yes   No

7. Did you recite the Surrender Prayer? *(Found in Appendix D)*   Yes   No

8. What was your mood/feeling over the last 24hrs? *(Feelings Wheel in Appendix A)*

Encouraged   Discouraged   Hopeful   Defeated   Depressed   Other: _____

9. Fasting

Did you fast (give up) anything in the last 24hrs?   Yes   No

> If yes, describe: _____

Day 2

1. Did you violate any Primary Boundaries in the last 24hrs?　　Yes　　No

If No, go to **#2**, If Yes, then complete the following:

What Boundary did you violate? _____

What events led up to the behavior?

_____

_____

What Secondary Boundaries did you violate leading up to the Primary?

_____

_____

2. Did you violate any Secondary Boundaries in the last 24hrs?　　Yes　　No

If No, go to **#3**, If Yes, then complete the following:

What Boundaries did you violate?

_____

_____

3. How much time did you spend in prayer/meditation in the last 24hrs? (30-minute goal) _____

4. How much time did you spend reading scripture in the last 24hrs? _____

5. What **Gift of Self** did you perform in the last 24hrs?

_____

_____

6. Did you recite the 7 Cornerstones of Commitment? *(Found in Appendix B)*　　Yes　　No

7. Did you recite the Surrender Prayer? *(Found in Appendix D)*　　Yes　　No

8. What was your mood/feeling over the last 24hrs? *(Feelings Wheel in Appendix A)*

Encouraged　　Discouraged　　Hopeful　　Defeated　　Depressed　　Other: _____

9. Fasting

Did you fast (give up) anything in the last 24hrs?　　Yes　　No

If yes, describe: _____

Day 3

1. Did you violate any Primary Boundaries in the last 24hrs?   Yes   No

     If No, go to **#2**, If Yes, then complete the following:

     What Boundary did you violate? _____

     What events led up to the behavior?

     _____

     _____

     What Secondary Boundaries did you violate leading up to the Primary?

     _____

     _____

2. Did you violate any Secondary Boundaries in the last 24hrs?   Yes   No

     If No, go to **#3**, If Yes, then complete the following:

     What Boundaries did you violate?

     _____

     _____

3. How much time did you spend in prayer/meditation in the last 24hrs? (30-minute goal) _____

4. How much time did you spend reading scripture in the last 24hrs? _____

5. What **Gift of Self** did you perform in the last 24hrs?

_____

_____

6. Did you recite the 7 Cornerstones of Commitment? *(Found in Appendix B)*   Yes   No

7. Did you recite the Surrender Prayer? *(Found in Appendix D)*   Yes   No

8. What was your mood/feeling over the last 24hrs? *(Feelings Wheel in Appendix A)*

Encouraged   Discouraged   Hopeful   Defeated   Depressed   **Other:** _____

9. Fasting

Did you fast (give up) anything in the last 24hrs?   Yes   No

     If yes, describe: _____

Day 4

1. Did you violate any Primary Boundaries in the last 24hrs?   Yes   No

If No, go to **#2**, If Yes, then complete the following:

What Boundary did you violate? _____

What events led up to the behavior?

_____

_____

What Secondary Boundaries did you violate leading up to the Primary?

_____

_____

2. Did you violate any Secondary Boundaries in the last 24hrs?   Yes   No

If No, go to **#3**, If Yes, then complete the following:

What Boundaries did you violate?

_____

_____

3. How much time did you spend in prayer/meditation in the last 24hrs? (30-minute goal) _____

4. How much time did you spend reading scripture in the last 24hrs? _____

5. What **Gift of Self** did you perform in the last 24hrs?

_____

_____

6. Did you recite the 7 Cornerstones of Commitment? *(Found in Appendix B)*   Yes   No

7. Did you recite the Surrender Prayer? *(Found in Appendix D)*   Yes   No

8. What was your mood/feeling over the last 24hrs? *(Feelings Wheel in Appendix A)*

Encouraged   Discouraged   Hopeful   Defeated   Depressed   Other: _____

9. Fasting

Did you fast (give up) anything in the last 24hrs?   Yes   No

If yes, describe: _____

Day 5

1. Did you violate any Primary Boundaries in the last 24hrs?   Yes   No

    If No, go to **#2**, If Yes, then complete the following:

    What Boundary did you violate? _____

    What events led up to the behavior?

    _____

    _____

    What Secondary Boundaries did you violate leading up to the Primary?

    _____

    _____

2. Did you violate any Secondary Boundaries in the last 24hrs?   Yes   No

    If No, go to **#3**, If Yes, then complete the following:

    What Boundaries did you violate?

    _____

    _____

3. How much time did you spend in prayer/meditation in the last 24hrs? (30-minute goal) _____

4. How much time did you spend reading scripture in the last 24hrs? _____

5. What **Gift of Self** did you perform in the last 24hrs?

_____

_____

6. Did you recite the 7 Cornerstones of Commitment? *(Found in Appendix B)*   Yes   No

7. Did you recite the Surrender Prayer? *(Found in Appendix D)*   Yes   No

8. What was your mood/feeling over the last 24hrs? *(Feelings Wheel in Appendix A)*

Encouraged   Discouraged   Hopeful   Defeated   Depressed   Other: _____

9. Fasting

Did you fast (give up) anything in the last 24hrs?   Yes   No

If yes, describe: _____

Day 6

1. Did you violate any Primary Boundaries in the last 24hrs?   Yes   No

    If No, go to **#2**, If Yes, then complete the following:

    What Boundary did you violate? _____

    What events led up to the behavior?

    _____

    _____

    What Secondary Boundaries did you violate leading up to the Primary?

    _____

    _____

2. Did you violate any Secondary Boundaries in the last 24hrs?   Yes   No

    If No, go to **#3**, If Yes, then complete the following:

    What Boundaries did you violate?

    _____

    _____

3. How much time did you spend in prayer/meditation in the last 24hrs? (30-minute goal) _____

4. How much time did you spend reading scripture in the last 24hrs? _____

5. What **Gift of Self** did you perform in the last 24hrs?

_____

_____

6. Did you recite the 7 Cornerstones of Commitment? *(Found in Appendix B)*   Yes   No

7. Did you recite the Surrender Prayer? *(Found in Appendix D)*   Yes   No

8. What was your mood/feeling over the last 24hrs? *(Feelings Wheel in Appendix A)*

Encouraged   Discouraged   Hopeful   Defeated   Depressed   Other: _____

9. Fasting

Did you fast (give up) anything in the last 24hrs?   Yes   No

If yes, describe: _____

Day 7

1. Did you violate any Primary Boundaries in the last 24hrs?   Yes   No

    If No, go to **#2**, If Yes, then complete the following:

    What Boundary did you violate? _____

    What events led up to the behavior?

    _____

    _____

    What Secondary Boundaries did you violate leading up to the Primary?

    _____

    _____

2. Did you violate any Secondary Boundaries in the last 24hrs?   Yes   No

    If No, go to **#3**, If Yes, then complete the following:

    What Boundaries did you violate?

    _____

    _____

3. How much time did you spend in prayer/meditation in the last 24hrs? (30-minute goal) _____

4. How much time did you spend reading scripture in the last 24hrs? _____

5. What **Gift of Self** did you perform in the last 24hrs?

_____

_____

6. Did you recite the 7 Cornerstones of Commitment? *(Found in Appendix B)* Yes   No

7. Did you recite the Surrender Prayer? *(Found in Appendix D)* Yes   No

8. What was your mood/feeling over the last 24hrs? *(Feelings Wheel in Appendix A)*

Encouraged   Discouraged   Hopeful   Defeated   Depressed   Other: _____

9. Fasting

Did you fast (give up) anything in the last 24hrs?   Yes   No

If yes, describe: _____

Weekly Action Guide

Appendix G Work

Update the "**Fellowship with God – Beliefs**" section from **Week 17** as needed.

Complete the **Week 18 "River Under the River"** section.

Week 19 The Shame That Binds Me

Meeting Protocol

Group Invocation of the Holy Spirit
"Come Holy Spirit, renew me, dwell in me and protect me"

Facilitator Leads the Group in Prayer

Confidentiality Bond – group recites together
"I _____ pledge to honor each person present or not present today in this group. I will do so by keeping all comments and discussions offered here today and at all future meetings confidential. I also pledge to keep the identity of all members confidential. I also pledge to make no statements of judgmental nature about anyone in this group, including myself."

Welcome New Members

Check-in Round 1: Feelings/Mood
Check-in Round 2: Significant event since last meeting (30-60 seconds)
Check-in Round 3: Temptation Rating (On a scale of 1–10; 1 a low temptation, 10 a high temptation)
Check-in Round 4: Primary or Secondary Boundary Violations
   If a Primary Violation occurred, the following questions/factors need to be addressed:
   ✓ **What do you think led to acting out?** – life events 24+ hours before
   ✓ **What were your feelings before acting out?**
   ✓ **Did you call anyone?**
   ✓ **What Secondary Boundaries did you violate this week?** – include those that were prior to your Primary Boundary Violation if you had one.
   ✓ **Group affirmation and acceptance of sharing.**
Check-in Round 5: Victories

Scripture Verse

Psalm 94:11 *"The LORD knows the thoughts of man, that they are a mere breath."*

Group Discussion Question: How does this verse relate to your life and your battle with sexual sin?

Week 19 Recovery Foundation Lesson

As we discussed last week in the River Under the River lesson, all of us are formed by events in our lives, both positive and negative. These events begin to form our behaviors and reactions to various future events in our lives.

These experiences and behaviors that we experience from others, or even events that happen to us, can have an effect on our self-worth system. An effect can be so powerful that it begins to form perceptions about our self-identity. When these experiences are negative, they can create negative images about our self-image. This negative self-image, or self-identity, is referred to as shame.

For example, a mother may discipline her two-year-old child for writing on the wall with crayons. The child may feel embarrassed and even feel unloved or rejected by the mother's behavior. These feelings are rooted in shame.

Shame vs. Guilt

Guilt attaches to our behavior.

Shame attaches to our identity.

Guilt

Guilt is recognizing sin, recognizing we did something inappropriate, unethical, or unlawful. A confession and request for forgiveness or reconciliation is a normal process for resolving guilt.

Example of a guilt statement: "I stole a tool from my neighbor's garage – this action was wrong, and I shouldn't have done it. I need to confess and make amends."

Shame

Shame goes beyond guilt. Shame takes the offense, the sinful behavior and especially negative experiences, and internalizes them all as a component of our identity.

Example of a shame statement:
"I stole a tool from my neighbor's garage – I am a bad and evil person. I am a thief and I am not to be trusted."

"Shame looks to the outside for happiness and validation because the inside is flawed and defective." John Bradshaw – *Healing the Shame that Binds You*

Here are some common sources of shame that come from negative experiences:

1. **Emotional trauma** (death of a loved one, divorce, witnessing an act of violence, emotional abuse, personal failures)
2. **Physical trauma** (being in a car accident, experiencing physical abuse, military action, war, other physical accidents)
3. **Personal neglect** (a child with needs not met, being left alone at a young age, living in a poor or financially distressed family, ignored by a babysitter, uncared for properly from an absent parent possibly caused by poor behavior of the parent, such as due to alcoholism)
4. **Verbal abuse** (verbally abusive parents toward child or even one another, witnessing verbal abuse from a critical role model such as siblings or parents)
5. **Spiritual abuse** (discipline with guilt of God, using God to manipulate behaviors, a pastor or church member in authority abusing a child)
6. **Abandonment** (divorce, a parent leaving, death of a loved one, older sibling moving away or going to college, a parent taking a work shift in the evenings, a parent working two or more jobs that's keeping them away from the home.)

The following events may seem less significant and would be less likely to be the cause of trauma, but they can be significant to a young person who doesn't understand otherwise. With young children, the universe revolves around them and everything that happens can be perceived personally. They do not see the "big picture."

✓ Being left behind at home when others go to have fun
✓ Witnessing a sibling being abused
✓ Being ignored while a parent is doing something else (like watching TV, or on cell phone)

Here are some common quotes we have all heard and the resulting shame that can potentially be initiated.

Statement: Children are to be seen and not heard.
Unintended message: Be quiet, don't bother me. What you say doesn't matter. You are unimportant and insignificant.

Statement: Big boys don't cry.
Unintended message: Be tough, be strong, don't be an emotional wimp. Your feelings are not important or welcomed here. You are weak and don't measure up if you cry.

Statement: Don't do that, you are going to get hurt.
Unintended message: Be careful, don't take risks. You are not competent to do it. You are not capable.

Statement: Do it right the first time or don't bother trying.
Unintended message: Be perfect, don't just try. If you fail, you don't measure up and you're worthless. You are insignificant.

Most of these statements result in implying that you should stuff your emotions and that you should not express your thoughts or feelings.

Porn is a way to feel. It is a false sense of intimacy, but an intimacy, nonetheless.

"In the absence of a truth, the counterfeit will do."

Shame Inventory

Recall the earlier quote, "Shame looks to the outside for happiness and validation because the inside is flawed and defective."

Porn serves our shame, as we see in the following statements:

- ✓ We look at porn because the images are fantasy and they validate us.
- ✓ The intimacy we see (although false intimacy) validates us, makes us feel worthy.
- ✓ The control we fantasize about in the scenes makes us feel powerful, valuable, and worthy, and it hides our flawed view about ourselves.

Shame is probably the largest influence on our behavioral choices. Shame can also be referred to as spiritual bankruptcy.

As you dig during this process, you will discover that many of your behaviors are largely motivated by shame.

Take a look at the following statements. Circle any that you relate to, even mildly.

I am a loser.

I am not a good person.

I am not lovable.

I am undesirable.

I am evil.

I am a pervert.

I am pathetic.

I am stupid.

I am a bad person.

I am worthless.

I am a monster.

I am repulsive.

I am shameful.

I am a terrible person.

I am despicable.

I am ugly.

I can't change.

I am a failure.

I am incompetent.

I am insignificant.

I don't deserve love.

I am damaged goods.

I have to be perfect to deserve love.

I am wicked.

No one could ever understand me

I do not deserve _____

I am _____

I am _____

No matter what you have done in your life, no matter what you have been told, all of these statements and more are a lie. They are not you. God did not create you to be this way. Your behavior may represent characteristics of these statements, but at the core, this is not you. These statements ARE NOT your identity! This is fantastic news for you. Any statements that you may have circled or wrote in, are merely behavioral defects and can be changed and healed.

Another way of looking at these perceived imperfections is referred to as the "false self." The false self is a lifelong self-image one develops that does not reflect this true identity that God has created. The shame statements that you circled in the above exercise are one way of defining your false self.

In later lessons, we will address the false self and the shame you experience, as well as provide you with tools for healing these destructive traits.

Reflection

Here is a reflection that reveals the lies of worthlessness and inadequacy that fueled your addiction.

> *"God knows every hair on my head and knows what all my transgressions and sins were going to be before I was born (Jeremiah 1:5, Psalm 139:1-4, 1 John 4:19). He knew every sin I would commit, every person I would hurt, every time I would reject Him, every time I would knowingly turn my back on Him, and He created me anyway! He loves me anyway! I am that important to Him. Even with all the damage I have done, God still sees me as His beloved son (Col 3:12, 1 John 3:2, John 3:16, 1 Cor 3:16). This is absolutely with 100 percent certainty true for me. St. Therese of Lisieux said, "The most grievous sin is but a drop in the fiery furnace of God's mercy."*
>
> *YOU are good enough, YOU are worthy, YOU are significant, YOU are important, and that cannot be lost, ever! This is NOT a "No, well, maybe ...or "I'll think about it." YOU ARE WORTHY OF GOD'S LOVE! Just a plain fact – period!"*

Group Questions

Take about two minutes right now and close your eyes.

Imagine yourself with all of your sins and mistakes, no matter how many, all gone. See yourself as God sees you. See yourself wrapped in a blanket of His love and mercy. This is your true identity.

✓ What was your experience?

✓ How does this make you feel?

Meeting Close
Check Out

What do you need? – 5 min

Is there anything the group can offer any member?

– *Prayers*
– *Phone calls/texts*
– *Private meeting*
– *Ride to meetings*
– *Etc.*

Closing Prayers

Week 19 Homework

Exercise:

Take 10 minutes and meditate on the below facts. Say them as a prayer inspired from God. Do this in front of the blessed sacrament if possible. Imagine the experience of feeling His love pour over you like a blanket as you pray this. The overwhelming presence of His love is so powerful that it is impossible to ever be withdrawn.

"God knows every hair on my head and knows what all my transgressions and sins were going to be before I was born. He knew every sin I would commit, every person I would hurt, every time I would reject Him, every time I would knowingly turn my back on Him, and He created me anyway! He loves me anyway! I am that important to Him. Even with all the damage I have done, God still sees me as His beloved son.

This is absolutely, with 100 percent certainty, true for me.

St. Therese of Lisieux said, "The most grievous sin is but a drop in the fiery furnace of God's mercy."

The overwhelming presence of His love is so powerful that it was impossible to ever be withdrawn. I am good enough, I am worthy, I am significant, I am important, and that cannot be lost, ever! I AM WORTHY OF GOD'S LOVE!"

Write down the feelings you experience after completing this meditation.

_____

_____

_____

This meditation can be part of your Daily Action exercises.

Week 19 Recovery Action Guide

Daily Action Guide

(next page)

Day 1

1. Did you violate any Primary Boundaries in the last 24hrs?   Yes   No

  If No, go to **#2**, If Yes, then complete the following:

  What Boundary did you violate? _____

  What events led up to the behavior?

  _____

  _____

  What Secondary Boundaries did you violate leading up to the Primary?

  _____

  _____

2. Did you violate any Secondary Boundaries in the last 24hrs?   Yes   No

  If No, go to **#3**, If Yes, then complete the following:

  What Boundaries did you violate?

  _____

  _____

3. How much time did you spend in prayer/meditation in the last 24hrs? (30-minute goal) _____

4. How much time did you spend reading scripture in the last 24hrs? _____

5. What **Gift of Self** did you perform in the last 24hrs?

_____

_____

6. Did you recite the 7 Cornerstones of Commitment? *(Found in Appendix B)*   Yes   No

7. Did you recite the Surrender Prayer? *(Found in Appendix D)*   Yes   No

8. What was your mood/feeling over the last 24hrs? *(Feelings Wheel in Appendix A)*

Encouraged Discouraged Hopeful Defeated Depressed Other: _____

9. Fasting

Did you fast (give up) anything in the last 24hrs?   Yes   No

  If yes, describe: _____

Day 2

1. Did you violate any Primary Boundaries in the last 24hrs?   Yes   No

   If No, go to **#2**, If Yes, then complete the following:

   What Boundary did you violate? _____

   What events led up to the behavior?

   _____

   _____

   What Secondary Boundaries did you violate leading up to the Primary?

   _____

   _____

2. Did you violate any Secondary Boundaries in the last 24hrs?   Yes   No

   If No, go to **#3**, If Yes, then complete the following:

   What Boundaries did you violate?

   _____

   _____

3. How much time did you spend in prayer/meditation in the last 24hrs? (30-minute goal) _____

4. How much time did you spend reading scripture in the last 24hrs? _____

5. What **Gift of Self** did you perform in the last 24hrs?

_____

_____

6. Did you recite the 7 Cornerstones of Commitment? *(Found in Appendix B)*   Yes   No

7. Did you recite the Surrender Prayer? *(Found in Appendix D)*   Yes   No

8. What was your mood/feeling over the last 24hrs? *(Feelings Wheel in Appendix A)*

Encouraged   Discouraged   Hopeful   Defeated   Depressed   Other: _____

9. Fasting

Did you fast (give up) anything in the last 24hrs?   Yes   No

   If yes, describe: _____

Day 3

1. Did you violate any Primary Boundaries in the last 24hrs?   Yes   No

     If No, go to **#2**, If Yes, then complete the following:

     What Boundary did you violate? _____

     What events led up to the behavior?

     _____

     _____

     What Secondary Boundaries did you violate leading up to the Primary?

     _____

     _____

2. Did you violate any Secondary Boundaries in the last 24hrs?   Yes   No

     If No, go to **#3**, If Yes, then complete the following:

     What Boundaries did you violate?

     _____

     _____

3. How much time did you spend in prayer/meditation in the last 24hrs? (30-minute goal) _____

4. How much time did you spend reading scripture in the last 24hrs? _____

5. What **Gift of Self** did you perform in the last 24hrs?

_____

_____

6. Did you recite the 7 Cornerstones of Commitment? *(Found in Appendix B)*   Yes   No

7. Did you recite the Surrender Prayer? *(Found in Appendix D)*   Yes   No

8. What was your mood/feeling over the last 24hrs? *(Feelings Wheel in Appendix A)*

Encouraged   Discouraged   Hopeful   Defeated   Depressed   Other: _____

9. Fasting

Did you fast (give up) anything in the last 24hrs?   Yes   No

     If yes, describe: _____

Day 4

1. Did you violate any Primary Boundaries in the last 24hrs?   Yes   No

> If No, go to **#2**, If Yes, then complete the following:

> What Boundary did you violate? _____

> What events led up to the behavior?

> _____

> _____

> What Secondary Boundaries did you violate leading up to the Primary?

> _____

> _____

2. Did you violate any Secondary Boundaries in the last 24hrs?   Yes   No

> If No, go to **#3**, If Yes, then complete the following:

> What Boundaries did you violate?

> _____

> _____

3. How much time did you spend in prayer/meditation in the last 24hrs? (30-minute goal) _____

4. How much time did you spend reading scripture in the last 24hrs? _____

5. What **Gift of Self** did you perform in the last 24hrs?

_____

_____

6. Did you recite the 7 Cornerstones of Commitment? *(Found in Appendix B)*   Yes   No

7. Did you recite the Surrender Prayer? *(Found in Appendix D)*   Yes   No

8. What was your mood/feeling over the last 24hrs? *(Feelings Wheel in Appendix A)*

Encouraged   Discouraged   Hopeful   Defeated   Depressed   Other: _____

9. Fasting

Did you fast (give up) anything in the last 24hrs?   Yes   No

If yes, describe: _____

Day 5

1. Did you violate any Primary Boundaries in the last 24hrs?   Yes   No

   If No, go to **#2**, If Yes, then complete the following:

   What Boundary did you violate? _____

   What events led up to the behavior?

   _____

   _____

   What Secondary Boundaries did you violate leading up to the Primary?

   _____

   _____

2. Did you violate any Secondary Boundaries in the last 24hrs?   Yes   No

   If No, go to **#3**, If Yes, then complete the following:

   What Boundaries did you violate?

   _____

   _____

3. How much time did you spend in prayer/meditation in the last 24hrs? (30-minute goal) _____

4. How much time did you spend reading scripture in the last 24hrs? _____

5. What **Gift of Self** did you perform in the last 24hrs?

   _____

   _____

6. Did you recite the 7 Cornerstones of Commitment? *(Found in Appendix B)*   Yes   No

7. Did you recite the Surrender Prayer? *(Found in Appendix D)*   Yes   No

8. What was your mood/feeling over the last 24hrs? *(Feelings Wheel in Appendix A)*

Encouraged   Discouraged   Hopeful   Defeated   Depressed   Other: _____

9. Fasting

Did you fast (give up) anything in the last 24hrs?   Yes   No

If yes, describe: _____

Day 6

1. Did you violate any Primary Boundaries in the last 24hrs?   Yes   No

    If No, go to **#2**, If Yes, then complete the following:

    What Boundary did you violate? _____

    What events led up to the behavior?

    _____

    _____

    What Secondary Boundaries did you violate leading up to the Primary?

    _____

    _____

2. Did you violate any Secondary Boundaries in the last 24hrs?   Yes   No

    If No, go to **#3**, If Yes, then complete the following:

    What Boundaries did you violate?

    _____

    _____

3. How much time did you spend in prayer/meditation in the last 24hrs? (30-minute goal) _____

4. How much time did you spend reading scripture in the last 24hrs? _____

5. What **Gift of Self** did you perform in the last 24hrs?

_____

_____

6. Did you recite the 7 Cornerstones of Commitment? *(Found in Appendix B)*   Yes   No

7. Did you recite the Surrender Prayer? *(Found in Appendix D)*   Yes   No

8. What was your mood/feeling over the last 24hrs? *(Feelings Wheel in Appendix A)*

Encouraged   Discouraged   Hopeful   Defeated   Depressed   Other: _____

9. Fasting

Did you fast (give up) anything in the last 24hrs?   Yes   No

If yes, describe: _____

Day 7

1. Did you violate any Primary Boundaries in the last 24hrs?   Yes   No

If No, go to **#2**, If Yes, then complete the following:

What Boundary did you violate? _____

What events led up to the behavior?

_____

_____

What Secondary Boundaries did you violate leading up to the Primary?

_____

_____

2. Did you violate any Secondary Boundaries in the last 24hrs?   Yes   No

If No, go to **#3**, If Yes, then complete the following:

What Boundaries did you violate?

_____

_____

3. How much time did you spend in prayer/meditation in the last 24hrs? (30-minute goal) _____

4. How much time did you spend reading scripture in the last 24hrs? _____

5. What **Gift of Self** did you perform in the last 24hrs?

_____

_____

6. Did you recite the 7 Cornerstones of Commitment? *(Found in Appendix B)* Yes   No

7. Did you recite the Surrender Prayer? *(Found in Appendix D)* Yes   No

8. What was your mood/feeling over the last 24hrs? *(Feelings Wheel in Appendix A)*

Encouraged   Discouraged   Hopeful   Defeated   Depressed   Other: _____

9. Fasting

Did you fast (give up) anything in the last 24hrs?   Yes   No

If yes, describe: _____

Weekly Action Guide

Appendix G Work

- In **Appendix G**, within the space provided in the **Week 19 Guilt and Shame Inventory** section, write in each of the shame statements that you circled or wrote down.

- Answer the questions in **Appendix G** in the **Week 19 Guilt and Shame Inventory** section.

- Update the "**Fellowship with God – Beliefs**" section from **Week 17** as needed.

Week 20 Understanding Triggers and Early Warning Signs

Meeting Protocol

Group Invocation of the Holy Spirit
"Come Holy Spirit, renew me, dwell in me and protect me"

Facilitator Leads the Group in Prayer

Confidentiality Bond – group recites together
"I _____ pledge to honor each person present or not present today in this group. I will do so by keeping all comments and discussions offered here today and at all future meetings confidential. I also pledge to keep the identity of all members confidential. I also pledge to make no statements of judgmental nature about anyone in this group, including myself."

Welcome New Members

Check-in Round 1: Feelings/Mood
Check-in Round 2: Significant event since last meeting (30-60 seconds)
Check-in Round 3: Temptation Rating (On a scale of 1–10; 1 a low temptation, 10 a high temptation)
Check-in Round 4: Primary or Secondary Boundary Violations
   If a Primary Violation occurred, the following questions/factors need to be addressed:
   ✓ **What do you think led to acting out?** – life events 24+ hours before
   ✓ **What were your feelings before acting out?**
   ✓ **Did you call anyone?**
   ✓ **What Secondary Boundaries did you violate this week?** – include those that were prior to your Primary Boundary Violation if you had one.
   ✓ **Group affirmation and acceptance of sharing.**
Check-in Round 5: Victories

Scripture Verse

Sirach 23:19 "His fear is confined to human eyes and he does not realize that the eyes of the Lord are ten thousand times brighter than the sun; they look upon every aspect of human behavior and see into hidden corners.

Group Discussion Question: How does this verse relate to your life and your battle with sexual sin?

Week 20 Recovery Foundation Lesson

To understand how behaviors are fueled, we need to explore triggers and warning signs.

Remember the scripture in previous lessons:

Romans 7:15 (NRSVCE) *"I do not understand my own actions. For I do not do what I want, but I do the very thing I hate."*

We are going to use this scripture verse AGAIN this week. It is a strong catalyst for understanding our behavior. Only this time, when we discuss how it relates to our addiction, talk about what specific events in your life cause you to react by looking at porn, yet you don't understand why.

Triggers and Warning Signs

To begin to grasp why you act the way you do, we need to look at triggers.

Let's first establish the difference between triggers and warning signs. Very basically, triggers are clear events, items or people that always or nearly always trigger sexual arousal or lead to the desire of a sexual response. Either a direct temptation or craving, or a specific scenario that begins an attachment desire or a desire for connection. Triggers can be obvious or subtle. Everyone's triggers are different, especially the subtle ones.

Warning signs are current or future events, people or things that typically result in a situation or emotional trigger that commonly progress to a sexual response.

Obvious Triggers

Obvious triggers are those that are just that, obvious. They are common among men, and it's usually clear why they are triggers.

Examples of obvious triggers:

- Scantily clad women
- Women in tight/revealing clothing
- Covers of explicit magazines such as Playboy or Penthouse and even magazines like the Sports Illustrated swimsuit issue or Cosmopolitan
- Movies or TV shows with sexually suggestive content
- Particular categories with content of a sexual nature on social media sites
- Traveling on streets with strip clubs

Subtle Triggers

The subtle ones are those that sneak up on us—we don't even see them coming. In most cases, they are not obvious at the time we encounter them, but they affect us later. They can be the most powerful triggers. Here are a few examples of subtle triggers:

- a flirtatious waitress
- the sound of high heels
- the smell of a leather jacket
- blond hair
- certain color eyes
- a raspy woman's voice
- long hair
- a particular body part
- a confident woman
- a hippie van
- sandals and painted toenails
- a white ski parka
- a poodle

There are infinite possibilities. Identifying your triggers is a process that you as the addict need to investigate. Appendix A has space to begin to record your obvious and subtle triggers.

Here is an example of how one of the subtle triggers can work:

This a story of an actual client who came to recognize that, for some seemingly unknown reason, women in sandals or open-toed shoes with painted toenails were a huge trigger for him. Upon investigating this trigger through an entire session, we discovered that the man's mother was what he called "a well-kept woman." She was always put together, dressed nice, had her toenails painted, and commonly wore open-toe shoes. This client never had a good relationship with his mother. She was a professional and very busy. He felt neglected, rejected, and struggled with feelings of abandonment. He decided that she didn't love him enough to spend time with him and there was nothing he could do about it.

For this client, his desire to be loved by his mother revealed itself every time he saw a woman with open-toed shoes whose nails were painted. This unconsciously reminded him of his mother and the love that he so deeply craved. Now as a man growing up, as so many do, he improperly equated sex with love. Thus, when he saw a woman with painted nails and this type of shoe, it triggered the need to be wanted, to be cared for, to be valued ... and this translated into sexual cravings.

To identify subtle triggers, you need to identify nonsexual events or attributes of a person that trigger cravings for attention, attachment, or sex. As with the list above, smells, sounds, or particularly non-revealing articles of clothing can be triggers. Be aware of these and when you find them, take a mental note. You will be writing these down in **Appendix G** in the section **Week 20: Triggers and Warning Signs.**

Every time you feel tempted, or crave connection or intimacy, especially when it seems to "come out of nowhere," think back over the last 24 hours, or even a week, and see what may have brought on emotions or desires. It is also common for events that only trigger a desire for connection or intimacy and are not sexual, to later turn into sexual desires. Also find the non-sexual triggers that create a desire for connection, or even make you feel lonely. These are important to note and keep documented (Appendix A).

Looking Deeper, Looking at the River Under the River

Early Warning Signs

Early warning signs will come as an event or a series of circumstances – that when applied together will create a situation that triggers a desire for intimacy or connection and results in a craving for sexualized behavior.

Commonly the situation will represent the opposite of intimacy or connection: it will actually trigger negative emotions, which reflect the *absence* of intimacy or connection and, therefore, trigger the desire or deep need for intimacy or connection.

Here are several examples of how this can happen:

Example 1: In college, a professor who is not friendly or empathetic may serve as a reminder of a mean and critical teacher you had in grade school, which brings up old feelings of rejection, unworthiness, being unaccepted, etc. Here, the absence of a connection with the college professor stimulates memories of old feelings from the grade-school teacher who actually *was* mean. These feelings, unless you are looking for them, are likely to go unnoticed. Even though the college professor isn't a problem, he, unintentionally triggers your past woundedness. This stimulation of the need for connection can lead to a desire to artificially fulfill this need with porn or fantasy. This can go completely unnoticed, thus seeming like the urge to act out came from nowhere.

Here, the early warning sign is when you attend the first class with this professor, where you will likely get a "gut" feeling about the professor, and even some of the past feelings may already begin to rise up. Be aware of this experience already starting and take action to plan an exit strategy, as if you were already being tempted.

Example 2: You may be struggling financially, which may be a reminder of childhood at age six when your family was poor and tension among parents about paying bills was high. There were even times when you didn't have food and the heat was shut off. Now you are always very financially vigilant and frequently over-concerned about money and are overly penny-pinching. This is a result of fear of being without as a child, and you want to avoid that experience at all costs. At age 14 you discovered porn and that served as a medication to escape the family stress and soothe the pain of fearing being without. Now every time a bill comes, even though there is enough money to pay it, it's a reminder of when your family couldn't pay the bills. This triggers stress of finances, and then the old patterns of escaping with porn to soothe the financial problems come flooding back.

Here, the early warning sign is knowing that the bills come on the 20th of the month. Knowing this allows you to take action so you can plan for the stress experience: pre-plan an exit strategy or alternative health-coping mechanism, such as prayer, acknowledgement of the fear, talking to an accountability partner, etc. This can prevent the overwhelming desire to escape the past experience of the financial troubles and memories.

Example 3: You know at your job that your performance review at work is tomorrow, and it makes you feel like report card day in 5ᵗʰ grade, where your alcoholic father always punished you for getting C's. You can already feel the apprehension, the day before your performance review.

As an early warning sign, you know from past history that this performance review may cause feelings of rejection, unworthiness, insignificance, and general poor self-worth. You already feel the anxiety coming on. Stop – know that this is an early warning sign that may likely trigger a desire to medicate in order to soothe the feelings of possible rejection, unworthiness, etc. Take action now to redirect the choice of medication to something healthy and edifying. Use one or more of the exit strategies.

Example 4: You are going to a Christmas party alone because you don't have a spouse or partner. You will see many others you know who are with spouses or significant others.

You know before you attend the party that this experience will trigger you to realize that you are alone and wish you had someone for the holidays. Don't wait until the party is happening or over to then be in the depths of loneliness or despair. It will be extremely difficult then to choose a healthy alternative to combat these feelings because your past experience (your set neural pathways) will already be taking you down the path to use porn to escape these feelings and to attempt to give false connection through false intimacy – and ultimately make you feel even more alone and pile on the feelings of unworthiness because, after all, who would want to be with a porn addict, anyway? Stop this when you know the party is coming and the possible way it may trigger you. Discuss it with your accountability partner, and plan to also call your accountability partner right after the party to bring light into the feelings, keeping the darkness away and the enemy powerless. Increase prayer time the days before the event – ask Jesus to fill the emptiness and loneliness that comes with these events. Pre-plan a get together with single friends for immediately after the party, so you are not alone. These are action events to combat these early warning signs.

Ultimate Goals

While the action plans in the previous four examples are good strategies to re-direct the desire to medicate by looking at porn, the goal is to heal this wound that causes this stress, or the fear that comes with it from past experiences. Know that this plan to actually heal the underlying causes (the river under the river) comes in later lessons. However, these strategies are good to have experience with, because there are always events and experiences that come up in life, which you have not worked though the healing, yet.

This lesson is about identifying these triggers or events that bring up old, unpleasant memories, and we will work later on what to do with them.

Knowing these intimately will help you when a similar event or experience happens, so you can relate it to these feelings and not get caught unprepared. Instead, you will recognize them and know what to do.

Group Questions

✓ Do you frequently feel like the urge to act out suddenly just happens without warning?

✓ Look at the last time you had a strong desire to look at porn, or maybe did look at it. What event happened before the desire came up, and what feelings were associated with that event?

✓ Why do you think that event brought up these feelings?

✓ Is this event something you knew was going to happen?

Meeting Close
Check Out
What do you need? – 5 min
Is there anything the group can offer any member?
- *Prayers*
- *Phone calls/texts*
- *Private meeting*
- *Ride to meetings*
- *Etc.*

Closing Prayers

Week 20 Homework

This week's homework consists of the **Daily Action Guide** and the **Appendix G** questions.

Week 20 Recovery Action Guide

Daily Action Guide

(next page)

Day 1

1. Did you violate any Primary Boundaries in the last 24hrs?   Yes   No

If No, go to **#2**, If Yes, then complete the following:

What Boundary did you violate? _____

What events led up to the behavior?

_____

_____

What Secondary Boundaries did you violate leading up to the Primary?

_____

_____

2. Did you violate any Secondary Boundaries in the last 24hrs?   Yes   No

If No, go to **#3**, If Yes, then complete the following:

What Boundaries did you violate?

_____

_____

3. How much time did you spend in prayer/meditation in the last 24hrs? (30-minute goal) _____

4. How much time did you spend reading scripture in the last 24hrs? _____

5. What **Gift of Self** did you perform in the last 24hrs?

_____

_____

6. Did you recite the 7 Cornerstones of Commitment? *(Found in Appendix B)*   Yes   No

7. Did you recite the Surrender Prayer? *(Found in Appendix D)*   Yes   No

8. What was your mood/feeling over the last 24hrs? *(Feelings Wheel in Appendix A)*

Encouraged   Discouraged   Hopeful   Defeated   Depressed   **Other:** _____

9. Fasting

Did you fast (give up) anything in the last 24hrs?   Yes   No

If yes, describe: _____

Day 2

1. Did you violate any Primary Boundaries in the last 24hrs?   Yes   No

   If No, go to **#2**, If Yes, then complete the following:

   What Boundary did you violate? _____

   What events led up to the behavior?

   _____

   _____

   What Secondary Boundaries did you violate leading up to the Primary?

   _____

   _____

2. Did you violate any Secondary Boundaries in the last 24hrs?   Yes   No

   If No, go to **#3**, If Yes, then complete the following:

   What Boundaries did you violate?

   _____

   _____

3. How much time did you spend in prayer/meditation in the last 24hrs? (30-minute goal) _____

4. How much time did you spend reading scripture in the last 24hrs? _____

5. What **Gift of Self** did you perform in the last 24hrs?

   _____

   _____

6. Did you recite the 7 Cornerstones of Commitment? *(Found in Appendix B)*   Yes   No

7. Did you recite the Surrender Prayer? *(Found in Appendix D)*   Yes   No

8. What was your mood/feeling over the last 24hrs? *(Feelings Wheel in Appendix A)*

   Encouraged   Discouraged   Hopeful   Defeated   Depressed   Other: _____

9. Fasting

Did you fast (give up) anything in the last 24hrs?   Yes   No

   If yes, describe: _____

Day 3

1. Did you violate any Primary Boundaries in the last 24hrs?   Yes   No

    If No, go to **#2**, If Yes, then complete the following:

    What Boundary did you violate? _____

    What events led up to the behavior?

    _____

    _____

    What Secondary Boundaries did you violate leading up to the Primary?

    _____

    _____

2. Did you violate any Secondary Boundaries in the last 24hrs?   Yes   No

    If No, go to **#3**, If Yes, then complete the following:

    What Boundaries did you violate?

    _____

    _____

3. How much time did you spend in prayer/meditation in the last 24hrs? (30-minute goal) _____

4. How much time did you spend reading scripture in the last 24hrs? _____

5. What **Gift of Self** did you perform in the last 24hrs?

_____

_____

6. Did you recite the 7 Cornerstones of Commitment? *(Found in Appendix B)* Yes   No

7. Did you recite the Surrender Prayer? *(Found in Appendix D)* Yes   No

8. What was your mood/feeling over the last 24hrs? *(Feelings Wheel in Appendix A)*

Encouraged   Discouraged   Hopeful   Defeated   Depressed   Other: _____

9. Fasting

Did you fast (give up) anything in the last 24hrs?   Yes   No

    If yes, describe: _____

Day 4

1. Did you violate any Primary Boundaries in the last 24hrs?   Yes   No

If No, go to **#2**, If Yes, then complete the following:

What Boundary did you violate? _____

What events led up to the behavior?

_____

_____

What Secondary Boundaries did you violate leading up to the Primary?

_____

_____

2. Did you violate any Secondary Boundaries in the last 24hrs?   Yes   No

If No, go to **#3**, If Yes, then complete the following:

What Boundaries did you violate?

_____

_____

3. How much time did you spend in prayer/meditation in the last 24hrs? (30-minute goal) _____

4. How much time did you spend reading scripture in the last 24hrs? _____

5. What **Gift of Self** did you perform in the last 24hrs?

_____

_____

6. Did you recite the 7 Cornerstones of Commitment? *(Found in Appendix B)*   Yes   No

7. Did you recite the Surrender Prayer? *(Found in Appendix D)*   Yes   No

8. What was your mood/feeling over the last 24hrs? *(Feelings Wheel in Appendix A)*

Encouraged   Discouraged   Hopeful   Defeated   Depressed   Other: _____

9. Fasting

Did you fast (give up) anything in the last 24hrs?   Yes   No

If yes, describe: _____

Day 5

1. Did you violate any Primary Boundaries in the last 24hrs?   Yes   No

   If No, go to **#2**, If Yes, then complete the following:

   What Boundary did you violate? _____

   What events led up to the behavior?

   _____

   _____

   What Secondary Boundaries did you violate leading up to the Primary?

   _____

   _____

2. Did you violate any Secondary Boundaries in the last 24hrs?   Yes   No

   If No, go to **#3**, If Yes, then complete the following:

   What Boundaries did you violate?

   _____

   _____

3. How much time did you spend in prayer/meditation in the last 24hrs? (30-minute goal) _____

4. How much time did you spend reading scripture in the last 24hrs? _____

5. What **Gift of Self** did you perform in the last 24hrs?

   _____

   _____

6. Did you recite the 7 Cornerstones of Commitment? *(Found in Appendix B)*   Yes   No

7. Did you recite the Surrender Prayer? *(Found in Appendix D)*   Yes   No

8. What was your mood/feeling over the last 24hrs? *(Feelings Wheel in Appendix A)*

 Encouraged   Discouraged   Hopeful   Defeated   Depressed   Other: _____

9. Fasting

Did you fast (give up) anything in the last 24hrs?   Yes   No

If yes, describe: _____

Day 6

1. Did you violate any Primary Boundaries in the last 24hrs?   Yes   No

    If No, go to **#2**, If Yes, then complete the following:

    What Boundary did you violate? _____

    What events led up to the behavior?

    _____

    _____

    What Secondary Boundaries did you violate leading up to the Primary?

    _____

    _____

2. Did you violate any Secondary Boundaries in the last 24hrs?   Yes   No

    If No, go to **#3**, If Yes, then complete the following:

    What Boundaries did you violate?

    _____

    _____

3. How much time did you spend in prayer/meditation in the last 24hrs? (30-minute goal) _____

4. How much time did you spend reading scripture in the last 24hrs? _____

5. What **Gift of Self** did you perform in the last 24hrs?

_____

_____

6. Did you recite the 7 Cornerstones of Commitment? *(Found in Appendix B)*   Yes   No

7. Did you recite the Surrender Prayer? *(Found in Appendix D)*   Yes   No

8. What was your mood/feeling over the last 24hrs? *(Feelings Wheel in Appendix A)*

Encouraged   Discouraged   Hopeful   Defeated   Depressed   Other: _____

9. Fasting

Did you fast (give up) anything in the last 24hrs?   Yes   No

If yes, describe: _____

Day 7

1. Did you violate any Primary Boundaries in the last 24hrs?   Yes   No

 If No, go to **#2**, If Yes, then complete the following:

 What Boundary did you violate? _____

 What events led up to the behavior?

 _____

 _____

 What Secondary Boundaries did you violate leading up to the Primary?

 _____

 _____

2. Did you violate any Secondary Boundaries in the last 24hrs?   Yes   No

 If No, go to **#3**, If Yes, then complete the following:

 What Boundaries did you violate?

 _____

 _____

3. How much time did you spend in prayer/meditation in the last 24hrs? (30-minute goal) _____

4. How much time did you spend reading scripture in the last 24hrs? _____

5. What **Gift of Self** did you perform in the last 24hrs?

_____

_____

6. Did you recite the 7 Cornerstones of Commitment? *(Found in Appendix B)*   Yes   No

7. Did you recite the Surrender Prayer? *(Found in Appendix D)*   Yes   No

8. What was your mood/feeling over the last 24hrs? *(Feelings Wheel in Appendix A)*

Encouraged Discouraged Hopeful Defeated Depressed Other: _____

9. Fasting

Did you fast (give up) anything in the last 24hrs? Yes No

 If yes, describe: _____

Weekly Action Guide

Feelings triggered by events:

There are likely many events that continually happen in your life that trigger unpleasant memories, and many times fuel the desire to escape the negative feelings. Using the examples in this weeks lesson, try to find and document some of these events that happen in your life. Here are some examples:

- "Every time I see my sister I feel _____"
- "Every time I go home for the holidays, I am reminded of _____ and I feel _____"
- "Every time my coworker tells me something I did wrong, it reminds me of when_____ and I feel _____"
- "Every time my wife criticizes me, it reminds me of when _____ and I feel _____"

Using this as a model, complete some "feelings triggered by events" statements. Attempt to find three examples. You may use events from the recent past or events that frequently come up in your life.

Every time I _____

I am reminded of _____

And I feel _____

Every time I _____

I am reminded of _____

And I feel _____

Every time I _____

I am reminded of _____

And I feel _____

Appendix G Work

Complete the additional exercises for **Week 20** in **Appendix G** on **Triggers and Loneliness.**

Update the "**Fellowship with God – Beliefs**" section from **Week 17** as needed.

Week 21 The 3-I's – What is it?

Meeting Protocol

Group Invocation of the Holy Spirit
"Come Holy Spirit, renew me, dwell in me and protect me"

Facilitator Leads the Group in Prayer

Confidentiality Bond – group recites together
"I _____ pledge to honor each person present or not present today in this group. I will do so by keeping all comments and discussions offered here today and at all future meetings confidential. I also pledge to keep the identity of all members confidential. I also pledge to make no statements of judgmental nature about anyone in this group, including myself."

Welcome New Members

Check-in Round 1: Feelings/Mood
Check-in Round 2: Significant event since last meeting (30-60 seconds)
Check-in Round 3: Temptation Rating (On a scale of 1–10; 1 a low temptation, 10 a high temptation)
Check-in Round 4: Primary or Secondary Boundary Violations
  If a Primary Violation occurred, the following questions/factors need to be addressed:
  ✓ **What do you think led to acting out?** – life events 24+ hours before
  ✓ **What were your feelings before acting out?**
  ✓ **Did you call anyone?**
  ✓ **What Secondary Boundaries did you violate this week?** – include those that were prior to your Primary Boundary Violation if you had one.
  ✓ **Group affirmation and acceptance of sharing.**
Check-in Round 5: Victories

Scripture Verse

Genesis 3:10-11: "...He [Adam] said, "I heard the sound of you in the garden, and I was afraid, because I was naked; and I hid myself." He [God] said, "Who told you that you were naked? Have you eaten from the tree of which I commanded you not to eat?"

Group Discussion Question: How does this verse relate to your life and your battle with sexual sin?

Week 21 Recovery Foundation Lesson

It is human nature to protect oneself. This is evident from the very beginning when, after eating the forbidden fruit, Adam said to God, "The woman gave it to me," and Eve said, "The serpent made me eat it." Looking back, these excuses almost seem amusing, but they clearly represent our human nature of self-protection.

Both science and psychology reveal self-protection mechanisms such as withdrawal, manipulation, rationalization, and denial. These protection behaviors seem to be instinctive; some call them animal instinct or the law of self-preservation. These behaviors can even at times be violent. Yes, God wired all his living creatures with some level of this instinct. However, in humans – God's divine creatures – it goes deeper than physical protection. There is also an instinctive wiring to protect our soul, our "self." In much the same way that a lion with a thorn in its paw will react violently to any that approach, humans will react in some way to anyone who touches his or her emotional wounds or personal brokenness.

This reaction is the basis of what was presented in **Lesson 18, "The River Under the River."** It's the pain in the analysis of: "If you don't transform your pain, you will transmit it."

As we have heard more than once before, even Paul refers to this two thousand years ago.

Romans 7:15 "I do not understand my own actions. For I do not do what I want, but I do the very thing I hate."

Paul recognized then that he tends to react and behave in ways he knows he shouldn't.

Many methods of dealing with this pain teach us tools and mechanisms to help us "react" in a different way to this pain, which is healthier than the old methods, such as addictions. These tools can help us manage our behaviors more effectively; although frequently, when we face serious adversity, the old wounds override the new tools we have learned, and we still react in our old addictive ways.

So, while these new tools and coping mechanisms can be helpful, they do not address the actual problem. The only real way to become free of the addictive behavior is to heal the underlying pain – heal the underlying shame and false beliefs about ourselves. Essentially, we need to dismantle the false self, our false identity. These next two lessons will help guide you on how to do that.

Feelings at the Root of Our Struggles

The core, or root, of the vast majority of our emotions that affect our behaviors can be reduced to three core feelings. These are the 3 I's:

Insignificance
Incompetence
Impotence (in this case, meaning "out of control")

Here is a real-life example of how these emotions come into play with sexual addiction.

Example

Jim prepares to leave for work in the morning. He is met by his wife, who is complaining that he did not do the dishes the day before, as he promised. She is annoyed and proceeds to point out that he does this frequently. Jim leaves for work and is feeling intensely angry. He says under his breath several expletives about his wife as he drives in his car. Emotionally, he is lashing out in self-defense because he is hurt by her comments. This, of course, ruins the rest of Jim's day. The anger he feels transmits itself in his commute to work and in his foul mood as he reacts to his coworkers for most of the day.

How do the 3-I's fit into this?

Jim feels **Incompetent** because his wife criticized his behavior, making him feel rejected and unworthy – that he can't do anything right. He also feels **Insignificant**, as his wife only seems to criticize the one thing he did wrong, but fails to recognize him for all that he does for the family. He feels worthless, unappreciated and unloved. Jim also feels **Impotent** because he has no control over the situation. Jim feels powerless and hopeless. His wife is reacting to her own set of issues and frustration, and he knows that for at least this one situation, she is right, and he can do nothing to change the fact that he forgot to do the dishes.

Jim is experiencing **i**ncompetence, **i**nsignificance and **i**mpotence.

He spends the rest of the day festering over how he feels and how unjustified his wife was with him. Jim is rude to other people on his way to work, driving aggressively and cutting other people off on the freeway (Note: Jim was the driver in Bob's story, in Example 2, in Lesson 18, "The River Under the River"). When Jim got to work, he was also rude to his coworkers. Jim had a difficult time doing his job, as he was constantly reliving the morning in his mind. Jim's feelings of the 3-I's grew throughout the day.

Jim also had a porn addiction. As the day continued, he was thinking about how looking at some pornography and masturbating would make him feel better. He began to fixate on the images he had seen in the past and planning his porn session when he got home – where he would do it, what excuses he would make to his wife for needing some time alone. He had it all planned. Jim got home and followed his plan.

Let's dismantle Jim's experience:

1. What did this behavior do for Jim?
Acting out to porn satisfied the 3-I's for Jim. When he was surfing for scenes on his favorite site, he chose images that made him feel worthy, respected, and desired—in other words, significant (opposite of **insignificant**).

Jim chose scenes where he felt that he was a good lover and the other woman was enjoying his lovemaking. This made Jim feel worthy and of value, he felt competent (opposite of **incompetent**).

He also chose scenes that made him feel like a powerful lover and in control of the situation and the other woman in the scene—in other words, competent and in control (the opposite of **impotent**).

2. Why did it seem to work?
With this porn binge, Jim countered the 3-I's feeling of the morning. The flood of dopamine provided an exhilaration and a high that Jim desired, and the serotonin after orgasm gave him a stress release and calming effect, and the oxytocin or bonding hormone helped him separate himself from the negative feelings he experienced all day while providing the brain the "illusion" of bonding with something else – the screen (even though that action actually failed because the brain cannot bond with an inanimate object).

3. What was wrong with this plan?
The real reason his wife's criticism hit him so hard was because, inside, Jim already feels unworthy, unwanted, rejected, and alone. He feels the 3-I's, which were developed from his childhood experiences with teachers and schoolmates. Essentially, there is pre-existing pain that gets triggered every time someone criticizes him. Through his porn introduction from neighborhood friends at age 11, Jim viewed sex as something that gave him worth, desire, and the ability to be in control.

This experience with porn at age 11 trained Jim's brain that women are objects to be used to make him feel better. Jim is so insecure with himself due to his childhood wounds that he is unable to open up and be vulnerable with a woman and give of his heart to her in a physically or emotionally intimate way. Complete transparency and vulnerability with a woman is terrifying to Jim.

Continued indulgence with pornography continues to write the neural pathways in Jim's brain to reinforce this. In Jim's mind, there is no other way to experience a woman. Until Jim realizes the pain he is experiencing is from his childhood, processes and heals that pain, learns what God's plan for sexuality really is, and learns what authentic intimacy is, he will continue to make his wife feel objectified, she will continue to criticize him, and the cycle of reaction to the pain Jim experiences and the pain that Jim transmits to others through his behaviors will not stop.

This is just one example of how seemingly simple life events can trigger emotions and lead to negative compensating desires and behavior.

As you can see, the urge to act out didn't "just happen." Although Jim experienced seemingly unconscious influences, other life events sparked his decision to act out – hence, "the river under the river." In this case, Jim's desire or craving to look at porn was not triggered by something or someone he saw. It wasn't even fueled by a subtle trigger. That's why the craving "seemed" to come out of nowhere.

In Jim's case, as is the real source for many of us: the urge to act out came from the need to compensate or medicate unpleasant feelings. The above example revealed a life event that triggered underlying, unresolved wounds that were developed in childhood. In Jim's youth and early adult years, Jim learned he could soothe these negative feelings by an act of false intimacy. Like most of us, Jim was never taught about God's plan for sexuality. He was never taught about authentic intimacy. Thus, he turned to what the world taught him. This teaching was seeking experiences of self-gratification: the act of "taking" to make him happy, rather than looking for the gift from God that was already present, or seeking true supportive relationships with others, including his spouse. Jim entered his marriage seeking to "take" love and acceptance from his spouse rather than "giving" fully of himself, thus inspiring his spouse to then "give" of herself to him. This giving of oneself is the only authentic fulfilling love. This backwards perception that Jim had, is the truth for nearly all of us!

Next week we will dive, in a visual way, into how these life events and underlying emotions actually lead us to false intimacy.

Group Questions

Name an event today that triggered some type of negative emotion. Take the time to seek every event that happened throughout the day and look deep to identify emotions that rose out of the event.

- What emotions were triggered?

- How did your behavior after this event reveal the manifestation of these emotions?

- When is the earliest time in your life that you can recall that you felt these same negative emotions?

- What caused it then?

Meeting Close
Check Out
What do you need? – 5 min
Is there anything the group can offer any member?
- *Prayers*
- *Phone calls/texts*
- *Private meeting*
- *Ride to meetings*
- *Etc.*

Closing Prayers

Week 21 Homework

Do This exercise 3 times this week:

Name an event today that triggered some type of negative emotion. Take the time to seek every event that happen throughout the day and look deep to identify emotions that rose out of the event.

- What emotions were triggered?

- How did your behavior after this event revel the manifestation of these emotions?

- When is the earliest time in your life that you can recall that you felt these same negative emotions?

- What caused it then?

Week 21 Recovery Action Guide

Daily Action Guide

(next page)

Day 1

1. Did you violate any Primary Boundaries in the last 24hrs?   Yes   No

If No, go to **#2**, If Yes, then complete the following:

What Boundary did you violate? _____

What events led up to the behavior?

_____

_____

What Secondary Boundaries did you violate leading up to the Primary?

_____

_____

2. Did you violate any Secondary Boundaries in the last 24hrs?   Yes   No

If No, go to **#3**, If Yes, then complete the following:

What Boundaries did you violate?

_____

_____

3. How much time did you spend in prayer/meditation in the last 24hrs? (30-minute goal) _____

4. How much time did you spend reading scripture in the last 24hrs? _____

5. What **Gift of Self** did you perform in the last 24hrs?

_____

_____

6. Did you recite the 7 Cornerstones of Commitment? *(Found in Appendix B)*   Yes   No

7. Did you recite the Surrender Prayer? *(Found in Appendix D)*   Yes   No

8. What was your mood/feeling over the last 24hrs? *(Feelings Wheel in Appendix A)*

Encouraged   Discouraged   Hopeful   Defeated   Depressed   Other: _____

9. Fasting

Did you fast (give up) anything in the last 24hrs?   Yes   No

If yes, describe: _____

Day 2

1. Did you violate any Primary Boundaries in the last 24hrs?   Yes   No

    If No, go to **#2**, If Yes, then complete the following:

    What Boundary did you violate? _____

    What events led up to the behavior?

    _____

    _____

    What Secondary Boundaries did you violate leading up to the Primary?

    _____

    _____

2. Did you violate any Secondary Boundaries in the last 24hrs?   Yes   No

    If No, go to **#3**, If Yes, then complete the following:

    What Boundaries did you violate?

    _____

    _____

3. How much time did you spend in prayer/meditation in the last 24hrs? (30-minute goal) _____

4. How much time did you spend reading scripture in the last 24hrs? _____

5. What **Gift of Self** did you perform in the last 24hrs?

_____

_____

6. Did you recite the 7 Cornerstones of Commitment? *(Found in Appendix B)*   Yes   No

7. Did you recite the Surrender Prayer? *(Found in Appendix D)*   Yes   No

8. What was your mood/feeling over the last 24hrs? *(Feelings Wheel in Appendix A)*

Encouraged   Discouraged   Hopeful   Defeated   Depressed   Other: _____

9. Fasting

Did you fast (give up) anything in the last 24hrs?   Yes   No

    If yes, describe: _____

Day 3

1. Did you violate any Primary Boundaries in the last 24hrs?   Yes   No

    If No, go to **#2**, If Yes, then complete the following:

    What Boundary did you violate? _____

    What events led up to the behavior?

    _____

    _____

    What Secondary Boundaries did you violate leading up to the Primary?

    _____

    _____

2. Did you violate any Secondary Boundaries in the last 24hrs?   Yes   No

    If No, go to **#3**, If Yes, then complete the following:

    What Boundaries did you violate?

    _____

    _____

3. How much time did you spend in prayer/meditation in the last 24hrs? (30-minute goal) _____

4. How much time did you spend reading scripture in the last 24hrs? _____

5. What **Gift of Self** did you perform in the last 24hrs?

_____

_____

6. Did you recite the 7 Cornerstones of Commitment? *(Found in Appendix B)*   Yes   No

7. Did you recite the Surrender Prayer? *(Found in Appendix D)*   Yes   No

8. What was your mood/feeling over the last 24hrs? *(Feelings Wheel in Appendix A)*

Encouraged   Discouraged   Hopeful   Defeated   Depressed   Other: _____

9. Fasting

Did you fast (give up) anything in the last 24hrs?   Yes   No

    If yes, describe: _____

Day 4

1. Did you violate any Primary Boundaries in the last 24hrs?   Yes   No

      If No, go to **#2**, If Yes, then complete the following:

      What Boundary did you violate? _____

      What events led up to the behavior?

      _____

      _____

      What Secondary Boundaries did you violate leading up to the Primary?

      _____

      _____

2. Did you violate any Secondary Boundaries in the last 24hrs?   Yes   No

      If No, go to **#3**, If Yes, then complete the following:

      What Boundaries did you violate?

      _____

      _____

3. How much time did you spend in prayer/meditation in the last 24hrs? (30-minute goal) _____

4. How much time did you spend reading scripture in the last 24hrs? _____

5. What **Gift of Self** did you perform in the last 24hrs?

_____

_____

6. Did you recite the 7 Cornerstones of Commitment? *(Found in Appendix B)*   Yes   No

7. Did you recite the Surrender Prayer? *(Found in Appendix D)*   Yes   No

8. What was your mood/feeling over the last 24hrs? *(Feelings Wheel in Appendix A)*

Encouraged   Discouraged   Hopeful   Defeated   Depressed   Other: _____

9. Fasting

Did you fast (give up) anything in the last 24hrs?   Yes   No

If yes, describe: _____

Day 5

1. Did you violate any Primary Boundaries in the last 24hrs?   Yes   No

If No, go to **#2**, If Yes, then complete the following:

What Boundary did you violate? _____

What events led up to the behavior?

_____

_____

What Secondary Boundaries did you violate leading up to the Primary?

_____

_____

2. Did you violate any Secondary Boundaries in the last 24hrs?   Yes   No

If No, go to **#3**, If Yes, then complete the following:

What Boundaries did you violate?

_____

_____

3. How much time did you spend in prayer/meditation in the last 24hrs? (30-minute goal) _____

4. How much time did you spend reading scripture in the last 24hrs? _____

5. What **Gift of Self** did you perform in the last 24hrs?

_____

_____

6. Did you recite the 7 Cornerstones of Commitment? *(Found in Appendix B)* Yes   No

7. Did you recite the Surrender Prayer? *(Found in Appendix D)* Yes   No

8. What was your mood/feeling over the last 24hrs? *(Feelings Wheel in Appendix A)*

Encouraged   Discouraged   Hopeful   Defeated   Depressed   Other: _____

9. Fasting

Did you fast (give up) anything in the last 24hrs?   Yes   No

If yes, describe: _____

Day 6

1. Did you violate any Primary Boundaries in the last 24hrs?   Yes   No

      If No, go to **#2**, If Yes, then complete the following:

      What Boundary did you violate? _____

      What events led up to the behavior?

      _____

      _____

      What Secondary Boundaries did you violate leading up to the Primary?

      _____

      _____

2. Did you violate any Secondary Boundaries in the last 24hrs?   Yes   No

      If No, go to **#3**, If Yes, then complete the following:

      What Boundaries did you violate?

      _____

      _____

3. How much time did you spend in prayer/meditation in the last 24hrs? (30-minute goal) _____

4. How much time did you spend reading scripture in the last 24hrs? _____

5. What **Gift of Self** did you perform in the last 24hrs?

_____

_____

6. Did you recite the 7 Cornerstones of Commitment? *(Found in Appendix B)*   Yes   No

7. Did you recite the Surrender Prayer? *(Found in Appendix D)*   Yes   No

8. What was your mood/feeling over the last 24hrs? *(Feelings Wheel in Appendix A)*

Encouraged   Discouraged   Hopeful   Defeated   Depressed   Other: _____

9. Fasting

Did you fast (give up) anything in the last 24hrs?   Yes   No

If yes, describe: _____

Day 7

1. Did you violate any Primary Boundaries in the last 24hrs? Yes No

 If No, go to **#2**, If Yes, then complete the following:

 What Boundary did you violate? _____

 What events led up to the behavior?

 _____

 _____

 What Secondary Boundaries did you violate leading up to the Primary?

 _____

 _____

2. Did you violate any Secondary Boundaries in the last 24hrs? Yes No

 If No, go to **#3**, If Yes, then complete the following:

 What Boundaries did you violate?

 _____

 _____

3. How much time did you spend in prayer/meditation in the last 24hrs? (30-minute goal) _____

4. How much time did you spend reading scripture in the last 24hrs? _____

5. What **Gift of Self** did you perform in the last 24hrs?

_____

_____

6. Did you recite the 7 Cornerstones of Commitment? *(Found in Appendix B)* Yes No

7. Did you recite the Surrender Prayer? *(Found in Appendix D)* Yes No

8. What was your mood/feeling over the last 24hrs? *(Feelings Wheel in Appendix A)*

Encouraged Discouraged Hopeful Defeated Depressed Other: _____

9. Fasting

Did you fast (give up) anything in the last 24hrs? Yes No

If yes, describe: _____

Weekly Action Guide

Feelings triggered by events:

Similar to the exercise you did in Week 20 homework, find events this past week that fit in this format. Here are some examples:

- "When my boss said _____ it made me feel _____"

- "When my wife/girlfriend criticizes me _____, I am reminded of _____and I feel _____"

- "Every time my coworker tells me something I did wrong, it reminds me of when_____ and I feel _____"

Using this as a model, complete some "feelings triggered by events" statements. Attempt to find three examples. You may use events from the recent past or events that frequently come up in your life.

When (name event)_____

I am reminded of _____

And I feel _____

When (name event)_____

I am reminded of _____

And I feel _____

When (name event)_____

I am reminded of _____

And I feel _____

Appendix G Work

Recall triggers that may have come up while working on the exercises this week. **In Appendix G, add as needed to the Triggers sections.** Also, in **Week 20** of **Appendix G,** add **two** more events this past week that **invoked feelings of loneliness.**

Update the "**Fellowship with God – Beliefs**" section from **Week 17** as needed.

Week 22   3-I's Part 2: How it Works

This week's lesson is fairly lengthy and is also very important. As a result, we will be shortening the Check-in rounds to only Round 4, the Boundary Violation round.

Meeting Protocol

Group Invocation of the Holy Spirit
"Come Holy Spirit, renew me, dwell in me and protect me."

Facilitator Leads the Group in Prayer

Confidentiality Bond – group recites together
"I _____ pledge to honor each person present or not present today in this group. I will do so by keeping all comments and discussions offered here today and at all future meetings confidential. I also pledge to keep the identity of all members confidential. I also pledge to make no statements of judgmental nature about anyone in this group, including myself."

Welcome New Members

Check-in Round 4: Primary or Secondary Boundary Violations
  If a Primary Violation occurred, the following questions/factors need to be addressed:
  ✓ **What do you think led to acting out?** – life events 24+ hours before
  ✓ **What were your feelings before acting out?**
  ✓ **Did you call anyone?**
  ✓ **What Secondary Boundaries did you violate this week?** – include those that were prior to your Primary Boundary Violation if you had one.
  ✓ **Group affirmation and acceptance of sharing.**

Scripture Verse

Psalm 107:19-20 "Then they cried to the Lord in their trouble, and he saved them from their distress; he sent out his word and healed them, and delivered them from destruction."

Group Discussion Question: How does this verse relate to your life and your battle with sexual sin?

Week 22 Recovery Foundation Lesson

Addressing Everyday Life

The 3-I's that we began discussing last week can be called "pre-early warning signs." They, in many cases, come before the triggers to act out. Below is an exercise or process that you are encouraged to use daily in your healing journey.

We saw that life events (like a spouse complaining) can trigger emotions. These emotions can be mostly categorized under one or more of the 3-I's. They trigger a need to fulfill or counteract these unpleasant emotions or experiences (for example, porn makes the addict feel significant, competent, and in control, or it is simply an escape from unpleasant emotions). These needs trigger rationalization thoughts, such as "What's one more time?" or, "I need this." In turn, these thoughts allow temptations (such as a short skirt, painted toenails, or the sound of high heels) to have an impact on us. This leads us to choosing False Intimacy (as discussed in Week 13, "What is Intimacy") because that's what we learned is pleasurable and fulfills what we "think" we need.

Understand that EVERY person seeks to be accepted, appreciated, validated, desired, wanted, loved, affirmed, respected, and made to feel significant. Seeking this can involve "false" intimacy or "true" intimacy.

The 3-I's: Visually

Let's take a graphic look at this process—kind of a flowchart.

We have a **LIFE EVENT** (bad day at work, car break down, getting cut off in traffic, etc.)

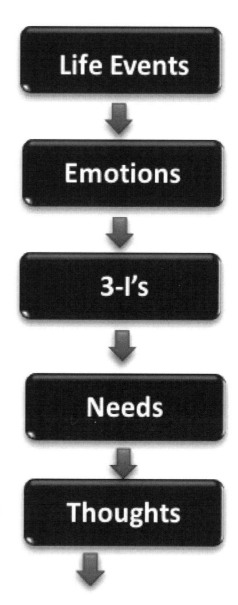

This event triggers **EMOTIONS** (anger, fear, rejection, abandonment, etc.)

Which drill down to the **3-I's:**
Insignificance
Incompetence
Impotence

Here, we are in a state of emotional discomfort. It may be lack of fulfillment, or emptiness, need for connection, etc. In reality, we have a **NEED** for authentic intimacy. The craving for dopamine to stimulate pleasure begins to creep in.

THOUGHTS get triggered of old pleasurable experiences, such as porn, eating, or shopping. Thoughts like "I could look at porn later" or "I should go get a Cinnabon roll" may begin to pop into your head

TEMPTATIONS

This is precisely when we are most
receptive to temptations of all kinds.
New counterfeit methods of intimacy
can be suggested by the world or by Satan,
or the dopamine will invoke memories
of past events that we've indulged in
as it begins to flood the brain. Just like
when you are hungry or thirsty, the brain
guides you on what to do to satisfy this "need."
Here additional thoughts begin to come in.
These thoughts are usually
moral battle thoughts, such as "I shouldn't do this,
it isn't right, but what's one more time?"
or, "I need this," kind of thinking.
The brain treats this "craving" like a primal
need. At this point, depending on how deep
the neural pathways are, due to
past repeated experiences, our moral
judgment gets trumped by the
"I gotta have it" sensation.

FALSE INTIMACY

These thoughts and temptations
will typically be ones of False Intimacy.
We have made choices of False Intimacy
in the past; it's what's been shown to
us and it's the path we are familiar with.

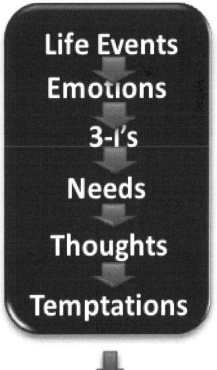

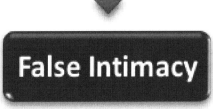

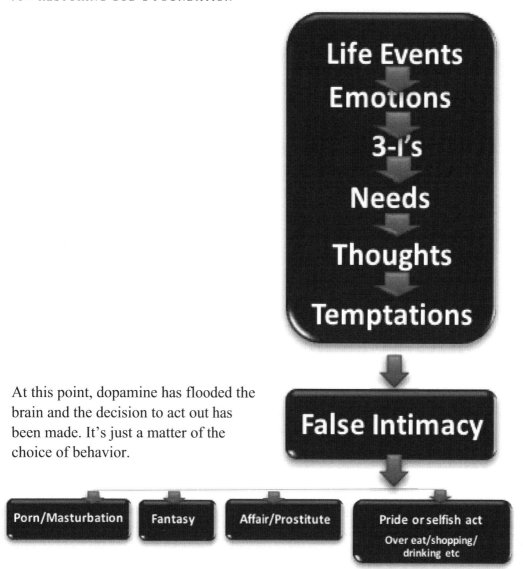

At this point, dopamine has flooded the brain and the decision to act out has been made. It's just a matter of the choice of behavior.

You can take nearly any behavior and backtrack it into this formula for action. Drinking, eating, gambling, overachieving, and so on, can all be put into this formula. If you really look closely at yourself, you will see that many times per week or even per day, you unconsciously seek False Intimacy for satisfaction. These behaviors ultimately result in guilt and shame or at least unfulfillment. Why? It's False Intimacy; it's not God's plan; it's not how we are designed. We are not being obedient to our biological, psychological, and spiritual design. We are not being authentic to God's purpose for us. It's like eating from the dumpster, and when we eat out of the dumpster, we get sick. We ultimately are left feeling empty and unsatisfied or even riddled with guilt and shame; and in many cases, physical manifestations such as depression, irritability, and the urge to isolate oneself are common.

Ezekiel 14:3 *"... these men have taken their idols into their hearts, and set the stumbling block of their iniquity before their faces..."*

Now that the guilt, shame, and/or un-fulfillment have set in, these deep-rooted feelings BECOME the LIFE EVENT, and the process starts all over—an endless loop. "We attempt the same behavior expecting a different result." These are characteristics of addiction and, according to Albert Einstein, this behavior is the definition of insanity. Remember, addiction is a brain disease! As we saw in **Week 15, "How Porn Damages Us,"** this repeated behavior done in a response to a stimulus (the river under the river) creates the deep neural pathways in the brain that lead to an almost instinctive behavior. It's much like Pavlov's law, only in this case "bad personal experience or feeling = acting out." It's automatic, it's instinctual.

Recall the stories of John and Bob in **Week 18, "The River Under the River."** Observe how both men's behaviors resulted in seeking False Intimacy. Now look at the example of Lisa and her compulsive desire to serve. Notice how this is also an act of seeking False Intimacy. While Lisa's behavior is not immoral, it's still an unhealthy response for Lisa because it's feeding the emotional disorder rather than being motivated simply by the desire to serve. Are you beginning to see a pattern of behavior and causes?

By now you are probably saying, "I'm stuck! Neural pathways have been established, my brain wants this behavior, I will always be tempted. What do I do?"

The only surefire way to become free of this cycle is to rewrite your neural pathways. Because of neuroplasticity, the brain can change and heal itself. This is where understanding intimacy, the river under the river, understanding God's plan for sexuality, accountability partners, self-awareness, and everything else you learned thus far, comes in.

Let's take a look in a similar graphic diagram, at how this works.

At any of these three places in this Path:
Life Events
Emotions
3-I's
we want to
make an intentional decision
to seek True Intimacy.
(This takes practice
and self-awareness.)

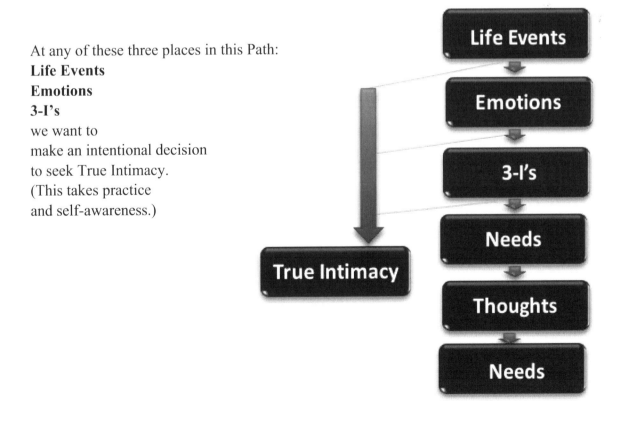

Investigating the Path of TRUE INTIMACY and Redirecting Behavior Choices

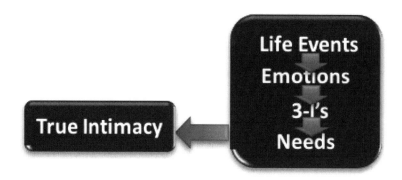

You will be doing this exercise on a daily basis with the revised Daily Inventory Tracker in your homework. Ideally, as you become proficient in this exercise, you may find yourself working through this several times per day—indefinitely. It may become your new "go to" instinctive behavior rather than turning to porn or any other behavior that is unhealthy.

For the best chance of success, you must learn to practice true intimacy at any of the stages of **Life Events, Emotions, or 3-I's**. The earlier the better.

If you miss this opportunity, you end up in the middle of the **Needs** phase, and then you are battling your current habits or old neural pathways to change course. This is much more difficult, but not impossible. At first, you will notice that you are catching yourself at the **Need**s phase and in the middle of the battle of **Thoughts** to act out, possibly even resulting in a fall. This is normal. You may experience feelings of defeat or, more appropriately, **Incompetence**. Aptly enough, that presents a perfect opportunity to practice this exercise.

True Intimacy

In the **True Intimacy Exercise,** there are *three phases of intimacy* that you will practice. You will be actively bringing God and the Holy Spirit into much of this. The goal is to find intimacy in self, God, and others, while dismantling the false self.

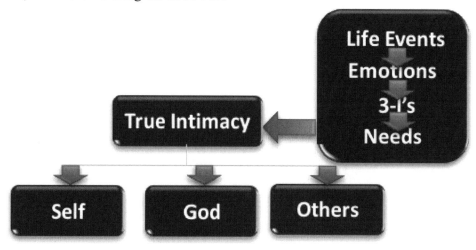

In this **True Intimacy Exercise**, you will be setting aside some time in a quiet place, 10–15 minutes is ideal. In prayer or meditation, ask the Holy Spirit to reveal to you any events that happened today or in the last 24 hours and the emotions that those events brought about. This includes both good emotions and bad emotions.

(If you're uncomfortable with prayer or don't know what to say, you may use this prayer: "Come Holy Spirit, bring peace to my heart. Please reveal to me events and emotions that were recently present in my life." Be with this thought for a few minutes and observe what comes to you.)

You will be writing these events and corresponding emotions in the space provided in your Daily Inventory Tracker.

Good or Healthy Emotions

Good emotions are just as important to recognize as bad or unpleasant ones. Some samples of good events can be a stranger holding a door open for you, a close friend sharing challenges he was having in his marriage, your spouse sitting down with you and asking about your day, someone on the freeway letting you merge in, the bank teller smiling at you, or getting a raise or promotion at your job. Try and think of how these events could counter any of the 3-I's. For example, the stranger opening the door for you could make you feel acknowledged or significant. The raise at work may make you feel wanted, valued, and worthy—which is competent and significant. Your friend sharing his marital troubles might make you feel valued, needed, and that your council was welcomed—thus, significant and competent. The teller smiling at you could make you feel significant (this one is tricky, as the teller smiling at you—especially if you find this person attractive—could also trigger awareness of desire and trigger thoughts, such as, "Maybe she likes me," and lead to fantasy; pay special attention to these events).

Intimacy Reflection

Reflect on these events, and try and see where authentic intimacy was present. Your friend sharing his relationship troubles and asking advice could be a form of emotional and intellectual intimacy. Your raise or promotion could be professional intimacy. Your spouse sitting by you and asking about your day might be proximal, emotional, and intellectual intimacy.

God's Presence

Take a minute or two and meditate on the events, related emotions, and presence of intimacy. Ask the Holy Spirit to reveal where God was present in these situations. Maybe He inspired the stranger to open the door, making you feel valued and significant. Your spouse asking how your day went reveals that you are important and significant, making you feel closer to your spouse. God constantly uses others to influence us, our decisions, and our feelings. It's a matter of recognizing it when it happens.

Gift of Self

The stranger opening the door, your spouse asking about your day, the teller smiling, and the job promotion are all gifts from another to you. In each of these situations, the other party practiced a gift of self to you.

Look back over the last 24 hours. Did you practice a gift of yourself to anyone else?

When you do give of yourself to others in this way, and you do so consciously, you are actually allowing the existence of Christ within you to shine through to others. You are reflecting His love to others. Living in love, mercy, and sacrifice is BEING Christ as HE created you to be. It's there—find it, recognize it, and celebrate it.

Bad Events and Unpleasant Emotions

Maybe you didn't get the promotion you were expecting, making you feel unappreciated, unworthy, and rejected; and you have no control over the boss's decision, which leaves you feeling *insignificant, incompetent,* and *impotent.* Your wife didn't ask about your day; instead she complained about the dishes, also yielding feelings of *insignificance* and *incompetence.* And the stranger who was supposed to hold the door for you actually let it slam in your face as if you weren't even there, making you feel *insignificant.* Whatever it is that happened, see if you can trace the emotion back to one or more of the 3-I's; find how they may be "underneath" the first emotion you sense.

Your natural tendency will be to try and ignore the unpleasant feelings you just discovered. It is very common to experience irritation, frustration, or even anger when faced with negative events. These responses are actually learned coping mechanisms to cover the unpleasantness of the underlying negative feelings. Anger may be the responsive behavior, but unworthiness and rejection are the true feelings underneath.

Instead of avoiding or ignoring the underlying feelings, focus on these negative emotions; don't ignore them or push them back in the dark. That is where Satan has his power. That's what triggers thoughts of seeking your addictive behavior to medicate or soothe your pain. We must do something with these feelings. We must bring them to the light where Christ can heal them. The three places or methods—God, self, and others—are where we do this.

Steps to Practice True Intimacy

True Intimacy Step: *Self*

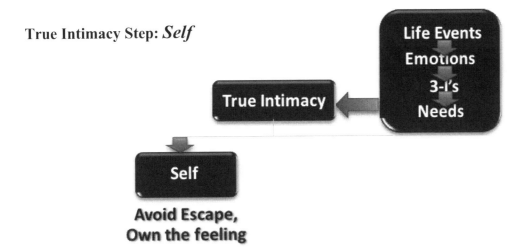

Be with the emotions in the **Self** step. Allow them to be present. Reject any desire to let them flow to a higher emotion (letting the insignificant feelings stimulate anger, for example). Running from the emotions and feelings triggers the old neural pathways and starts the dopamine craving, thus leading to old methods of self-medication. Allowing the emotions to exist in the light will begin to diffuse their power.

After identifying the emotion and owning it, being with it, we also acknowledge that this emotion and any shame we felt was not from God.

True Intimacy Step: *God*

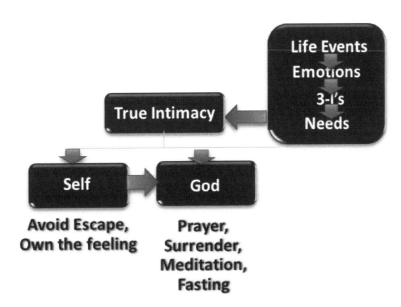

Now that we have been guided by the Holy Spirit and have identified the emotion, we bring God back in.

I suggest three options of doing this. Choose any or all.

Option 1: Meditation Image

Take the emotions, the shame, and the 3-I's that match, as well as any other corresponding emotions (rejection, pride, lust, etc.), and reflect on how these have become part of your identity. Consider how you perceive these emotions as part of who you think you are. Since these emotions are not of God, they are part of the false self. You may find yourself experiencing emotions and false identities like worthlessness, rejection and being unwanted. You may want to refer back to the shame exercise to see what fits, as well.

Take this emotion or shame identity. See it out in front of you like an object; see its shape, its color. Notice if it has a smell, a texture, any weight. Notice that Jesus is standing in front of you. Then picture yourself grabbing and handing over to Jesus the feeling and self-image that relates to it—essentially, surrendering it.

--------------- See Him willingly take it.
--------------- Hear Him say, "Good job, my son."

Next, identify the feelings that come forward when you surrender to Christ. These are usually feelings of peace, relief, freedom, and so on.

Option 2: Decisive Statement

Make a statement out loud (whispering is okay) that this shame belief or 3-I belief (name it) is not me; it is not who I am.

"Lord, this emotion of (name it) is not who I am; it is not who You created me to be. In the name of Jesus Christ, I reject and renounce the emotion of (name it) into Your hands."

Do this one by one for each emotion that you experience or think you may experience, even if you are not sure.

Option 3: Imagery

Here is another option that works for many.

See yourself sitting on the side of a stream. Leaves are lying on the water floating by. See yourself placing each of the negative or unpleasant emotions, one at a time, on a floating leaf. Watch it float down the stream as it goes away forever.

In all three exercises, our goal is to seek the emotion on purpose, to go into the dark places and face the unpleasantness rather than instinctively escaping it. This brings light to the emotions, thus taking the power of darkness away and helps prevent us from finding ourselves too far in the battle to turn back. And then taking these emotions and disposing of them removes the power and influence they have over you.

True Intimacy Step: *Others*

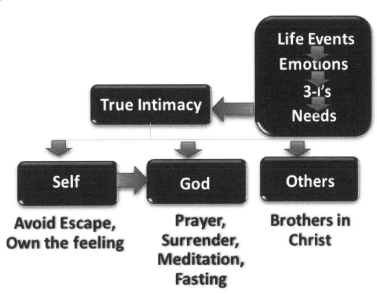

Refer to your list of accountability partners or brothers in Christ. Contact them, by phone or in person if possible, and discuss the events, related feelings, and even your experience in the first two intimacy experiences.

Remember, you cannot do this work alone!

Take a look at **Matthew 27:32** (NRSVCE), "As they went out, they came upon a man from Cyrene named Simon; they compelled this man to carry his cross."

If Jesus had help to carry His cross, why do we think we can carry ours alone? That's exactly what Satan wants, but if we go it alone, we will absolutely lose—every time!

We must look at the process of changing any addictive behavior like going through drug detox. Relying on God alone is not what He asks us to do. God does not want us to be alone; not only does He want us to have others in our lives for companionship, but He also wants our brothers to hold us up in times of struggle. We are the body of Christ, and we are here to help one another.

We are God's children. Experiencing intimacy with each other—in this case spiritual, intellectual, and emotional intimacy—is a form of being with God Himself. Spiritual and emotional intimacy are the deepest and most revealing forms we can share. This is where healing and fulfillment will happen. Trust in the people God has put in your life. This is one of many ways He reveals Himself to you.

Below, take one last look at the entire path of this process.

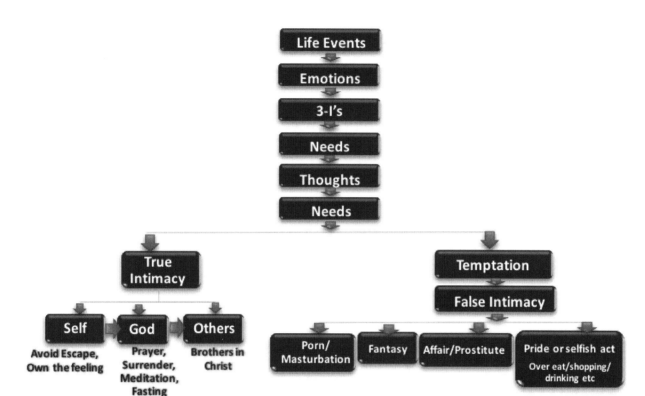

Additional Meditation

Another exercise you can do daily is to find an experience in your life that is or was life-giving or holy, something that may have been a euphoric experience. Even a fantasy along these lines is fine if it's healthy or holy. Think about what brings you peace, such as fishing, camping, biking, listening to music, etc. Create a meditation of that experience. You can also bring Jesus into the experience and use this in the God portion, of the True Intimacy section of the 3-I's.

It is amazing how when this process becomes the focus of your life, that outside temptations, needs, or desires seem to simply vanish.

Group Questions

As a group, discuss how you see this process fitting into your

- ✓ Recovery

- ✓ Healing of past woundedness

- ✓ And, how the 3-I's can pre-empt the need to seek sexual sin as a medication

NOTE: Please make sure you do the homework, because next week we will practice this process using your homework answers.

Meeting Close
Check Out
What do you need? – 5 min
Is there anything the group can offer any member?
- *Prayers*
- *Phone calls/texts*
- *Private meeting*
- *Ride to meetings*
- *Etc.*

Closing Prayers

Week 22 Homework

There are no journaling questions this week. Please complete the **Recovery Action Guide** and the **Weekly Action Guide**.

Week 22 Recovery Action Guide

Daily Action Guide

(next page)

Day 1

1. Did you violate any Primary Boundaries in the last 24hrs?   Yes   No

    If No, go to **#2**, If Yes, then complete the following:

    What Boundary did you violate? _____

    What events led up to the behavior?

    _____

    _____

    What Secondary Boundaries did you violate leading up to the Primary?

    _____

    _____

2. Did you violate any Secondary Boundaries in the last 24hrs?   Yes   No

    If No, go to **#3**, If Yes, then complete the following:

    What Boundaries did you violate?

    _____

    _____

3. How much time did you spend in prayer/meditation in the last 24hrs? (30-minute goal) _____

4. How much time did you spend reading scripture in the last 24hrs? _____

5. What **Gift of Self** did you perform in the last 24hrs?

_____

_____

6. Did you recite the 7 Cornerstones of Commitment? *(Found in Appendix B)*   Yes   No

7. Did you recite the Surrender Prayer? *(Found in Appendix D)*   Yes   No

8. What was your mood/feeling over the last 24hrs? *(Feelings Wheel in Appendix A)*

Encouraged   Discouraged   Hopeful   Defeated   Depressed   Other: _____

9. Fasting

Did you fast (give up) anything in the last 24hrs?   Yes   No

    If yes, describe: _____

Day 2

1. Did you violate any Primary Boundaries in the last 24hrs?   Yes   No

    If No, go to **#2**, If Yes, then complete the following:

    What Boundary did you violate? _____

    What events led up to the behavior?

    _____

    _____

    What Secondary Boundaries did you violate leading up to the Primary?

    _____

    _____

2. Did you violate any Secondary Boundaries in the last 24hrs?   Yes   No

    If No, go to **#3**, If Yes, then complete the following:

    What Boundaries did you violate?

    _____

    _____

3. How much time did you spend in prayer/meditation in the last 24hrs? (30-minute goal) _____

4. How much time did you spend reading scripture in the last 24hrs? _____

5. What **Gift of Self** did you perform in the last 24hrs?

_____

_____

6. Did you recite the 7 Cornerstones of Commitment? *(Found in Appendix B)*   Yes   No

7. Did you recite the Surrender Prayer? *(Found in Appendix D)*   Yes   No

8. What was your mood/feeling over the last 24hrs? *(Feelings Wheel in Appendix A)*

Encouraged   Discouraged   Hopeful   Defeated   Depressed   Other: _____

9. Fasting

Did you fast (give up) anything in the last 24hrs?   Yes   No

    If yes, describe: _____

Day 3

1. Did you violate any Primary Boundaries in the last 24hrs?   Yes   No

> If No, go to **#2**, If Yes, then complete the following:
>
> What Boundary did you violate? _____
>
> What events led up to the behavior?

_____

_____

> What Secondary Boundaries did you violate leading up to the Primary?

_____

_____

2. Did you violate any Secondary Boundaries in the last 24hrs?   Yes   No

> If No, go to **#3**, If Yes, then complete the following:
>
> What Boundaries did you violate?

_____

_____

3. How much time did you spend in prayer/meditation in the last 24hrs? (30-minute goal) _____

4. How much time did you spend reading scripture in the last 24hrs? _____

5. What **Gift of Self** did you perform in the last 24hrs?

_____

_____

6. Did you recite the 7 Cornerstones of Commitment? *(Found in Appendix B)* Yes   No

7. Did you recite the Surrender Prayer? *(Found in Appendix D)* Yes   No

8. What was your mood/feeling over the last 24hrs? *(Feelings Wheel in Appendix A)*

Encouraged   Discouraged   Hopeful   Defeated   Depressed   Other: _____

9. Fasting

Did you fast (give up) anything in the last 24hrs?   Yes   No

> If yes, describe: _____

Day 4

1. Did you violate any Primary Boundaries in the last 24hrs?   Yes   No

    If No, go to **#2**, If Yes, then complete the following:

    What Boundary did you violate? _____

    What events led up to the behavior?

    _____

    _____

    What Secondary Boundaries did you violate leading up to the Primary?

    _____

    _____

2. Did you violate any Secondary Boundaries in the last 24hrs?   Yes   No

    If No, go to **#3**, If Yes, then complete the following:

    What Boundaries did you violate?

    _____

    _____

3. How much time did you spend in prayer/meditation in the last 24hrs? (30-minute goal) _____

4. How much time did you spend reading scripture in the last 24hrs? _____

5. What **Gift of Self** did you perform in the last 24hrs?

_____

_____

6. Did you recite the 7 Cornerstones of Commitment? *(Found in Appendix B)*   Yes   No

7. Did you recite the Surrender Prayer? *(Found in Appendix D)*   Yes   No

8. What was your mood/feeling over the last 24hrs? *(Feelings Wheel in Appendix A)*

Encouraged   Discouraged   Hopeful   Defeated   Depressed   Other: _____

9. Fasting

Did you fast (give up) anything in the last 24hrs?   Yes   No

If yes, describe: _____

Day 5

1. Did you violate any Primary Boundaries in the last 24hrs?   Yes   No

     If No, go to **#2**, If Yes, then complete the following:

     What Boundary did you violate? _____

     What events led up to the behavior?

     _____

     _____

     What Secondary Boundaries did you violate leading up to the Primary?

     _____

     _____

2. Did you violate any Secondary Boundaries in the last 24hrs?   Yes   No

     If No, go to **#3**, If Yes, then complete the following:

     What Boundaries did you violate?

     _____

     _____

3. How much time did you spend in prayer/meditation in the last 24hrs? (30-minute goal) _____

4. How much time did you spend reading scripture in the last 24hrs? _____

5. What **Gift of Self** did you perform in the last 24hrs?

_____

_____

6. Did you recite the 7 Cornerstones of Commitment? *(Found in Appendix B)* Yes   No

7. Did you recite the Surrender Prayer? *(Found in Appendix D)* Yes   No

8. What was your mood/feeling over the last 24hrs? *(Feelings Wheel in Appendix A)*

Encouraged   Discouraged   Hopeful   Defeated   Depressed   Other: _____

9. Fasting

Did you fast (give up) anything in the last 24hrs?   Yes   No

If yes, describe: _____

Day 6

1. Did you violate any Primary Boundaries in the last 24hrs?   Yes   No

If No, go to **#2**, If Yes, then complete the following:

What Boundary did you violate? _____

What events led up to the behavior?

_____

_____

What Secondary Boundaries did you violate leading up to the Primary?

_____

_____

2. Did you violate any Secondary Boundaries in the last 24hrs?   Yes   No

If No, go to **#3**, If Yes, then complete the following:

What Boundaries did you violate?

_____

_____

3. How much time did you spend in prayer/meditation in the last 24hrs? (30-minute goal) _____

4. How much time did you spend reading scripture in the last 24hrs? _____

5. What **Gift of Self** did you perform in the last 24hrs?

_____

_____

6. Did you recite the 7 Cornerstones of Commitment? *(Found in Appendix B)*   Yes   No

7. Did you recite the Surrender Prayer? *(Found in Appendix D)*   Yes   No

8. What was your mood/feeling over the last 24hrs? *(Feelings Wheel in Appendix A)*

Encouraged   Discouraged   Hopeful   Defeated   Depressed   Other: _____

9. Fasting

Did you fast (give up) anything in the last 24hrs?   Yes   No

If yes, describe: _____

Day 7

1. Did you violate any Primary Boundaries in the last 24hrs?   Yes   No

If No, go to **#2**, If Yes, then complete the following:

What Boundary did you violate? _____

What events led up to the behavior?

_____

_____

What Secondary Boundaries did you violate leading up to the Primary?

_____

_____

2. Did you violate any Secondary Boundaries in the last 24hrs?   Yes   No

If No, go to **#3**, If Yes, then complete the following:

What Boundaries did you violate?

_____

_____

3. How much time did you spend in prayer/meditation in the last 24hrs? (30-minute goal) _____

4. How much time did you spend reading scripture in the last 24hrs? _____

5. What **Gift of Self** did you perform in the last 24hrs?

_____

_____

6. Did you recite the 7 Cornerstones of Commitment? *(Found in Appendix B)*   Yes   No

7. Did you recite the Surrender Prayer? *(Found in Appendix D)*   Yes   No

8. What was your mood/feeling over the last 24hrs? *(Feelings Wheel in Appendix A)*

Encouraged   Discouraged   Hopeful   Defeated   Depressed   Other: _____

9. Fasting

Did you fast (give up) anything in the last 24hrs?   Yes   No

If yes, describe: _____

Weekly Action Guide

1. Review the 3-I's process and attempt to fully understand and memorize it. Next week this will begin to be a daily part of your growth and healing.

2. Write down three events that happened this week that triggered emotions, and which of the 3-I's you can relate them to; then list these emotions and how they affected your day. Next week we will use these events and practice the 3-I's process with them.

Event 1

Describe event

_____

_____

_____

Related emotions

_____

_____

Which of the 3-I's did these emotions relate to?

_____

_____

Subsequent behavior

_____

_____

Was this behavior choice True Intimacy or False Intimacy? _____

Event 2

Describe event

_____

_____

_____

Related emotions

_____

_____

Which of the 3-I's did these emotions relate to?

_____

_____

Subsequent behavior

_____

_____

Was this behavior choice True Intimacy or False Intimacy? _____

Event 3

Describe event

_____

_____

_____

Related emotions

_____

_____

Which of the 3-I's did these emotions relate to?

_____

_____

Subsequent behavior

_____

_____

Was this behavior choice True Intimacy or False Intimacy? _____

Appendix G Work

Recall triggers that may have come up while working on the exercises this week. **In Appendix G, add as needed to the Triggers sections.** Also, in **Week 20** of **Appendix G,** add **two** more events this past week that **invoked feelings of loneliness.**

Update the "**Fellowship with God – Beliefs**" section from **Week 17** as needed.

Week 23 The 3-I's Part 3 – Using the 3-I's Going Deeper

Meeting Protocol

Group Invocation of the Holy Spirit
"Come Holy Spirit, renew me, dwell in me and protect me"

Facilitator Leads the Group in Prayer

Confidentiality Bond – group recites together
"I _____ pledge to honor each person present or not present today in this group. I will do so by keeping all comments and discussions offered here today and at all future meetings confidential. I also pledge to keep the identity of all members confidential. I also pledge to make no statements of judgmental nature about anyone in this group, including myself."

Welcome New Members

Check-in Round 1: Feelings/Mood
Check-in Round 2: Significant event since last meeting (30-60 seconds)
Check-in Round 3: Temptation Rating (On a scale of 1–10; 1 a low temptation, 10 a high temptation)
Check-in Round 4: Primary or Secondary Boundary Violations
   If a Primary Violation occurred, the following questions/factors need to be addressed:
   ✓ **What do you think led to acting out?** – life events 24+ hours before
   ✓ **What were your feelings before acting out?**
   ✓ **Did you call anyone?**
   ✓ **What Secondary Boundaries did you violate this week?** – include those that were prior to your Primary Boundary Violation if you had one.
   ✓ **Group affirmation and acceptance of sharing.**
Check-in Round 5: Victories

Scripture Verse

Jeremiah 17:14 "Heal me, O Lord, and I shall be healed; save me, and I shall be saved."

Group Discussion Question: How does this verse relate to your life and your battle with sexual sin?

Week 23 Recovery Foundation Lesson

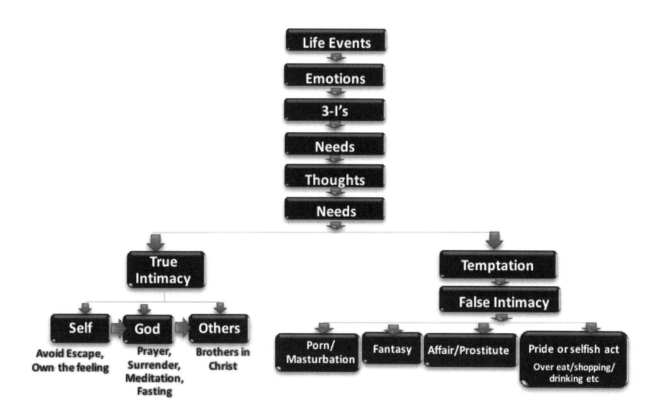

The last two weeks we discussed the process of the 3-I's: Insignificance, Incompetence, Impotence and the choices of True Intimacy and False Intimacy.

This week we will put these lessons into practice.

In last week's homework, you were asked to document three events, their related emotions, how they connect to the 3-I's, and the behaviors that resulted.

Let's do a practice example; then we will go to group participation and work on your individual experiences from last week's homework.

Example

George graduated over a year ago with a business degree. He has been working in sales for the last six years supporting himself and paying his way through college. George has had multiple interviews for business positions without success. He just heard news from his recent interview that he, again, was not chosen for this position.

George was very disappointed and felt completely rejected. After hearing the news, George left his current job early in the day claiming he didn't feel well. He stopped by a bar and had a few drinks to ease the pain. He couldn't stop thinking about how he was a failure and wasted all that time and money on the college education. He recalled his father (who was also in sales) telling him he was wasting his time in school when his sales career would do him just fine for a career. He knew that if his father knew about his several failed attempts to get a job using his new education, he would think he was a failure. George felt incompetent.

Feeling very low and in need of companionship, George attempted to pick up one of the girls at the bar. He was shot down. This of course didn't help matters. Now, being completely depressed and also feeling the effects of the alcohol, George's willpower was also down, and he proceeded home and binged on porn and masturbation.

How did George's behavior fit into the 3-I's flow?
1. **Life Event:** George was turned down for another job interview.
2. **Emotions:** George felt rejected and worthless and a failure.
3. **3-I's:** *Incompetent* because he failed again to get a job, *Insignificant* because no one wanted him, *Impotent* because he was helpless and powerless in achieving his goal.
4. **Needs:** George needed to feel worthy and wanted.
5. **Thoughts:** George was recalling how his father thought he was wasting his time going to college. He was desperate to feel needed and accepted, as his father had made him feel insignificant and incompetent – so he tried to pick up the girl at the bar. With that failed attempt, George recalled his only past option to make him feel better, which was porn.
6. **Needs:** at this point, the dopamine craving was so high that George felt a desperation for the pornography almost as much as he needed air.
Intimacy Choice:
At this point, the craving for porn (the dopamine rush and soothing effects of the serotonin), and the reduced willpower from the alcohol was so great that he couldn't fight the urges any longer and went home and watched porn.

George's life event of being turned down for the job ultimately led to the false intimacy selection of looking at porn. This could be considered the selfish act of drinking, on the flow chart. And if the woman at the bar happened to be a prostitute, who knows what could have happened.

It is important to note that in the flow of False Intimacy, George could have chosen to go shopping for something like a new electronic device for himself. While this would not have been a sinful choice like the pornography was, it still would have been a False Intimacy choice.

Group discussion: Can you all see why the choice of going shopping was still a choice of false intimacy?

What could George have done differently?

Considering the above 6 steps outlined, George could have chosen at any of steps (1. Life Event; 2. Emotions; 3. The 3-I's; or 4. Needs) to do the following:

1. Taken 5 minutes to evaluate the event of not getting the job, Invite the Holy Spirit to guide him in reflection on how it makes him feel, note the feelings, and think back on past times when he felt this way. Note the times and people in the past who triggered these feelings. **(SELF step in true intimacy)**

2. Take these feelings and the 3-I's they relate to, do the meditation exercise described in last week's lesson and see Jesus take the emotions. **(GOD step in true intimacy)**

3. After noting the emotions and the 3-I's relationship, George could make these statements out loud (in his car, as that was the safest place after he heard the news). "Lord, this emotion of incompetence is not who I am! It is NOT who you created me to be. In your name I REJECT and RENOUNCE the feelings of incompetence into your hands for You to do with as You will! He repeats this statement 3 times for each feeling of Incompetence, Insignificance, and Impotence, as well as the rejection, worthless, and all other emotions that he experiences **(also, GOD step in true intimacy)**

4. He calls his accountability partner, or even just his best friend to talk about the situation and get emotional support and to just vent about his dissatisfaction about life, in general. **(OTHERS step in true intimacy)**

Group Questions

Individual Experiences

For each person in the group, take one of the events that were documented in last week's homework and do the following:

1. Describe the event that happened.
2. Name the emotions that were revealed.
3. Name the 3-I emotions that were related.
4. What behavior was engaged in after this event and emotions happened?
5. Was this an expression of True Intimacy or False Intimacy?

If False Intimacy was chosen:
(a) describe where in the process you could have made a different decision and followed True Intimacy.
And...
(b) What True Intimacy steps would you have personally engaged in?

If True Intimacy was chosen:
(a) What True Intimacy steps did you engage in?

As time permits, continue with additional events that were recorded in the previous week's homework by each member of the group.

Meeting Close
Check Out
What do you need? – 5 min
Is there anything the group can offer any member?
- *Prayers*
- *Phone calls/texts*
- *Private meeting*
- *Ride to meetings*
- *Etc.*

Closing Prayers

Week 23 Homework

Beginning this week, your **Recovery Action Guide** again changes. Your entire homework for the week is following the Tracker which engages the 3-I's in evaluating events and responses in your life.

Week 23 Recovery Action Guide

Daily Action Guide

(next page)

Use the chart for reference while doing your homework.

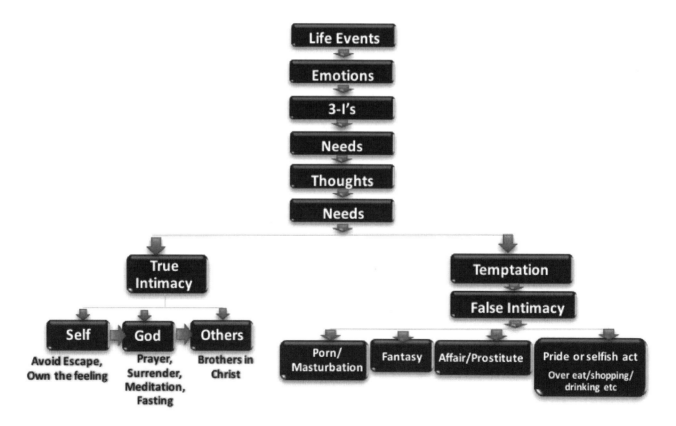

Day 1

1. Did you violate any Primary Boundaries in the last 24hrs?   Yes   No

If No, go to **#2**, If Yes, then complete the following:

What Boundary did you violate? _____

What events led up to the behavior?

_____

_____

What Secondary Boundaries did you violate leading up to the Primary?

_____

_____

2. Did you violate any Secondary Boundaries in the last 24hrs?   Yes   No

If No, go to **#3**, If Yes, then complete the following:

What Boundaries did you violate?

_____

_____

3. What **Gift of Self** did you perform in the last 24hrs?

_____

_____

At this point in the program, we will stop tracking the below listed items. Although for your recovery and ongoing spiritual growth, these should be daily disciplined practices for the rest of your life.

- ✓ Prayer/meditation for 30 or more minutes per day.
- ✓ Read Scripture every day.
- ✓ Recite the 7 Cornerstones of Commitment.
- ✓ Recite the Surrender Prayer.
- ✓ Practice some type of intentional fast every day.

Day 1 continued:

4. 3-I's Evaluation of a Daily Event

There will be an event EVERY day. Big or small. Anything from the Starbucks barista who was rude to you, to your car breaking down, to your spouse leaving you. At any level. Any of these events created an emotion that resulted in a reaction on your part: anything from simple anger or frustration to a sinful behavior. Find it, pray about it, and document it.

Day 1: Describe the event that happened:

_____

_____

Name the emotions that were revealed: _____

Name the 3-I emotions that were related: _____

What behavior was engaged in after this event and emotions happened?

_____

_____

Was this an expression of True Intimacy or False Intimacy? _____

__If False Intimacy was chosen:__
 (a) Describe where in the process you could have made a different decision and followed True Intimacy. (Event, Thought, Emotions, 3-I's, Needs, etc.)

_____

_____

And:
(b) What True Intimacy steps would you have personally engaged in? Can you do it now?

Self _____

God _____

Others _____

__If True Intimacy was chosen__:
(a) What True Intimacy steps did you engage in?

Self _____

God _____

Day 1 continued:

OR

<u>*If True Intimacy was chosen*</u>:
(a) What True Intimacy steps did you engage in?

Self
_____

God
_____

Others
_____

Day 2

1. Did you violate any Primary Boundaries in the last 24hrs?   Yes   No

    If No, go to **#2**, If Yes, then complete the following:

    What Boundary did you violate? _____

    What events led up to the behavior?

    _____

    _____

    What Secondary Boundaries did you violate leading up to the Primary?

    _____

    _____

2. Did you violate any Secondary Boundaries in the last 24hrs?   Yes   No

    If No, go to **#3**, If Yes, then complete the following:

    What Boundaries did you violate?

    _____

    _____

3. What **Gift of Self** did you perform in the last 24hrs?

_____

_____

4. 3-I's Evaluation of a Daily Event *(Remember, big or small event. Find it, pray about it, document it.)*

    Describe the event that happened:

    _____

    _____

    Name the emotions that were revealed: _____

    Name the 3-I emotions that were related: _____

Day 2 continued:

What behavior was engaged in after this event and the emotions happened?

_____

_____

Was this an expression of True Intimacy or False Intimacy? _____

If False Intimacy was chosen:
(a) Describe where in the process you could have made a different decision and followed True Intimacy. (Event, Thought, Emotions, 3-I's, Needs, etc.)

_____

_____

And:
(b) What True Intimacy steps would you have personally engaged in? Can you do it now?

Self _____

God _____

Others _____

_OR_

If True Intimacy was chosen:
(a) What True Intimacy steps did you engage in?

Self _____

God _____

Others _____

Day 3

1. Did you violate any Primary Boundaries in the last 24hrs?   Yes   No

If No, go to **#2**, If Yes, then complete the following:

What Boundary did you violate? _____

What events led up to the behavior?

_____

_____

What Secondary Boundaries did you violate leading up to the Primary?

_____

_____

2. Did you violate any Secondary Boundaries in the last 24hrs?   Yes   No

If No, go to **#3**, If Yes, then complete the following:

What Boundaries did you violate?

_____

_____

3. What **Gift of Self** did you perform in the last 24hrs?

_____

_____

4. 3-I's Evaluation of a Daily Event *(Remember, big or small event. Find it, pray about it, document it.)*

Describe the event that happened:

_____

_____

Name the emotions that were revealed: _____

Name the 3-I emotions that were related: _____

Day 3 continued:

What behavior was engaged in after this event and emotions happened:

_____

_____

Was this an expression of True Intimacy or False Intimacy? _____

If False Intimacy was chosen:

(a) Describe where in the process you could have made a different decision and followed True Intimacy. (Event, Thought, Emotions, 3-I's, Needs, etc.)

_____

_____

And:

(b) What True Intimacy steps would you have personally engaged in? Can you do it now?

Self _____

God _____

Others _____

OR

If True Intimacy was chosen:

(a) What True Intimacy steps did you engage in?

Self _____

God _____

Others _____

Day 4

1. Did you violate any Primary Boundaries in the last 24hrs?   Yes   No

If No, go to **#2**, If Yes, then complete the following:

What Boundary did you violate? _____

What events led up to the behavior?

_____

_____

What Secondary Boundaries did you violate leading up to the Primary?

_____

_____

2. Did you violate any Secondary Boundaries in the last 24hrs?   Yes   No

If No, go to **#3**, If Yes, then complete the following:

What Boundaries did you violate?

_____

_____

3. What **Gift of Self** did you perform in the last 24hrs?

_____

_____

4. 3-I's Evaluation of a Daily Event *(Remember, big or small event. Find it, pray about it, document it.)*

Describe the event that happened:

_____

_____

Name the emotions that were revealed: _____

Name the 3-I emotions that were related: _____

Day 4 continued:

What behavior was engaged in after this event and emotions happened?

_____

_____

Was this an expression of True Intimacy or False Intimacy? _____

<u>*If False Intimacy was chosen:*</u>
(a) Describe where in the process you could have made a different decision and followed True Intimacy. (Event, Thought, Emotions, 3-I's, Needs, etc.)

_____

_____

And:

(b) What True Intimacy steps would you have personally engaged in? Can you do it now?

Self _____

God _____

Others _____

OR

<u>*If True Intimacy was chosen*</u>:
(a) What True Intimacy steps did you engage in?

Self _____

God _____

Others _____

Day 5

1. Did you violate any Primary Boundaries in the last 24hrs?   Yes   No

      If No, go to **#2,** If Yes, then complete the following:

      What Boundary did you violate? _____

      What events led up to the behavior?

      _____

      _____

      What Secondary Boundaries did you violate leading up to the Primary?

      _____

      _____

2. Did you violate any Secondary Boundaries in the last 24hrs?   Yes   No

      If No, go to **#3**, If Yes, then complete the following:

      What Boundaries did you violate?

      _____

      _____

3. What **Gift of Self** did you perform in the last 24hrs?

_____

_____

4. 3-I's Evaluation of a Daily Event *(Remember, big or small event. Find it, pray about it, document it.)*

    Describe the event that happened:

    _____

    _____

    Name the emotions that were revealed: _____

    Name the 3-I emotions that were related: _____

Day 5 continued:

What behavior was engaged in after this event and emotions happened:

_____

_____

Was this an expression of True Intimacy or False Intimacy? _____

If False Intimacy was chosen:
(a) Describe where in the process you could have made a different decision and followed True Intimacy. (Event, Thought, Emotions, 3-I's, Needs, etc.)

_____

_____

And:
(b) What True Intimacy steps would you have personally engaged in? Can you do it now?

Self _____

God _____

Others _____

OR

If True Intimacy was chosen:
(a) What True Intimacy steps did you engage in?

Self _____

God _____

Others _____

Day 6

1. Did you violate any Primary Boundaries in the last 24hrs?   Yes   No

    If No, go to **#2,** If Yes, then complete the following:

    What Boundary did you violate? _____

    What events led up to the behavior?

    _____

    _____

    What Secondary Boundaries did you violate leading up to the Primary?

    _____

    _____

2. Did you violate any Secondary Boundaries in the last 24hrs?   Yes   No

    If No, go to **#3**, If Yes, then complete the following:

    What Boundaries did you violate?

    _____

    _____

3. What **Gift of Self** did you perform in the last 24hrs?

_____

_____

4. 3-I's Evaluation of a Daily Event *(Remember, big or small event. Find it, pray about it, document it.)*

    Describe the event that happened:

    _____

    _____

    Name the emotions that were revealed: _____

    Name the 3-I emotions that were related: _____

Day 6 continued:

What behavior was engaged in after this event and emotions happened?

_____

_____

Was this an expression of True Intimacy or False Intimacy? _____

<u>*If False Intimacy was chosen:*</u>
(a) Describe where in the process you could have made a different decision and followed True Intimacy. (Event, Thought, Emotions, 3-I's, Needs, etc.)

_____

_____

And:
(b) What True Intimacy steps would you have personally engaged in? Can you do it now?

Self _____

God _____

Others _____

OR

<u>*If True Intimacy was chosen*</u>:
(a) What True Intimacy steps did you engage in?

Self _____

God _____

Others _____

Day 7

1. Did you violate any Primary Boundaries in the last 24hrs?   Yes   No

If No, go to **#2**, If Yes, then complete the following:

What Boundary did you violate? _____

What events led up to the behavior?

_____

_____

What Secondary Boundaries did you violate leading up to the Primary?

_____

_____

2. Did you violate any Secondary Boundaries in the last 24hrs?   Yes   No

If No, go to **#3**, If Yes, then complete the following:

What Boundaries did you violate?

_____

_____

3. What **Gift of Self** did you perform in the last 24hrs?

_____

_____

4. 3-I's Evaluation of a Daily Event *(Remember, big or small event. Find it, pray about it, document it.)*

Describe the event that happened:

_____

_____

Name the emotions that were revealed: _____

Name the 3-I emotions that were related: _____

Day 7 continued:

What behavior was engaged in after this event and emotions happened?

_____

_____

Was this an expression of True Intimacy or False Intimacy? _____

If False Intimacy was chosen:
(a) Describe where in the process you could have made a different decision and followed True Intimacy. (Event, Thought, Emotions, 3-I's, Needs, etc.)

_____

_____

And:
(b) What True Intimacy steps would you have personally engaged in? Can you do it now?

Self _____

God _____

Others _____

OR

If True Intimacy was chosen:
(a) What True Intimacy steps did you engage in?

Self _____

God _____

Others _____

Weekly Action Guide

Appendix G Work

Recall triggers that may have come up while working on the exercises this week. **In Appendix G, add as needed to the Triggers sections.**

Update the "**Fellowship with God – Beliefs**" section from **Week 17** as needed.

Week 24 True Intimacy and Rewiring Neural Pathways

Meeting Protocol

Group Invocation of the Holy Spirit
"Come Holy Spirit, renew me, dwell in me and protect me."

Facilitator Leads the Group in Prayer

Confidentiality Bond – group recites together
"I _____ pledge to honor each person present or not present today in this group. I will do so by keeping all comments and discussions offered here today and at all future meetings confidential. I also pledge to keep the identity of all members confidential. I also pledge to make no statements of judgmental nature about anyone in this group, including myself."

Welcome New Members

Check-in Round 1: Feelings/Mood
Check-in Round 2: Significant event since last meeting (30-60 seconds)
Check-in Round 3: Temptation Rating (On a scale of 1–10; 1 a low temptation, 10 a high temptation)
Check-in Round 4: Primary or Secondary Boundary Violations
  If a Primary Violation occurred, the following questions/factors need to be addressed:
  ✓ **What do you think led to acting out?** – life events 24+ hours before
  ✓ **What were your feelings before acting out?**
  ✓ **Did you call anyone?**
  ✓ **What Secondary Boundaries did you violate this week?** – include those that were prior to your Primary Boundary Violation if you had one.
  ✓ **Group affirmation and acceptance of sharing.**
Check-in Round 5: Victories

Scripture Verse

2 Cor 10:5 "…and every proud obstacle raised up against the knowledge of God, and we take every thought captive to obey Christ."

Group Discussion Question: How does this verse relate to your life and your battle with sexual sin?

Week 24 Recovery Foundation Lesson

In the lesson several weeks ago, **"How Porn Damages Us"** we learned how our neural pathways have been re-written to desire False Intimacy behaviors that we have repeatedly engaged in. Porn is only one of these behaviors. It happens with things like food, video games, gambling, shopping and even things like anger.

If you recall, we discussed how each time we react to a stimulus we create a new "on ramp" to the neural pathway superhighway.

Stimuli can be anything, like choosing porn after a bad day at work, choosing porn when you feel lonely, choosing porn when you feel down or depressed, choosing porn when life gets hard or when you experience stress, and so many more.

This repeated behavior of choosing porn for all kinds of situations and feelings creates the deep neural pathways that make you feel like you're falling into a rut. Then when adversity strikes, we just "go there," the mere thoughts about looking at porn already begin to relax us and soothe us. This mere thought of indulging in porn is, itself, an onramp to the porn neural pathway superhighway. It has happened so much that the desire is almost instinctive. So how do we stop it?

We react to our established behaviors via stimuli and desires. To change the reaction, we must re-wire our brains. No, not brain surgery. It's a matter of knowing when and where to change a behavior and what behavior to engage in. It's not extremely difficult, but it takes time, deep self-awareness and patience.

The knowledge and awareness to accomplish this is fairly extensive, which is why this lesson is so far into the program. If you have done your homework each week and attended each meeting, then you already have the tools and knowledge to begin to make this happen. Let's look at how it works.

Here we will combine the following:

- exit strategies
- self-awareness of triggers
- self-awareness of emotions
- knowledge of your shame that binds you
- gift of self-practices
- knowledge and practice of the 3-I's process
- understanding false intimacy vs. true intimacy

Rewriting neural pathways means creating new paths and replacing old thoughts with new ones.

Take a look at these two concepts along with scripture support:

Stopping thoughts: 2 Cor 10:5 "…and every proud obstacle raised up against the knowledge of God, and we take every thought captive to obey Christ."

Replacement thoughts: Philippians 4:8 "Finally, beloved, whatever is true, whatever is honorable, whatever is just, whatever is pure, whatever is pleasing, whatever is commendable, if there is any excellence and if there is anything worthy of praise, think about these things."

Amazingly, God has already laid a path for us to follow.

As we learned in the 3-I's exercise, we take an event, its related thoughts and emotions, and choose a behavior in response. That's everything in life. This is precisely how we once created the neural pathways that capture us and take us to false intimacy. We just need to change the patterns. We create replacement thoughts and actions and, in effect, re-write the neural pathways.

This 3-I's exercise is an invaluable tool for helping to rewrite neural pathways, create new habits, and develop healthy alternatives for negative emotions and experiences.

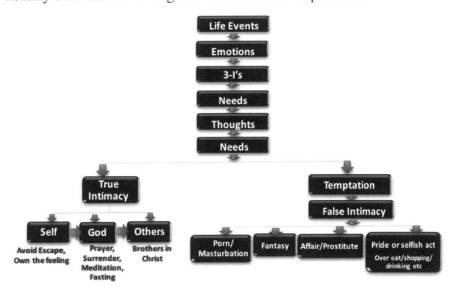

As we practiced last week, at any of the first 4 stages is the optimum time to intentionally make a choice of **TRUE INTIMACY**. The Thoughts and the second Needs stages are possible, but at that point you're reversing the existing neural pathway that has been established and, in a matter of speaking, need to take an "off ramp" to get off the neural pathway superhighway. This is much more difficult. The easiest option is always to never get on the old neural pathway superhighway to begin with.

As part of your homework this week, you will be creating a list of True Intimacy choices you can easily select from. This is much the same as engaging exit strategies. Practicing them, essentially doing fire drills, will accelerate the modification of your behavior choices; in technical terms, this will accelerate the re-writing of your neural pathways.

To get you started, begin with an existing exit strategy as an **action** that you already engage in when you sense a battle. Essentially, we are taking the 3-I's process you just learned and inserting the exit strategy action in front of the plan. The Self, God, and Others list below is slightly more detailed.

Action
- Choose an exit strategy you already have in place to break the current cycle.
- Next, begin the Self, God, and Others actions.

Self
- Name the negative or unpleasant emotions or feelings you are experiencing, or even any temptations.
- Identify any shame feelings that are present.
- Focus on recognizing them and not denying them.
- Ask the Holy Spirit to reveal to you why they are there.
- Meditate on these feelings and separate them from yourself – maybe even imagine them in a trash can in front of you.

God
- Meditate on taking the emotions and giving them to Christ (see Lesson 22 for full example).
- Engage in specific prayers you like.
- Choose scripture verses that help you refocus or that motivate you.
- Make a decisive statement to deny negative identity thoughts or feelings.
- Create your own surrender imagery (see Lesson 22 for full example).
- Go to an adoration chapel and silently pray to and talk with Jesus.
- Choose whatever actions, imagery, or even fantasy that brings God or Jesus to you, and potentially brings euphoria.

Others
- Make a list of people you can contact to discuss the event that is triggering your negative experience.
- Accountability partner, friend, priest, counselor, spouse, significant other, etc.

Here is another word picture that can help understand this process and modify the behavior.

Recall on a hot summer day, when you were doing an activity outside such as a sport or working in the yard. You suddenly have this insatiable craving for lemonade. You can't have lemonade because you are diabetic, and the high sugar is not healthy for you. So, what do you do? You're suddenly craving the lemonade, but you shouldn't have it? Being outside has created a situation where your body is getting dehydrated and the sudden sugar and fluid is craved. This is like porn where you "suddenly out of nowhere" find yourself very tempted.

Remember that we always keep saying to "back up" and look earlier in life for the event that started it all. In this case it was the combination of being in the heat and the physical exertion. The life event was this activity. But you knew in advance that this was going to happen. So, being pro-active, you could drink plenty of water before you start and continue to drink water as you're engaged outside in your activity. When doing this, you never get to the point where you have the huge craving for the lemonade. You prevent the trigger from ever happening. Your brain never says it needs the lemonade because it recalls how to correct for the dehydration and heat experience.

In the same way, the act of engaging intentionally in true intimacy after a negative experience means your brain never reaches the "thoughts" and "needs" stage to be triggered to demand the old established sinful behaviors of coping with these feelings by engaging in false intimacy or sinful choices.

Repeating this plan over and over and over, you begin to "re-wire" your brain to desire and choose the True Intimacy actions. In time, self-awareness, seeking God, and sharing yourself will be your automatic "go to" behaviors to satisfy the need for connection, acceptance, and affirmation instead of porn or other historical False intimacy choices.

In a few weeks, we will discuss forgiveness and healing of the brokenness and false identity issues that we all have. In theory, if you eliminate or reduce the "need" to escape, the "desire" to escape nearly disappears. While this healing can take a lifetime, the rewiring of the neural pathways is something that can always work to help you choose healthy behaviors and help with avoiding the impact of impeding grace by choosing sinful behaviors, throughout your entire life.

Group Questions

Individual Experiences

For each person in the group, take one of the events that were documented in last week's homework (you should have one for each of seven days this time) and complete the following questions: (*Note, this may seem like a repeat, but hearing another man's experience, his path, and solutions, is empowering for others in the group.*)

1. Describe an event that happened.
2. Name the emotions that were revealed.
3. Name the 3-I emotions that were related.
4. What behavior was engaged in after this event and emotions happened?
5. Was this an expression of True Intimacy or False Intimacy?
6. What True Intimacy steps did (if you chose True Intimacy) or could (if you chose False Intimacy) you have engaged in?
7. Are you finding it easier to become self-aware of events throughout your day?
8. As you progressed through the seven days of doing the exercise, did you find yourself being more able to choose True Intimacy rather than False Intimacy?

As time permits, continue with additional events that were recorded in the previous week's homework by each member of the group.

Meeting Close

Check Out

What do you need? – 5 min

Is there anything the group can offer any member?
- *Prayers*
- *Phone calls/texts*
- *Private meeting*
- *Ride to meetings*
- *Etc.*

Closing Prayers

Week 24 Homework

In **Appendix G** complete the TRUE INTIMACY worksheet for Lesson 24.

Week 24 Recovery Action Guide

Daily Action Guide

(next page)

Use the chart for reference while doing your homework.

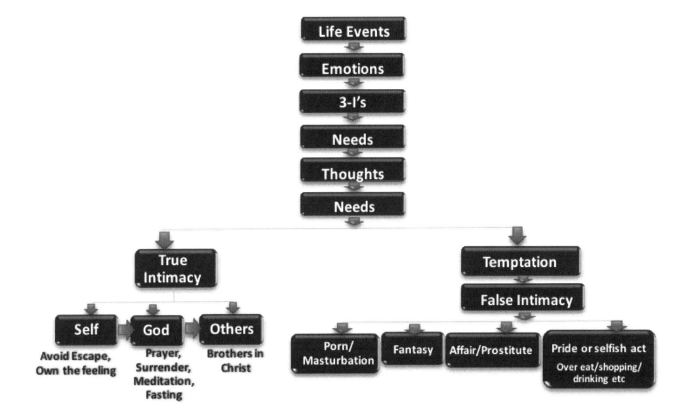

Day 1

1. Did you violate any Primary Boundaries in the last 24hrs?   Yes   No

If No, go to **#2**, If Yes, then complete the following:

What Boundary did you violate? _____

What events led up to the behavior?

_____

_____

What Secondary Boundaries did you violate leading up to the Primary?

_____

_____

2. Did you violate any Secondary Boundaries in the last 24hrs?   Yes   No

If No, go to **#3**, If Yes, then complete the following:

What Boundaries did you violate?

_____

_____

3. What **Gift of Self** did you perform in the last 24hrs?

_____

_____

At this point in the program, we will stop tracking the below listed items. Although for your recovery and ongoing spiritual growth, these should be daily disciplined practices for the rest of your life.

- ✓ Prayer/meditation for 30 or more minutes per day.
- ✓ Read Scripture every day.
- ✓ Recite the 7 Cornerstones of Commitment.
- ✓ Recite the Surrender Prayer.
- ✓ Practice some type of intentional fast every day.

Day 1 continued:

4. 3-I's Evaluation of a Daily Event

There will be an event EVERY day. Big or small. Anything from the Starbucks barista who was rude to you, to your car breaking down, to your spouse leaving you. Any level. Any of these events created an emotion that resulted in a reaction on your part. Anything from simple anger or frustration to a sinful behavior. Find it, pray about it, and document it.

Day 1: Describe the event that happened:

_____

_____

Name the emotions that were revealed: _____

Name the 3-I emotions that were related: _____

What behavior was engaged in after this event and emotions happened?

_____

_____

Was this an expression of True Intimacy or False Intimacy? _____

If False Intimacy was chosen:

(a) Describe where in the process you could have made a different decision and followed True Intimacy. (Event, Thought, Emotions, 3-I's, Needs, etc.)

_____

_____

And:

(b) What True Intimacy steps would you have personally engaged in? Can you do it now?

Self _____

God _____

Others _____

Day 1 continued:

OR

If True Intimacy was chosen:

(a) What True Intimacy steps did you engage in?

Self
_____

God
_____

Others
_____

Day 2

1. Did you violate any Primary Boundaries in the last 24hrs?   Yes   No

If No, go to **#2,** If Yes, then complete the following:

What Boundary did you violate? _____

What events led up to the behavior?

_____

_____

What Secondary Boundaries did you violate leading up to the Primary?

_____

_____

2. Did you violate any Secondary Boundaries in the last 24hrs?   Yes   No

If No, go to **#3**, If Yes, then complete the following:

What Boundaries did you violate?

_____

_____

3. What **Gift of Self** did you perform in the last 24hrs?

_____

_____

4. 3-I's Evaluation of a Daily Event *(Remember, big or small event. Find it, pray about it, document it.)*

Describe the event that happened:

_____

_____

Name the emotions that were revealed: _____

Name the 3-I emotions that were related: _____

Day 2 continued:

What behavior was engaged in after this event and emotions happened?

_____

_____

Was this an expression of True Intimacy or False Intimacy? _____

If False Intimacy was chosen:
(a) Describe where in the process you could have made a different decision and followed True Intimacy. (Event, Thought, Emotions, 3-I's, Needs, etc.)

_____

_____

And:

(b) What True Intimacy steps would you have personally engaged in? Can you do it now?

Self _____

God _____

Others _____

OR

If True Intimacy was chosen:
(a) What True Intimacy steps did you engage in?

Self _____

God _____

Others _____

Day 3

1. Did you violate any Primary Boundaries in the last 24hrs?   Yes   No

      If No, go to **#2,** If Yes, then complete the following:

      What Boundary did you violate? _____

      What events led up to the behavior?

      _____

      _____

      What Secondary Boundaries did you violate leading up to the Primary?

      _____

      _____

2. Did you violate any Secondary Boundaries in the last 24hrs?   Yes   No

      If No, go to **#3**, If Yes, then complete the following:

      What Boundaries did you violate?

      _____

      _____

3. What **Gift of Self** did you perform in the last 24hrs?

_____

_____

4. 3-I's Evaluation of a Daily Event *(Remember, big or small event. Find it, pray about it, document it.)*

    Describe the event that happened:

    _____

    _____

    Name the emotions that were revealed: _____

    Name the 3-I emotions that were related: _____

Day 3 continued:

What behavior was engaged in after this event and emotions happened?

_____

_____

Was this an expression of True Intimacy or False Intimacy? _____

<u>If False Intimacy was chosen:</u>
(a) Describe where in the process you could have made a different decision and followed True Intimacy. (Event, Thought, Emotions, 3-I's, Needs, etc.)

_____

_____

And:

(b) What True Intimacy steps would you have personally engaged in? Can you do it now?

Self _____

God _____

Others _____

OR

<u>If True Intimacy was chosen</u>:
(a) What True Intimacy steps did you engage in?

Self _____

God _____

Others _____

Day 4

1. Did you violate any Primary Boundaries in the last 24hrs?   Yes   No

If No, go to **#2,** If Yes, then complete the following:

What Boundary did you violate? _____

What events led up to the behavior?

_____

_____

What Secondary Boundaries did you violate leading up to the Primary?

_____

_____

2. Did you violate any Secondary boundaries in the last 24hrs?   Yes   No

If No, go to **#3**, If Yes, then complete the following:

What Boundaries did you violate?

_____

_____

3. What **Gift of Self** did you perform in the last 24hrs?

_____

_____

4. 3-I's Evaluation of a Daily Event *(Remember, big or small event. Find it, pray about it, document it.)*

Describe the event that happened:

_____

_____

Name the emotions that were revealed: _____

Name the 3-I emotions that were related: _____

Day 4 continued:

What behavior was engaged in after this event and emotions happened

_____

_____

Was this an expression of True Intimacy or False Intimacy? _____

If False Intimacy was chosen:
(a) Describe where in the process you could have made a different decision and followed True Intimacy. (Event, Thought, Emotions, 3-I's, Needs, etc.)

_____

_____

And:

(b) What True Intimacy steps would you have personally engaged in? Can you do it now?

Self _____

God _____

Others _____

OR

If True Intimacy was chosen:
(a) What True Intimacy steps did you engage in?

Self _____

God _____

Others _____

Day 5

1. Did you violate any Primary Boundaries in the last 24hrs?   Yes   No

If No, go to **#2,** If Yes, then complete the following:

What Boundary did you violate? _____

What events led up to the behavior?

_____

_____

What Secondary Boundaries did you violate leading up to the Primary?

_____

_____

2. Did you violate any Secondary Boundaries in the last 24hrs?   Yes   No

If No, go to **#3**, If Yes, then complete the following:

What Boundaries did you violate?

_____

_____

3. What **Gift of Self** did you perform in the last 24hrs?

_____

_____

4. 3-I's Evaluation of a Daily Event *(Remember, big or small event. Find it, pray about it, document it.)*

Describe the event that happened:

_____

_____

Name the emotions that were revealed: _____

Name the 3-I emotions that were related: _____

Day 5 continued:

What behavior was engaged in after this event and emotions happened?

_____

_____

Was this an expression of True Intimacy or False Intimacy? _____

<u>*If False Intimacy was chosen:*</u>
(a) Describe where in the process you could have made a different decision and followed True Intimacy. (Event, Thought, Emotions, 3-I's, Needs, etc.)

_____

_____

And:

(b) What True Intimacy steps would you have personally engaged in? Can you do it now?

Self _____

God _____

Others _____

OR

<u>*If True Intimacy was chosen*</u>:
(a) What True Intimacy steps did you engage in?

Self _____

God _____

Others _____

Day 6

1. Did you violate any Primary Boundaries in the last 24hrs?   Yes   No

    If No, go to **#2,** If Yes, then complete the following:

    What Boundary did you violate? _____

    What events led up to the behavior?

    _____

    _____

    What Secondary Boundaries did you violate leading up to the Primary?

    _____

    _____

2. Did you violate any Secondary Boundaries in the last 24hrs?   Yes   No

    If No, go to **#3**, If Yes, then complete the following:

    What Boundaries did you violate?

    _____

    _____

3. What **Gift of Self** did you perform in the last 24hrs?

_____

_____

4. 3-I's Evaluation of a Daily Event *(Remember, big or small event. Find it, pray about it, document it.)*

    Describe the event that happened:

    _____

    _____

    Name the emotions that were revealed: _____

    Name the 3-I emotions that were related: _____

Day 6 continued:

What behavior was engaged in after this event and emotions happened?

_____

_____

Was this an expression of True Intimacy or False Intimacy? _____

__If False Intimacy was chosen:__
(a) Describe where in the process you could have made a different decision and followed True Intimacy. (Event, Thought, Emotions, 3-I's, Needs, etc.)

_____

_____

And:

(b) What True Intimacy steps would you have personally engaged in? Can you do it now?

Self _____

God _____

Others _____

OR

__If True Intimacy was chosen__:
(a) What True Intimacy steps did you engage in?

Self _____

God _____

Others _____

Day 7

1. Did you violate any Primary Boundaries in the last 24hrs?   Yes   No

      If No, go to **#2,** If Yes, then complete the following:

      What Boundary did you violate? _____

      What events led up to the behavior?

      _____

      _____

      What Secondary Boundaries did you violate leading up to the Primary?

      _____

      _____

2. Did you violate any Secondary Boundaries in the last 24hrs?   Yes   No

      If No, go to **#3**, If Yes, then complete the following:

      What Boundaries did you violate?

      _____

      _____

3. What **Gift of Self** did you perform in the last 24hrs?

_____

_____

4. 3-I's Evaluation of a Daily Event *(Remember, big or small event. Find it, pray about it, document it.)*

    Describe the event that happened:

    _____

    _____

    Name the emotions that were revealed: _____

    Name the 3-I emotions that were related: _____

Day 7 continued:

What behavior was engaged in after this event and emotions happened?

_____

_____

Was this an expression of True Intimacy or False Intimacy? _____

<u>*If False Intimacy was chosen:*</u>
(a) Describe where in the process you could have made a different decision and followed True Intimacy. (Event, Thought, Emotions, 3-I's, Needs, etc.)

_____

_____

And:

(b) What True Intimacy steps would you have personally engaged in? Can you do it now?

Self _____

God _____

Others _____

OR

<u>*If True Intimacy was chosen*</u>:
(a) What True Intimacy steps did you engage in?

Self _____

God _____

Others _____

Weekly Action Guide

Appendix G Work

Recall triggers that may have come up while working on the exercises this week. **In Appendix G, add as needed to the Triggers sections.**

Update the "**Fellowship with God – Beliefs**" section from **Week 17** as needed.

Week 25 Identity Part 1 – Discovering the False Self

Meeting Protocol

Group Invocation of the Holy Spirit
"Come Holy Spirit, renew me, dwell in me and protect me"

Facilitator Leads the Group in Prayer

Confidentiality Bond – group recites together
"I _____ pledge to honor each person present or not present today in this group. I will do so by keeping all comments and discussions offered here today and at all future meetings confidential. I also pledge to keep the identity of all members confidential. I also pledge to make no statements of judgmental nature about anyone in this group, including myself."

Welcome New Members

Check-in Round 1: Feelings/Mood
Check-in Round 2: Significant event since last meeting (30-60 seconds)
Check-in Round 3: Temptation Rating (On a scale of 1–10; 1 a low temptation, 10 a high temptation)
Check-in Round 4: Primary or Secondary Boundary Violations
   If a Primary Violation occurred, the following questions/factors need to be addressed:
   ✓ **What do you think led to acting out?** – life events 24+ hours before
   ✓ **What were your feelings before acting out?**
   ✓ **Did you call anyone?**
   ✓ **What Secondary Boundaries did you violate this week?** – include those that were prior to your Primary Boundary Violation if you had one.
   ✓ **Group affirmation and acceptance of sharing.**
Check-in Round 5: Victories

Scripture Verse

Jeremiah 1:5 "Before I formed you in the womb, I knew you, and before you were born, I consecrated you; I appointed you a prophet to the nations."

Group Discussion Question: How does this verse relate to your life and your battle with sexual sin?

Week 25 Recovery Foundation Lesson

Most people are unaware that a large part of life's choices and behaviors are rooted in identity. How we see ourselves, our identity, plays a huge part in how we react to most all of life's events. It impacts how we choose careers, our choices in cars, our attraction to worldly things, and how we generally present ourselves. It even dictates how we perceive the words that others use when speaking to us.

This self-identity is built from our life's experiences, the majority of which are from childhood and the early years of development. These experiences are also responsible for the majority of our shame that we carry. Recall the 'Shame That Binds Me' lesson in Week 19. These statements of shame impact to a great extent our life's choices and reactions.

Here is an example:
A person who circled the statements: "I am a loser, I am worthless, I am unworthy, I am not good enough, I am unwanted," or any similar statement, may be constantly beating themselves up, have a low self-esteem, be an underachiever, be perceived as someone who doesn't care or won't try, doesn't keep good hygiene and generally has a personal disposition of being a very introverted person. This person may be constantly angry and everything someone says is interpreted to be a criticism about him. He is very self-focused. This person believes the shame statement and is owned by it and feels hopeless to try to be anything else. He lives what he believes is his identity.

The other option may be that this person will overcompensate by being out-going, extroverted, over-confident, choose expensive cars, wear expensive clothes, and always try to "one up" everyone else. A characteristic of perfectionism or materialism is present. He may be successful in his work and have the belief that if he "makes it" that he will be good enough or worthy of his father's love. He even is unlikely to recognize that this internal belief is what drives his success. This person knows what he believes is the truth and tries to hide it from the outside world by faking a different identity.

In both cases, these men are living with a false identity, a false self. Both are desperate for the love, acceptance, affirmation, feelings of being wanted and known. So desperate is this need, they are willing to accept the counterfeit love that the world promises: promiscuous sex, porn, acquiring things, success, status, etc. These behaviors are a desperate method to cover their inner pain.

In most cases, the false self is built from the absence of authentic unconditional love in young formative years, the absence of the authentic teaching of God, of His love, and the teaching of authentic sexuality. Without these critical parts of our formation as children of God, we are desperate and become open to the presentation of false intimacy ideals from the world, as formed by the enemy. We look to the world and the examples of others, who are also living in false intimacy, to attempt to acquire the love that God created us for. Unfortunately, this love that God created us for is not found in the pleasures of the world.

In the example above, both persons were very self-focused and even narcissistic. If you look at it from Satan's perspective and motivation, his goal is to keep you from God. The more focused you are on your life, either from a pity perspective or an earning love and acceptance perspective, the more you become focused on self. The false identity that you carry (with the enemy's help) keeps you in bondage. Not only to sinful behaviors like porn, but also in bondage to the endless attempts to satisfy self with worldly things, success, status, etc.

God's entire focus is for us to give of ourselves, as He has given everything to us. He even gave us His Son to pay for our sins with His blood on the cross. Think about it. When another person genuinely gives of themselves to you, it makes you feel valued and accepted: the very thing you starve for. It's because God wired you that way. But we need to receive it authentically. Not from false items like things, success, or status. Even porn. Those are all things that are taken. Think about it, can you take love from another person, or do they have to give it to you?

We live our lives trying to take or earn something that can only be given. No wonder we're never satisfied!

Consider this quote by Fr. Ralph Drendel, SJ, who was the 2nd main confessor of St. John Vianney:

"We don't grow up until we think for ourselves, but then we must put off self for God's way. The more I know and experience Him, the more I know myself, and empty myself. God always asks what I don't want. When I give up my own thinking, that's when I am crucified, and that is humility. His way is the best way, even if I don't understand it – then we begin to make progress. God uses different ways to empty ourselves of ourselves."

This "emptying" of ourselves is part of the conversion process. This false identity, the false self that we have lived with all of our lives, is the very thing that erodes our ability to do the thing what we want to do, rather than causing us to do the thing that we don't want. – remember Romans 7:15?

"**Romans 7:15** "I do not understand my own actions. For I do not do what I want, but I do the very thing I hate."

We live our lives trying to take the thing we can never get. But, when we surrender ourselves, our very existence (remember the Surrender Prayer that you are supposed to be reciting daily?), we then empty ourselves so God can fill us with His grace; and our true identity in Him is revealed. The "**Gift of Self**" exercise that is in your daily plan also serves to reverse the self-focused behavior and help you give to others, helping them to receive the love, acceptance, respect, etc., that they desperately crave. You likely don't even know the people you give to, but you know by now that they desperately crave the love, too.

The difficulty at this point is that just knowing that you carry this shame and how it affects your identity isn't enough to simply "turn it off" and be different. Your brain is set, your neural pathways are established, and instincts of self-preservation will take you to the false intimacy choices that you so concretely learned your whole life. You would rather accept the counterfeit because it's familiar, it's comfortable, and any other choice brings tremendous fear.

This is where the 3-I's Exercise helps to redirect these behaviors and re-wire your brain away from the old harmful behavior choices, towards healthy, loving, and Godly choices. It slowly helps you "wean" yourself from the counterfeit false intimacy experiences to the authentic Godly choices He created you for.

Next Week, we will dismantle each of our false self-identities through scripture.

Let's take some time and let each of us explore our identities.

Group Questions

✓ How do you see yourself; what is your self-image?
(copy some of the shame statements you circled in lesson 19 to the space below)

_____

_____

_____

✓ How do you believe others see you (parents, siblings, peers, co-workers, other influential persons such as teachers/bosses)?

✓ How have experiences from these people shaped your self-image? What events were most significant?

✓ What poor life choices have you made to counteract or satisfy this self-image?

✓ Do events in your day-to-day life remind you of this unpleasant identity? – How? Give examples.

✓ How do you think God sees you?

✓ Do you believe that you have to be "good enough" to earn God's love? Are you "good enough?"

Meeting Close
Check Out
What do you need? – 5 min
Is there anything the group can offer any member?
- *Prayers*
- *Phone calls/texts*
- *Private meeting*
- *Ride to meetings*
- *Etc.*

Closing Prayers

Week 25 Homework

Week 25 Recovery Action Guide

Daily Action Guide

(next page)

Use the chart for reference while doing your homework.

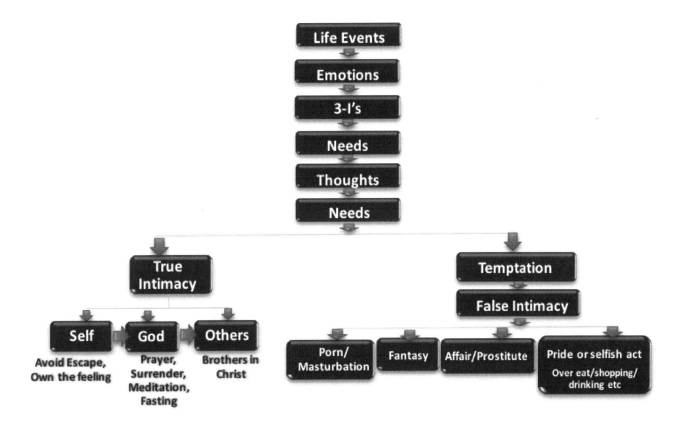

Day 1

1. Did you violate any Primary Boundaries in the last 24hrs?   Yes   No

   If No, go to **#2**, If Yes, then complete the following:

   What Boundary did you violate? _____

   What events led up to the behavior?

   _____

   _____

   What Secondary Boundaries did you violate leading up to the Primary?

   _____

   _____

2. Did you violate any Secondary Boundaries in the last 24hrs?   Yes   No

   If No, go to **#3**, If Yes, then complete the following:

   What Boundaries did you violate?

   _____

   _____

3. What **Gift of Self** did you perform in the last 24hrs?

   _____

   _____

At this point in the program, we will stop tracking the below listed items. Although for your recovery and ongoing spiritual growth, these should be daily disciplined practices for the rest of your life.

- ✓ Prayer/meditation for 30 or more minutes per day.
- ✓ Read Scripture every day.
- ✓ Recite the 7 Cornerstones of Commitment.
- ✓ Recite the Surrender Prayer.
- ✓ Practice some type of intentional fast every day.

Day 1 continued:

4. 3-I's Evaluation of a Daily Event

There will be an event EVERY day. Big or small. Anything from the Starbucks barista who was rude to you, to your car breaking down, to your spouse leaving you. Any level. Any of these events created an emotion that resulted in a reaction on your part. Anything from simple anger or frustration to a sinful behavior. Find it, pray about it, and document it.

Day 1: Describe the event that happened:

_____

_____

Name the emotions that were revealed: _____

Name the 3-I emotions that were related: _____

What behavior was engaged in after this event and emotions happened?

_____

_____

Was this an expression of True Intimacy or False Intimacy? _____

If False Intimacy was chosen:

(a) Describe where in the process you could have made a different decision and followed True Intimacy. (Event, Thought, Emotions, 3-I's, Needs, etc.)

_____

_____

And:

(b) What True Intimacy steps would you have personally engaged in? Can you do it now?

Self _____

God _____

Others _____

Day 1 continued:

OR

If True Intimacy was chosen:

(a) What True Intimacy steps did you engage in?

Self
_____

God
_____

Others
_____

Day 2

1. Did you violate any Primary Boundaries in the last 24hrs?   Yes   No

If No, go to **#2,** If Yes, then complete the following:

What Boundary did you violate? _____

What events led up to the behavior?

_____

_____

What Secondary Boundaries did you violate leading up to the Primary?

_____

_____

2. Did you violate any Secondary Boundaries in the last 24hrs?   Yes   No

If No, go to **#3**, If Yes, then complete the following:

What Boundaries did you violate?

_____

_____

3. What **Gift of Self** did you perform in the last 24hrs?

_____

_____

4. 3-I's Evaluation of a Daily Event *(Remember, big or small event. Find it, pray about it, document it.)*

Describe the event that happened:

_____

_____

Name the emotions that were revealed: _____

Name the 3-I emotions that were related: _____

Day 2 continued:

What behavior was engaged in after this event and emotions happened?

_____

_____

Was this an expression of True Intimacy or False Intimacy? _____

If False Intimacy was chosen:
(a) Describe where in the process you could have made a different decision and followed True Intimacy. (Event, Thought, Emotions, 3-I's, Needs, etc.)

_____

_____

And:

(b) What True Intimacy steps would you have personally engaged in? Can you do it now?

Self _____

God _____

Others _____

OR

If True Intimacy was chosen:
(a) What True Intimacy steps did you engage in?

Self _____

God _____

Others _____

Day 3

1. Did you violate any Primary Boundaries in the last 24hrs?   Yes   No

     If No, go to #**2,** If Yes, then complete the following:

     What Boundary did you violate? _____

     What events led up to the behavior?

     _____

     _____

     What Secondary Boundaries did you violate leading up to the Primary?

     _____

     _____

2. Did you violate any Secondary Boundaries in the last 24hrs?   Yes   No

     If No, go to #**3**, If Yes, then complete the following:

     What Boundaries did you violate?

     _____

     _____

3. What **Gift of Self** did you perform in the last 24hrs?

_____

_____

4. 3-I's Evaluation of a Daily Event *(Remember, big or small event. Find it, pray about it, document it.)*

     Describe the event that happened:

     _____

     _____

     Name the emotions that were revealed: _____

     Name the 3-I emotions that were related: _____

Day 3 continued:

What behavior was engaged in after this event and emotions happened?

_____

_____

Was this an expression of True Intimacy or False Intimacy? _____

If False Intimacy was chosen:
(a) Describe where in the process you could have made a different decision and followed True Intimacy. (Event, Thought, Emotions, 3-I's, Needs, etc.)

_____

_____

And:

(b) What True Intimacy steps would you have personally engaged in? Can you do it now?

Self _____

God _____

Others _____

OR

If True Intimacy was chosen:
(a) What True Intimacy steps did you engage in?

Self _____

God _____

Others _____

Day 4

1. Did you violate any Primary Boundaries in the last 24hrs?   Yes   No

      If No, go to **#2,** If Yes, then complete the following:

      What Boundary did you violate? _____

      What events led up to the behavior?

      _____

      _____

      What Secondary Boundaries did you violate leading up to the Primary?

      _____

      _____

2. Did you violate any Secondary Boundaries in the last 24hrs?   Yes   No

      If No, go to **#3**, If Yes, then complete the following:

      What Boundaries did you violate?

      _____

      _____

3. What **Gift of Self** did you perform in the last 24hrs?

_____

_____

4. 3-I's Evaluation of a Daily Event *(Remember, big or small event. Find it, pray about it, document it.)*

    Describe the event that happened:

    _____

    _____

    Name the emotions that were revealed: _____

    Name the 3-I emotions that were related: _____

Day 4 continued:

What behavior was engaged in after this event and emotions happened?

_____

_____

Was this an expression of True Intimacy or False Intimacy? _____

<u>*If False Intimacy was chosen:*</u>
(a) Describe where in the process you could have made a different decision and followed True Intimacy. (Event, Thought, Emotions, 3-I's, Needs, etc.)

_____

_____

And:

(b) What True Intimacy steps would you have personally engaged in? Can you do it now?

Self _____

God _____

Others _____

OR

<u>*If True Intimacy was chosen:*</u>
(a) What True Intimacy steps did you engage in?

Self _____

God _____

Others _____

Day 5

1. Did you violate any Primary Boundaries in the last 24hrs?   Yes   No

    If No, go to **#2,** If Yes, then complete the following:

    What Boundary did you violate? _____

    What events led up to the behavior?

    _____

    _____

    What Secondary Boundaries did you violate leading up to the Primary?

    _____

    _____

2. Did you violate any Secondary Boundaries in the last 24hrs?   Yes   No

    If No, go to **#3**, If Yes, then complete the following:

    What Boundaries did you violate?

    _____

    _____

3. What **Gift of Self** did you perform in the last 24hrs?

_____

_____

4. 3-I's Evaluation of a Daily Event *(Remember, big or small event. Find it, pray about it, document it.)*

    Describe the event that happened:

    _____

    _____

    Name the emotions that were revealed: _____

    Name the 3-I emotions that were related: _____

Day 5 continued:

What behavior was engaged in after this event and emotions happened?

_____

_____

Was this an expression of True Intimacy or False Intimacy? _____

If False Intimacy was chosen:
(a) Describe where in the process you could have made a different decision and followed True Intimacy. (Event, Thought, Emotions, 3-I's, Needs, etc.)

_____

_____

And:

(b) What True Intimacy steps would you have personally engaged in? Can you do it now?

Self _____

God _____

Others _____

OR

If True Intimacy was chosen:
(a) What True Intimacy steps did you engage in?

Self _____

God _____

Others _____

Day 6

1. Did you violate any Primary Boundaries in the last 24hrs?   Yes   No

If No, go to **#2,** If Yes, then complete the following:

What Boundary did you violate? _____

What events led up to the behavior?

_____

_____

What Secondary Boundaries did you violate leading up to the Primary?

_____

_____

2. Did you violate any Secondary Boundaries in the last 24hrs?   Yes   No

If No, go to **#3**, If Yes, then complete the following:

What Boundaries did you violate?

_____

_____

3. What **Gift of Self** did you perform in the last 24hrs?

_____

_____

4. 3-I's Evaluation of a Daily Event *(Remember, big or small event. Find it, pray about it, document it.)*

Describe the event that happened:

_____

_____

Name the emotions that were revealed: _____

Name the 3-I emotions that were related: _____

Day 6 continued:

What behavior was engaged in after this event and emotions happened?

_____

_____

Was this an expression of True Intimacy or False Intimacy? _____

If False Intimacy was chosen:
(a) Describe where in the process you could have made a different decision and followed True Intimacy. (Event, Thought, Emotions, 3-I's, Needs, etc.)

_____

_____

And:

(b) What True Intimacy steps would you have personally engaged in? Can you do it now?

Self _____

God _____

Others _____

OR

If True Intimacy was chosen:
(a) What True Intimacy steps did you engage in?

Self _____

God _____

Others _____

Day 7

1. Did you violate any Primary Boundaries in the last 24hrs?   Yes   No

If No, go to **#2,** If Yes, then complete the following:

What Boundary did you violate? _____

What events led up to the behavior?

_____

_____

What Secondary Boundaries did you violate leading up to the Primary?

_____

_____

2. Did you violate any Secondary Boundaries in the last 24hrs?   Yes   No

If No, go to **#3**, If Yes, then complete the following:

What Boundaries did you violate?

_____

_____

3. What **Gift of Self** did you perform in the last 24hrs?

_____

_____

4. 3-I's Evaluation of a Daily Event *(Remember, big or small event. Find it, pray about it, document it.)*

Describe the event that happened:

_____

_____

Name the emotions that were revealed: _____

Name the 3-I emotions that were related: _____

Day 7 continued:

What behavior was engaged in after this event and emotions happened?

_____

_____

Was this an expression of True Intimacy or False Intimacy? _____

If False Intimacy was chosen:

(a) Describe where in the process you could have made a different decision and followed True Intimacy. (Event, Thought, Emotions, 3-I's, Needs, etc.)

_____

_____

And:

(b) What True Intimacy steps would you have personally engaged in? Can you do it now?

Self _____

God _____

Others _____

OR

If True Intimacy was chosen:

(a) What True Intimacy steps did you engage in?

Self _____

God _____

Others _____

Weekly Action Guide

Look ahead to next week's lesson. Circle each shame or identity belief that you have.

Appendix G Work

Recall triggers that may have come up while working on the exercises this week. **In Appendix G, add as needed to the Triggers sections.**

Update the "**Fellowship with God – Beliefs**" section from **Week 17** as needed.

Week 26 Dismantling the False Self

Meeting Protocol

Group Invocation of the Holy Spirit
   "Come Holy Spirit, renew me, dwell in me and protect me"

Facilitator Leads the Group in Prayer

Confidentiality Bond – group recites together
   "I _____ pledge to honor each person present or not present today in this group. I will do so by keeping all comments and discussions offered here today and at all future meetings confidential. I also pledge to keep the identity of all members confidential. I also pledge to make no statements of judgmental nature about anyone in this group, including myself."

Welcome New Members

Check-in Round 1: Feelings/Mood
Check-in Round 2: Significant event since last meeting (30-60 seconds)
Check-in Round 3: Temptation Rating (On a scale of 1–10; 1 a low temptation, 10 a high temptation)
Check-in Round 4: Primary or Secondary Boundary Violations
   If a Primary Violation occurred, the following questions/factors need to be addressed:
   ✓ **What do you think led to acting out?** – life events 24+ hours before
   ✓ **What were your feelings before acting out?**
   ✓ **Did you call anyone?**
   ✓ **What Secondary Boundaries did you violate this week?** – include those that were prior to your Primary Boundary Violation if you had one.
   ✓ **Group affirmation and acceptance of sharing.**
Check-in Round 5: Victories

Scripture Verse

1 Corinthians 3:16 "Do you not know that you are God's temple and that God's Spirit dwells in you?"

Group Discussion Question: How does this verse relate to your life and your battle with sexual sin?

Week 26 Recovery Foundation Lesson

Dismantling the False Self

While we work to modify behaviors, we need to work at dismantling our false identity, finding the source of the woundedness and seeking to heal those false identities and beliefs. This dismantling will aid us in more easily allowing the False Intimacy behaviors to be surrendered.

Your homework from last week (Week 25) asked you to circle below, the shame and identity statements you expressed in the **"Shame that Binds Me"** Week 19 Lesson.

As a group, let's discuss the statements that you circled and see how scripture reveals that your beliefs are false, and not rooted in God and His undeniable love for you.

Each person in the group, select one Shame/Identity belief that you circled and read the accompanying scripture verses.

Many of the beliefs are similar and can be disproven with the same scripture, so we combined them.

Shame/Identity Beliefs #1
- o I am a loser
- o I am unworthy
- o I am a bad person
- o I am worthless
- o I am insignificant
- o I am a terrible person

Scripture shows these beliefs are lies.

- o **1 Peter 5:7** "Cast all your anxiety on him, because he cares for you."

- o **Romans 8:11** "If the Spirit of him who raised Jesus from the dead dwells in you, he who raised Christ from the dead will give life to your mortal bodies also through his Spirit that dwells in you."

- o **Ephesians 3:17** "...and that Christ may dwell in your hearts through faith, as you are being rooted and grounded in love."

Shame/Identity Beliefs #2

- o I am evil
- o I am a bad person
- o I am a sinner
- o I am pathetic
- o I am a terrible person
- o I am a monster

Scripture shows these beliefs are lies.

- o **Romans 3:24** "...they are now justified by his grace as a gift, through the redemption that is in Christ Jesus."

- o **1 Corinthians 6:11** "And this is what some of you used to be. But you were washed, you were sanctified, you were justified in the name of the Lord Jesus Christ and in the Spirit of our God."

- o **Hebrews 10:14** "For by a single offering he has perfected for all time those who are sanctified."

- o **Colossians 2:13** "And when you were dead in trespasses and the uncircumcision of your flesh, God made you alive together with him, when he forgave us all our trespasses."

Shame/Identity Beliefs #3

- o I am not good enough
- o I am not perfect
- o I am incompetent
- o I am damaged goods
- o I am a failure
- o I am hopeless

Scripture shows these beliefs are lies.

- o **2 Corinthians 3:5-6** "Not that we are competent of ourselves to claim anything as coming from us; our competence is from God, Who has made us competent to be ministers of a new covenant, not of letter but of spirit; for the letter kills, but the Spirit gives life."

- o **Philippians 4:13** "I can do all things through him who strengthens me."

- o **Romans 15:13** "May the God of hope fill you with all joy and peace in believing, so that you may abound in hope by the power of the Holy Spirit."

- o **Psalm 31:24** "Be strong, and let your heart take courage, all you who wait for the Lord."

Shame/Identity Beliefs #4

- o I am unloved
- o I am unwanted
- o I am unlovable
- o I am undesirable
- o I have been abandoned
- o I don't deserve love
- o I am ugly
- o I am hopeless

Scripture shows these beliefs are lies.

- o **Galatians 4:5** "…in order to redeem those who were under the law, so that we might receive adoption as children."

- o **1 Peter 5:7** "…casting all your anxieties on him, because he cares for you."

- o **Ephesians 1:5** "He destined us for adoption as his children through Jesus Christ, according to the good pleasure of his will."

- **John 15:9** "As the Father has loved me, so I have loved you; abide in my love."

- **Romans 8:38-39** "For I am convinced that neither death, nor life, nor angels, nor rulers, nor things present, nor things to come, nor powers, nor height, nor depth, nor anything else in all creation, will be able to separate us from the love of God in Christ Jesus our Lord."

- **Ephesians 5:1** "Therefore be imitators of God, as beloved children."

- **Rom 15:13** "May the God of hope fill you with all joy and peace in believing, so that you may abound in hope by the power of the Holy Spirit."

Shame/Identity Beliefs #5

- I am alone
- I am abandoned
- I am unwanted
- I have no purpose

Scripture shows these beliefs are lies.

- **Romans 8:38-39** "For I am convinced that neither death, nor life, nor angels, nor rulers, nor things present, nor things to come, nor powers, nor height, nor depth, nor anything else in all creation, will be able to separate us from the love of God in Christ Jesus our Lord."

- **Psalm 145:9** "The Lord is good to all, and his mercy is over all that he has made."

- **Isiah 41:10** "Do not fear, for I am with you, do not be afraid, for I am your God; I will strengthen you, I will help you, I will uphold you with my victorious right hand."

Shame/Identity Beliefs #6

- I am stupid
- I am not smart enough

Scripture shows these beliefs are lies.

- o **Daniel 1:17** "To these four young men God gave knowledge and skill in every aspect of literature and wisdom; Daniel also had insight into all visions and dreams."

- o **Proverbs 2:1 & 9-10** "My child, if you accept my words and treasure up my commandments within you,.....Then you will understand righteousness and justice and equity, every good path; for wisdom will come into your heart, and knowledge will be pleasant to your soul."

- o **James 3:13** "Who among you is wise and understanding? Let him show by his good behavior his deeds in the gentleness of wisdom."

- o **1 Corinthians 3:20** "The Lord knows the reasonings of the wise, that they are useless."

Shame/Identity Beliefs #7

- o I am in bondage
- o I can never be free

Scripture shows these beliefs are lies.

- o **Psalms 32:7** "You are a hiding place for me; you preserve me from trouble; you surround me with glad cries of deliverance."

- o **2 Corinthians 3:17** "Now the Lord is the Spirit, and where the Spirit of the Lord is, there is freedom."

- o **John 8:36** "So if the Son makes you free, you will be free indeed."

- o **Philippians 4:13** "I can do all things through him who strengthens me."

Shame/Identity Beliefs #8

- o I am a weak person
- o I have no control
- o I am impotent
- o I have no power

Scripture shows these beliefs are lies.

- **Psalms 37:34** "Wait for the Lord, and keep to his way, and he will exalt you to inherit the land; you will look on the destruction of the wicked."

- **Philippians 4:13** "I can do all things through him who strengthens me."

Shame/Identity Beliefs #9

- I am a fearful person
- I am an anxious person

Scripture shows these beliefs are lies.

- **Psalms 34:4** "I sought the Lord, and he answered me, and delivered me from all my fears."

- **2 Timothy1:7** "…for God did not give us a spirit of cowardice, but rather a spirit of power and of love and of self-discipline."

- **Psalm 23:4** "Even though I walk through the valley of the shadow of death, I will fear no evil, for you are with me; your rod and your staff, they comfort me."

Shame/Identity Beliefs #10

- I can't reach God

Scripture shows this belief is a lie.

- **Ephesians 2:6** "…and raised us up with him and seated us with him in the heavenly places in Christ Jesus."

- **Psalm 94:11** "The LORD knows the thoughts of man, that they are a mere breath."

Shame/Identity Beliefs #11

- I am afraid of Satan

Scripture shows this belief is a lie.

o **Mk 16:16-18** "The one who believes and is baptized will be saved; but the one who does not believe will be condemned. And these signs will accompany those who believe: by using my name they will cast out demons; they will speak in new tongues; they will pick up snakes in their hands and if they drink any deadly thing, it will not hurt them; they will lay their hands on the sick, and they will recover."

Shame/Identity Beliefs #12

o Sin overpowers me
o I am unforgiveable

Scripture shows these beliefs are lies.

o **Romans 6:11** "So you also must consider yourselves dead to sin and alive to God in Christ Jesus."

o **1 John 1:9** "If we confess our sins, he who is faithful and just will forgive us our sins and cleanse us from all unrighteousness."

Scripture on the value of every person and human dignity

o **Jeremiah 1:5** "Before I formed you in the womb, I knew you, and before you were born, I consecrated you; I appointed you a prophet to the nations."

o **Mark 2:17** "Those who are well have no need of a physician, but those who are sick. I came not to call the righteous, but sinners."

o **1 Corinthians 3:16** "Do you not know that you are God's temple and that God's Spirit dwells in you?"

o **Psalm 139:13** "For you formed my inward parts; you knitted me together in my mother's womb."

While we have discovered many of our beliefs that cause us to behave the way we do and see ourselves as less than the cherished child of God that we are, there still needs to be healing around the causes or triggers of these beliefs. The lessons in the next few weeks will dive deeper into this healing.

For now, take each of the Shame/Identity statements that you circled, include the entire category that this belief is in, then do the true intimacy exercise of the 3-I exercise using Self, God and Others. This will be part of your homework for this week.

Group Questions

✓ What did you experience, or how did it feel when you read the scripture verse that rebuked your shame or identity belief?

✓ Did some of the shame or identity beliefs of others in the group trigger any thoughts for you? Could you relate to some that you didn't connect with previously?

Meeting Close
Check Out
What do you need? – 5 min
Is there anything the group can offer any member?
- *Prayers*
- *Phone calls/texts*
- *Private meeting*
- *Ride to meetings*
- *Etc.*

Closing Prayers

Week 26 Homework

This week only, we will modify the 3-I's exercise. Each day this week take each of the shame and identity beliefs that you have and follow the True Intimacy steps in the 3-I's exercise. This will provide you with seven times to implement the act of dismantling each False Identity beliefs you have. The homework will guide you through it. Space will be provided for three groups. If you identify with items in more than two of the groups, then you may combine groups.

Week 26 Recovery Action Guide

Daily Action Guide

(next page)

Use the chart for reference while doing your homework.

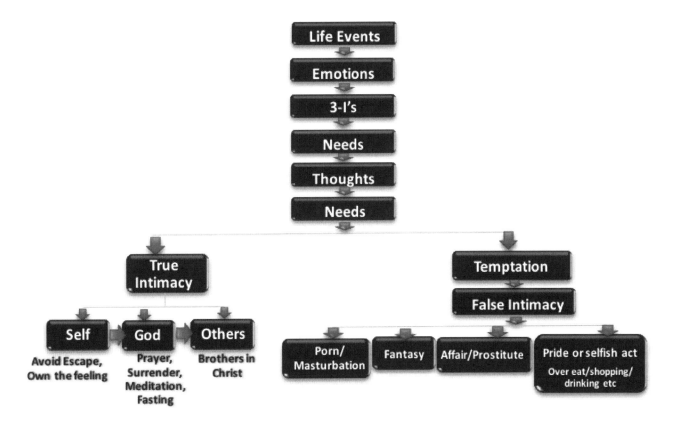

Day 1

1. Did you violate any Primary Boundaries in the last 24hrs?   Yes   No

    If No, go to **#2**, If Yes, then complete the following:

    What Boundary did you violate? _____

    What events led up to the behavior?

    _____

    _____

    What Secondary Boundaries did you violate leading up to the Primary?

    _____

    _____

2. Did you violate any Secondary Boundaries in the last 24hrs?   Yes   No

    If No, go to **#3**, If Yes, then complete the following:

    What Boundaries did you violate?

    _____

    _____

3. What **Gift of Self** did you perform in the last 24hrs?

_____

_____

Remember, we will stop tracking the below listed items. Although for your recovery and ongoing spiritual growth, these should be daily disciplined practices for the rest of your life.

- ✓ Prayer/meditation for 30 or more minutes per day.
- ✓ Read Scripture every day.
- ✓ Recite the 7 Cornerstones of Commitment.
- ✓ Recite the Surrender Prayer.
- ✓ Practice some type of intentional fast every day.

Day 1 continued:

4. Using 3-I's True Intimacy to Dismantle False Self

Recall again, the implementation suggestions of each step of True Intimacy:

Self
- Name the negative or unpleasant emotions or feelings that you experience when this Identity/False Self belief is experienced.
- Focus on recognizing them and not denying them.
- Note which of the 3-I's that fit with your emotions.
- Ask the Holy Spirit to reveal to you why they are there.
- Meditate on these feelings and separate them from yourself – maybe even imagine them in a trash can in front of you.

God
- Meditate on taking the emotions and giving them to Christ (see Lesson 22 for full example).
- Engage specific prayers you like.
- Choose scripture verses that help you refocus or motivate you.
- Make a decisive statement to deny negative identity thoughts or feelings.
- Create your own surrender imagery (see Lesson 22 for full example).
- Go to an adoration chapel and silently pray to and talk with Jesus.
- Choose whatever actions, imagery or even fantasy that brings God or Jesus to you, and potentially brings euphoria.

Others
- Make a list of people you can contact to discuss the event that is triggering your negative experience.
- Accountability partner, friend, priest, counselor, spouse, significant other, etc.

Day 1 continued:

Choose one or more of the Shame/Identity belief groups in this week's lesson and write below the shame statements that fit for you:

_____

_____

Do the True Intimacy exercise for this group of Shame/Identity beliefs and write your actions and experience for each.

Self

_____

_____

_____

_____

God

(Recite the scriptures that relate to this belief from the lesson, then proceed with the remainder of the God exercise portion.)

_____

_____

_____

_____

Others

_____

_____

_____

_____

Choose another of the Shame/Identity belief groups in this week's lesson and write below, the shame statements that fit for you:

_____

_____

Do the True Intimacy exercise for this group of Shame/Identity beliefs and write your actions and experience for each.

Self

_____

_____

_____

_____

God
(Recite the scriptures that relate to this belief from the lesson, then proceed with the remainder of the God exercise portion.)

_____

_____

_____

Others

_____

_____

_____

Day 2

1. Did you violate any Primary Boundaries in the last 24hrs?   Yes   No

If No, go to **#2**, If Yes, then complete the following:

What Boundary did you violate? _____

What events led up to the behavior?

_____

_____

What Secondary Boundaries did you violate leading up to the Primary?

_____

_____

2. Did you violate any Secondary Boundaries in the last 24hrs?   Yes   No

If No, go to **#3**, If Yes, then complete the following:

What Boundaries did you violate?

_____

_____

3. What **Gift of Self** did you perform in the last 24hrs?

_____

_____

Remember, this point in the program, we will stop tracking the below listed items. Although for your recovery and ongoing spiritual growth, these should be daily disciplined practices for the rest of your life.

- ✓ Prayer/meditation for 30 or more minutes per day.
- ✓ Read Scripture every day.
- ✓ Recite the 7 Cornerstones of Commitment.
- ✓ Recite the Surrender Prayer.
- ✓ Practice some type of intentional fast every day.

4. Using 3-I's True Intimacy to Dismantle False Self

Choose one or more of the Shame/Identity belief groups in this week's lesson and write below the shame statements that fit for you:

_____

_____

Do the True Intimacy exercise for this group of Shame/Identity beliefs and write your actions and experience for each:

Self

_____

_____

_____

_____

God
(Recite the scriptures that relate to this belief from the lesson, then proceed with the remainder of the God exercise portion)

_____

_____

_____

_____

Others

_____

_____

_____

_____

Choose another of the Shame/Identity belief groups in this week's lesson and write below the shame statements that fit for you:

_____

_____

Do the True Intimacy exercise for this group of Shame/Identity beliefs and write your actions and experience for each:

Self

_____

_____

_____

_____

God

(Recite the scriptures that relate to this belief from the lesson, then proceed with the remainder of the God exercise portion.)

_____

_____

_____

_____

Others

_____

_____

_____

_____

Day 3

1. Did you violate any Primary Boundaries in the last 24hrs?   Yes   No

     If No, go to **#2**, If Yes, then complete the following:

     What Boundary did you violate? _____

     What events led up to the behavior?

     _____

     _____

     What Secondary Boundaries did you violate leading up to the Primary?

     _____

     _____

2. Did you violate any Secondary Boundaries in the last 24hrs?   Yes   No

     If No, go to **#3**, If Yes, then complete the following:

     What Boundaries did you violate?

     _____

     _____

3. What **Gift of Self** did you perform in the last 24hrs?

_____

_____

Remember, at this point in the program, we will stop tracking the below listed items. Although for your recovery and ongoing spiritual growth, these should be daily disciplined practices for the rest of your life.

- ✓ Prayer/meditation for 30 or more minutes per day.
- ✓ Read Scripture every day.
- ✓ Recite the 7 Cornerstones of Commitment.
- ✓ Recite the Surrender Prayer.
- ✓ Practice some type of intentional fast every day.

4. Using 3-I's True Intimacy to Dismantle False Self

Choose one or more of the Shame/Identity belief groups in this week's lesson and write below the shame statements that fit for you:

_____

_____

Do the True Intimacy exercise for this group of Shame/Identity beliefs and write your actions and experience for each:

Self

_____

_____

_____

_____

God
(Recite the scriptures that relate to this belief from the lesson, then proceed with the remainder of the God exercise portion.)

_____

_____

_____

_____

Others

_____

_____

_____

_____

Choose another of the Shame/Identity belief groups in this week's lesson and write below the shame statements that fit for you:

_____

_____

Do the True Intimacy exercise for this group of Shame/Identity beliefs and write your actions and experience for each:

Self

_____

_____

_____

_____

God
(Recite the scriptures that relate to this belief from the lesson, then proceed with the remainder of the God exercise portion.)

_____

_____

_____

_____

Others

_____

_____

_____

_____

Day 4

1. Did you violate any Primary Boundaries in the last 24hrs?   Yes   No

If No, go to **#2**, If Yes, then complete the following:

What Boundary did you violate? _____

What events led up to the behavior?

_____

_____

What Secondary Boundaries did you violate leading up to the Primary?

_____

_____

2. Did you violate any Secondary Boundaries in the last 24hrs?   Yes   No

If No, go to **#3**, If Yes, then complete the following:

What Boundaries did you violate?

_____

_____

3. What **Gift of Self** did you perform in the last 24hrs?

_____

_____

Remember, at this point in the program, we will stop tracking the below listed items. Although for your recovery and ongoing spiritual growth, these should be daily disciplined practices for the rest of your life.

- ✓ Prayer/meditation for 30 or more minutes per day.
- ✓ Read Scripture every day.
- ✓ Recite the 7 Cornerstones of Commitment.
- ✓ Recite the Surrender Prayer.
- ✓ Practice some type of intentional fast every day.

Day 4 continued:

4. Using 3-I's True Intimacy to Dismantle False Self

Choose one or more of the Shame/Identity belief groups in this week's lesson and write below the shame statements that fit for you:

_____

_____

Do the True Intimacy exercise for this group of Shame/Identity beliefs and write your actions and experience for each:

Self

_____

_____

_____

_____

God
(Recite the scriptures that relate to this belief from the lesson, then proceed with the remainder of the God exercise portion.)

_____

_____

_____

_____

Others

_____

_____

_____

_____

Choose another of the Shame/Identity belief groups in this week's lesson and write below the shame statements that fit for you:

_____

_____

Do the True Intimacy exercise for this group of Shame/Identity beliefs and write your actions and experience for each:

Self

_____

_____

_____

_____

God
(Recite the scriptures that relate to this belief from the lesson, then proceed with the remainder of the God exercise portion.)

_____

_____

_____

_____

Others

_____

_____

_____

_____

Day 5

1. Did you violate any Primary Boundaries in the last 24hrs?   Yes   No

If No, go to **#2**, If Yes, then complete the following:

What Boundary did you violate? _____

What events led up to the behavior?

_____

_____

What Secondary Boundaries did you violate leading up to the Primary?

_____

_____

2. Did you violate any Secondary Boundaries in the last 24hrs?   Yes   No

If No, go to **#3**, If Yes, then complete the following:

What Boundaries did you violate?

_____

_____

3. What **Gift of Self** did you perform in the last 24hrs?

_____

_____

Remember, at this point in the program, we will stop tracking the below listed items. Although for your recovery and ongoing spiritual growth, these should be daily disciplined practices for the rest of your life.

- ✓ Prayer/meditation for 30 or more minutes per day.
- ✓ Read Scripture every day.
- ✓ Recite the 7 Cornerstones of Commitment.
- ✓ Recite the Surrender Prayer.
- ✓ Practice some type of intentional fast every day.

Day 5 continued:

4. Using 3-I's True Intimacy to Dismantle False Self

Choose one or more of the Shame/Identity belief groups in this week's lesson and write below the shame statements that fit for you:

_____

_____

Do the True Intimacy exercise for this group of Shame/Identity beliefs and write your actions and experience for each:

Self

_____

_____

_____

_____

God
(Recite the scriptures that relate to this belief from the lesson, then proceed with the remainder of the God exercise portion.)

_____

_____

_____

_____

Others

_____

_____

_____

_____

Choose another of the Shame/Identity belief groups in this week's lesson and write below the shame statements that fit for you:

_____

_____

Do the True Intimacy exercise for this group of Shame/Identity beliefs and write your actions and experience for each:

Self

_____

_____

_____

_____

God
(Recite the scriptures that relate to this belief from the lesson, then proceed with the remainder of the God exercise portion.)

_____

_____

_____

_____

Others

_____

_____

_____

_____

Day 6

1. Did you violate any Primary Boundaries in the last 24hrs?   Yes   No

If No, go to **#2**, If Yes, then complete the following:

What Boundary did you violate? _____

What events led up to the behavior?

_____

_____

What Secondary Boundaries did you violate leading up to the Primary?

_____

_____

2. Did you violate any Secondary Boundaries in the last 24hrs?   Yes   No

If No, go to **#3**, If Yes, then complete the following:

What Boundaries did you violate?

_____

_____

3. What **Gift of Self** did you perform in the last 24hrs?

_____

_____

Remember at this point in the program, we will stop tracking the below listed items. Although for your recovery and ongoing spiritual growth, these should be daily disciplined practices for the rest of your life.

- ✓ Prayer/meditation for 30 or more minutes per day.
- ✓ Read Scripture every day.
- ✓ Recite the 7 Cornerstones of Commitment.
- ✓ Recite the Surrender Prayer.
- ✓ Practice some type of intentional fast every day.

Day 6 continued:

4. Using 3-I's True Intimacy to Dismantle False Self

Choose one or more of the Shame/Identity belief groups in this week's lesson and write below the shame statements that fit for you:

_____

_____

Do the True Intimacy exercise for this group of Shame/Identity beliefs and write your actions and experience for each.

Self

_____

_____

_____

_____

God
(Recite the scriptures that relate to this belief from the lesson, then proceed with the remainder of the God exercise portion.)

_____

_____

_____

_____

Others

_____

_____

_____

_____

Choose another of the Shame/Identity belief groups in this week's lesson and write below the shame statements that fit for you:

_____

_____

Do the True Intimacy exercise for this group of Shame/Identity beliefs and write your actions and experience for each.

Self

_____

_____

_____

_____

God
(Recite the scriptures that relate to this belief from the lesson, then proceed with the remainder of the God exercise portion.)

_____

_____

_____

_____

Others

_____

_____

_____

_____

Day 7

1. Did you violate any Primary Boundaries in the last 24hrs?   Yes   No

> If No, go to **#2**, If Yes, then complete the following:
>
> What Boundary did you violate? _____
>
> What events led up to the behavior?
>
> _____
>
> _____
>
> What Secondary Boundaries did you violate leading up to the Primary?
>
> _____
>
> _____

2. Did you violate any Secondary Boundaries in the last 24hrs?   Yes   No

> If No, go to **#3**, If Yes, then complete the following:
>
> What Boundaries did you violate?
>
> _____
>
> _____

3. What **Gift of Self** did you perform in the last 24hrs?

_____

_____

Remember, at this point in the program, we will stop tracking the below listed items. Although for your recovery and ongoing spiritual growth, these should be daily disciplined practices for the rest of your life.

- ✓ Prayer/meditation for 30 or more minutes per day.
- ✓ Read Scripture every day.
- ✓ Recite the 7 Cornerstones of Commitment.
- ✓ Recite the Surrender Prayer.
- ✓ Practice some type of intentional fast every day.

Day 7 continued:

4. Using 3-I's True Intimacy to Dismantle False Self.

Choose one or more of the Shame/Identity belief groups in this week's lesson and write below the shame statements that fit for you:

_____

_____

Do the True Intimacy exercise for this group of Shame/Identity beliefs and write your actions and experience for each:

Self

_____

_____

_____

_____

God
(Recite the scriptures that relate to this belief from the lesson, then proceed with the remainder of the God exercise portion.)

_____

_____

_____

_____

Others

_____

_____

_____

_____

Choose another of the Shame/Identity belief groups in this week's lesson and write below the shame statements that fit for you:

_____

_____

Do the True Intimacy exercise for this group of Shame/Identity beliefs and write your actions and experiences for each:

Self

_____

_____

_____

_____

God
(Recite the scriptures that relate to this belief from the lesson, then proceed with the remainder of the God exercise portion.)

_____

_____

_____

_____

Others

_____

_____

_____

_____

There is no additional Weekly Action Guide this week.

Week 27 Sources of Wounds: Mother, Father, Historical Events

Meeting Protocol

Group Invocation of the Holy Spirit
"Come Holy Spirit, renew me, dwell in me and protect me"

Facilitator Leads the Group in Prayer

Confidentiality Bond – group recites together
"I _____ pledge to honor each person present or not present today in this group. I will do so by keeping all comments and discussions offered here today and at all future meetings confidential. I also pledge to keep the identity of all members confidential. I also pledge to make no statements of judgmental nature about anyone in this group, including myself."

Welcome New Members

Check-in Round 1: Feelings/Mood
Check-in Round 2: Significant event since last meeting (30-60 seconds)
Check-in Round 3: Temptation Rating (On a scale of 1–10; 1 a low temptation, 10 a high temptation)
Check-in Round 4: Primary or Secondary Boundary Violations
   If a Primary Violation occurred, the following questions/factors need to be addressed:
   ✓ **What do you think led to acting out?** – life events 24+ hours before
   ✓ **What were your feelings before acting out?**
   ✓ **Did you call anyone?**
   ✓ **What Secondary Boundaries did you violate this week?** – include those that were prior to your Primary Boundary Violation if you had one.
   ✓ **Group affirmation and acceptance of sharing.**
Check-in Round 5: Victories

Scripture Verse

Psalm 147:3 "He heals the brokenhearted, and binds up their wounds."

Group Discussion Question: How does this verse relate to your life and your battle with sexual sin?

Week 27 Recovery Foundation Lesson

In the past several weeks you have engaged in a significant effort at discovering and naming your shame and how it impacts your identity, as well as understanding the false self and learning paths to rewire the brain into true intimacy as originally designed by God.

While learning the lies of your beliefs about yourself and how they have led to unhealthy habits, this only aids in redirecting your behavior and learning new patterns. The truth is, each of these unhealthy or sinful habits and false beliefs are commonly rooted in emotional wounds that happened in earlier developmental times in your life. These events, at the time may not have been conscious. Also, looking back now, you can easily rationalize or justify the behavior of certain individuals, most commonly parents, that triggered the negative beliefs, or shame.

Here is an example of this:

Jim's father worked two jobs to make sure his family was properly taken care of. His three kids always had food on the table, their own bedrooms, and good clothes. Jim, now 35, would tell you that he had a good childhood and his relationship with his father was good and without events that would impact him in a negative way. However, Jim seems to be unable to explain his ongoing feelings of abandonment, unworthiness, and a general feeling of being unwanted. To put it simply, Jim doesn't feel loved. Jim also revealed that he feels he has an unreasonable attachment to forcing his family to be at home and together on Sunday – no matter the cost. In a deep examination of his childhood events, we find that as Jim's father worked his two jobs, he went directly from his day job to his evening job. Many times, his father also worked on Saturdays. Sunday was really the only time Jim had to see his father. In reflection, Jim discovered that he felt abandoned by his father because he only saw him one day a week. As a 5-year-old, he didn't understand that his father worked all the time as a sacrifice to make sure he was properly taken care of, so he developed the feelings of abandonment – thinking his father didn't want to be with him. These feelings naturally evolved into feelings of being unwanted and unworthy. Essentially, insignificance. Jim also transferred the Sunday that he did see his father to his own family requirement as a seemingly unjustified mandate for his own family to be together.

But now, at 35, how could he blame his father for these feelings, his negative self-worth, and his developed behaviors? His father did everything right for his family. Jim never even considered that his negative self-image partially stemmed from his father. Simply, all the five-year-old knew was that his father wasn't there, and it must be because he didn't want to be with him. Jim's father wasn't abusive, he wasn't neglectful – by all standards he was an outstanding father. But we see how even this "good" father experience resulted in significant woundedness. Many times, it is surprising how many of our significant beliefs of ourselves come from what seems like very minor experiences. As children, we are unable to logically rationalize behaviors of others. As children we are naturally very self-centered, and everything is about us or because of us.

Further to this example, it is extremely common for one or both parent to in some way express their own woundedness through their behaviors towards their children. A father who was actually abused by his father may be overly strict to his children, seemingly without cause. A mother who was told she wasn't worth anything by her own mother, may experience depression, withdraw in relationships and seem lazy to her husband and be uncaring to her children.

Now, beyond these typical and very common wounds that all of us have, are severe traumatic events. These can be anything from physical, emotional or spiritual abuse, to neglect, to serious events such as the divorce of parents or a death of one of your parents.

What follows is an outline of types of wounds, their typical impacts, and the resulting beliefs.

Father Wound

Common causes of woundedness from the father (many can be from the Mother, as well):

- **Neglect** – Father is self-focused (due to his own woundedness), his own addictions (alcohol, porn, drugs), depression, lack of supervision
- **Absence** – Divorce, separation, death, over-working, multiple jobs, travel
- **Abuse** – Mental, physical, sexual, spiritual – from anger, mental illness, lack of spiritual practice, excessive punishment or humiliating punishment, witness of abuse
- **Control** – Being oppressive, domination
- **Withholding** – Love and affirmation, these particular deficiencies lead to a profound lack of self-acceptance.

Any of these wounds can also result in possible gender confusion. These wounds serve to cause a broken role model and confusion, as the maturing male is seeking a model for his own identity and for his place in the world.

Low self-esteem or self-rejection is the most common result of both the father and the mother wound. Deep emotional pain and inner brokenness result, which often reveal themselves in some kind of performance orientation that makes us "doers" rather than "beings." Spiritual commitment and growth are a mandatory part of healing; however, this alone is not enough. God will use our commitment and connection to Him to reveal these wounds and the path toward healing them.

We tend to have four barriers that inhibit the healing of these wounds:

- **Pride** – No will to confront or change; "I'm alright"
- **Sin** – A blocked will that neither seeks to confess sin, nor to receive forgiveness
- **The wound itself** – Continuous emotional hurt inside
- **Lies** – Misconceptions about the Self, Birth Father, and God the Father.

Instead of going to the pain and receiving the healing we need, we tend to respond to life events by creating a misconception about our "Self." This is the false self and false identity that we have been working on for the past several sessions.

Relationship to our Birth Father

We discovered last week that several of these false self or false identity statements, essentially lies, are present in many of us. Most common are:

- I am unworthy
- I am unimportant
- I am stupid
- I am insignificant
- I am incompetent
- I am unloved or unlovable

As long as we accept these words *as truth*, we will likely experience depressed, anxious, and angry lives.

Relationship to God the Father

All too common, our experience with our birth fathers is translated to God the Father. When misconceptions about God are present (i.e., that He is angry, judgmental, unhappy with me, fearsome, legalistic, quick to punish and slow to forgive . . .) the identity that we tend to adopt is:

- I am not good enough
- I am not worthy
- I am guilty/shameful
- I must work harder to justify myself
- I must earn His love

When we accept these beliefs as truth, we will seek to perform and prove our worth through perfectionism and materialism. Recall previously, we defined shame as: "Shame looks to the outside for happiness and validation because the inside is flawed and defective."

Every person has a deep longing in their heart to hear from their father the same words Christ heard from His Father, "This is my beloved Son (or daughter), in whom I am well-pleased" (Matt 3:17; 17:5). It is a deep longing to know we have pleased our father.

The abandonment by the father, namely when the father is not in the picture at all, has very deep effects. Statistics from the **Fathers Unite Campaign at fathersunite.org** show that children from fatherless homes are:

- 5 times more likely to commit suicide
- 32 times more likely to run away
- 20 times more likely to have behavioral disorders
- 14 times more likely to commit rape
- 9 times more likely to drop out of high school
- 20 times more likely to end up in prison

In America we have a painful divorce rate of roughly 40-50 percent. Why is this? We have men growing up who don't know how to be husbands and fathers. We have women who are attempting to heal father issues with marriage, and think it is acceptable to remain in abusive relationships.

We have broken boys in the shells of men, leading broken relationships. We have wounded women looking for male approval in marriage. Many of these wounded women are looking to the broken men for approval. And when either of them can't get the love, approval and affirmation they so desperately need, they turn to fulfillment outside of the marriage.

Mother Wound

We all come into the world needing the tender presence of a mother's touch, nurture, care, and love. In fact, the mother's influence begins when we are in the womb. The absence of this mother love is a wound that is created in three ways:

- **Mother is separated from the child through:**
  - illness of the mother
  - mother's death
  - divorce

- **Child is separated from the mother through:**
  - illness of the child
  - incubator/hospitalization
  - adoption

- **Unhappy relationship with mother through:**
  - neglect
  - abuse
  - mother's mental and emotional distress
  - attempted abortion

When this motherly bond is interrupted, there are emotional consequences within the individual. These wounds reveal themselves as:

- Feelings of abandonment and dread of aloneness
- Loss of self and sense of being
- Powerful hunger for feminine touch that can be sexualized
- Emotional dependencies
- Possible gender confusion, fear, and insecurity

There are two main responses to a mother wound that affect one's ability to achieve healthy friendships and healthy married love:

- **Emotional detachment** – This defensive response to the breakdown in the mother's love causes a detachment from the mother. The legitimate need for love from the mother is repressed, leaving the child hungry but unable to secure relationships because of the emotional shutdown. The person fears the pain of attachment and therefore builds protective walls to hide behind.

- **Emotional dependency** – In this response, the person strives endlessly to fill the void, which often turns into co-dependency with grasping, clutching, and infantile tendencies. This striving for attachment is based in low self-confidence, fear, insecurity, and often confusion about self-worth.

Other Common Causes of Woundedness from the Mother

- **Lack of affection** - destroys the bonding necessary for a child to feel accepted, wanted, loved.

- **Rejection** – This is common when a mother's career is interrupted by an unplanned pregnancy, or as a single mother, or when a financial situation causes a child to be unwanted.

- **In the womb** – a mother may exhibit distress over an unwanted pregnancy, which studies show can be translated to the womb. Rejection in the infant, which is then carried forward to later life, is the most common manifestation of this.

Mother and father wounds can be present in both men and women. Common behavioral manifestations include:

- internalize a low view of women
- addictive, emotional and romantic dependencies
- infantile desire for union with women
- sexual confusion related to touch
- ambivalence towards women – need them but are very wary
- fixate on feminine objects of desire to fill the deprivation of mother love
- either detach or remain in toxic grip of a sinful alliance with mother
- sexual confusion related to touch
- separation anxiety that leads to striving, passivity, and depression
- fantasy bonding – attaching to fantasies
- fetish bonding – attaching to things, clothing, hair
- attachment to self – fantasy image of self
- emotional incest – meeting emotional needs of mother
- weak sense of identity and of one's being

Identities that are commonly adopted are:

- I am unworthy
- I am unimportant
- I am insignificant
- I am responsible for my own needs being met
- I am unwanted
- I am unlovable

Historical Wounds

While commonly the majority and deepest of wounds will result from events surrounding our mother or father, other sources can easily have a behavioral impact. These may include siblings, teachers, bosses, and other persons of authority such as scout leaders, group leaders, pastors, and civil leaders.

Common causes of woundedness from these individuals can be:

- Abuse – physical, verbal, sexual, or spiritual
- Control - being oppressive, domination
- Abandonment – leader leaving position, death, or illness

Revealing the Source

Up until now, you have been using the 3-I's exercise to reveal emotions and wounds that impact your behavior choices. A next step is during the true intimacy portion of the exercise, to ask the Holy Spirit to reveal the first time you experienced a particular emotion. Also, in that time of prayer and reflection, ask for any related memories and emotions that may be associated. Often times, we see a particular event as triggering a wound or emotional response when in reality, a closely related, almost displaced event actually had more impact on your response and ultimate emotional wound, and subsequent identity.

Feel free to use this prayer to help you start:

"Holy Spirit I ask You to come into my heart. I ask You to reveal to me the sources of my turmoil, my emotional and spiritual pain. I am experiencing feelings of_____ resulting from the event of _____. I ask You to bring forward memories of when in the past these same feelings were present. I ask You, Holy Spirit, to reveal to me the first time these emotions and feelings were present and who was present at that time, as well as the event that triggered these feelings and emotions. I surrender to You any fear and anxiety that arises from these past events and persons, as well as all current anxiety and fears that I am experiencing."

Here may be one example that could come up for you.

Your 3-I's exercise centered around the life event of your spouse criticizing you about not doing the dishes and not helping around the house enough. You determined that this event triggered emotions of rejection and belittlement, making you feel insignificant and incompetent. In prayer, the Holy Spirit reveals that your father frequently told you that you would never amount to anything and that you could never do anything right. Your spouse's criticism brings back old feelings of how your father made you feel.

Take the feelings that the past experience revealed to you, and the current experience, and offer them to Jesus Christ in your prayer.

Important distinction between the terms caused and triggered.

You will find in this and future lessons around sources of wounds that the term "triggered" is used rather than "caused." This is intentional. It is an important perspective to view the emotional wounds that you carry as your own, and your own choice to hold on to. It is a dangerous perspective to think of another person "causing" you to feel a certain way. This point of view takes the responsibility away from you and places it on someone else. This in effect lets you "off the hook" from being responsible for your behavior resulting from your wounds. This makes healing the wound and its resulting damage much more difficult, and in many cases can make it nearly impossible. Taking ownership of the reaction of the wound, particularly when you come to realize its source, is key to forgiveness as well as healing that wound and the ability to ultimately surrender it to Christ.

Group Questions

Reflecting back on the shame statements and identity work you did a few lessons ago,

- ✓ What wounds did your Father trigger in you?

- ✓ What events do you remember that resulted in these wounds?

- ✓ What wounds did your Mother trigger in you?

- ✓ What events do you remember that resulted in these wounds?

Meeting Close
Check Out
What do you need? – 5 min
Is there anything the group can offer any member?
- – *Prayers*
- – *Phone calls/texts*
- – *Private meeting*
- – *Ride to meetings*
- – *Etc.*

Closing Prayers

Week 27 Homework

In the 3-I's exercise, you will see an added section for "***Revealing the Source.***"
Using the Holy Spirit prayer, include this new part in your 3-I's exercise:

"Holy Spirit I ask You to come into my heart. I ask You to reveal to me the sources of my turmoil, my emotional and spiritual pain. I am experiencing feelings of_____ resulting from the event of _____. I ask You to bring forward memories of when in the past these same feelings were present. I ask You, Holy Spirit, to reveal to me the first time these emotions and feelings were present and who was present at that time, as well as the event that triggered these feelings and emotions. I surrender to You any fear and anxiety that arises from these past events and persons, as well as all current anxiety and fears that I am experiencing."

Week 27 Recovery Action Guide

Daily Action Guide

(next page)

Use the chart for reference while doing your homework.

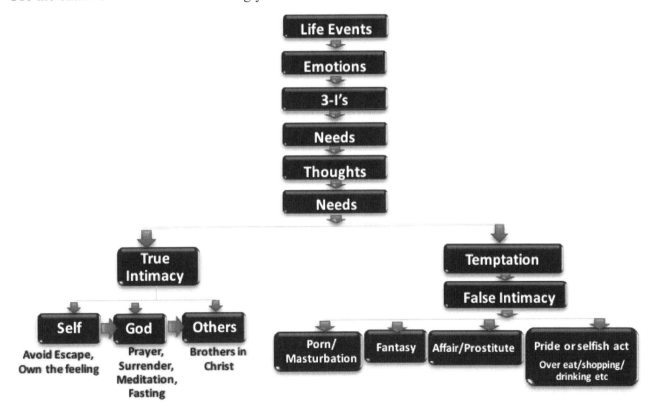

Day 1

1. Did you violate any Primary Boundaries in the last 24hrs?   Yes   No

   If No, go to **#2**, If Yes, then complete the following:

   What Boundary did you violate? _____

   What events led up to the behavior?

   _____

   _____

   What Secondary Boundaries did you violate leading up to the Primary?

   _____

   _____

2. Did you violate any Secondary Boundaries in the last 24hrs?   Yes   No

   If No, go to **#3**, If Yes, then complete the following:

   What Boundaries did you violate?

   _____

   _____

3. What **Gift of Self** did you perform in the last 24hrs?

   _____

   _____

Remember to continue these practices in your daily routine:

   ✓ Prayer/meditation for 30 or more minutes per day.
   ✓ Read Scripture every day.
   ✓ Recite the 7 Cornerstones of Commitment.
   ✓ Recite the Surrender Prayer.
   ✓ Practice some type of intentional fast every day.

Day 1 continued:

4. 3-I's Evaluation of a Daily Event

There will be an event EVERY day. Big or small. Anything from the Starbucks barista who was rude to you, to your car breaking down, to your spouse leaving you. Any level. Any of these events created an emotion that resulted in a reaction on your part. Anything from simple anger or frustration to a sinful behavior. Find it, pray about it, and document it.

Day 1: Describe the event that happened

_____

_____

Name the emotions that were revealed: _____

Revealing the Source: *When was the first time in your life (possibly childhood) when you recall these emotions and what was the event that triggered them? (pray the Holy Spirit prayer for guidance)*

_____

_____

Name the 3-I emotions that were related: _____

What behavior was engaged in after this event and emotions happened?

_____

_____

Was this an expression of True Intimacy or False Intimacy? _____

If False Intimacy was chosen:
(a) Describe where in the process you could have made a different decision and followed True Intimacy. (Event, Thought, Emotions, 3-I's, Needs, etc.)

_____

_____

And:
(b) What True intimacy steps would you have personally engaged in? Can you do it now?

Self _____

God _____

Others _____

Day 1 continued:

OR

If True Intimacy was chosen:
(a) What True Intimacy steps did you engage in?

Self
_____

God
_____

Others
_____

Day 2

1. Did you violate any Primary Boundaries in the last 24hrs?   Yes   No

    If No, go to **#2,** If Yes, then complete the following:

    What Boundary did you violate? _____

    What events led up to the behavior?

    _____

    _____

    What Secondary Boundaries did you violate leading up to the Primary?

    _____

    _____

2. Did you violate any Secondary Boundaries in the last 24hrs?   Yes   No

    If No, go to **#3,** If Yes, then complete the following:

    What Boundaries did you violate?

    _____

    _____

3. What **Gift of Self** did you perform in the last 24hrs?

    _____

    _____

4. 3-I's Evaluation of a Daily Event *(Remember, big or small event. Find it, pray about it, document it.)*

    Describe the event that happened:

    _____

    _____

    Name the emotions that were revealed: _____

Day 2 continued:

Revealing the Source: When was the first time in your life (possibly childhood) when you recall these emotions and what was the event that triggered them? (pray the Holy Spirit prayer for guidance)

_____

_____

Name the 3-I emotions that were related: _____

What behavior was engaged in after this event and emotions happened?

_____

_____

Was this an expression of True Intimacy or False Intimacy? _____

If False Intimacy was chosen:

(a) Describe where in the process you could have made a different decision and followed True Intimacy. (Event, Thought, Emotions, 3-I's, Needs, etc.)

_____

_____

And:

(b) What True Intimacy steps would you have personally engaged in? Can you do it now?

Self _____

God _____

Others _____

OR

If True Intimacy was chosen:

(a) What True Intimacy steps did you engage in?

Self _____

God _____

Others _____

Day 3

1. Did you violate any Primary Boundaries in the last 24hrs?   Yes   No

If No, go to **#2,** If Yes, then complete the following:

What Boundary did you violate? _____

What events led up to the behavior?

_____

_____

What Secondary Boundaries did you violate leading up to the Primary?

_____

_____

2. Did you violate any Secondary Boundaries in the last 24hrs?   Yes   No

If No, go to **#3**, If Yes, then complete the following:

What Boundaries did you violate?

_____

_____

3. What **Gift of Self** did you perform in the last 24hrs?

_____

_____

4. 3-I's Evaluation of a Daily Event *(Remember, big or small event. Find it, pray about it, document it.)*

Describe the event that happened

_____

_____

Name the emotions that were revealed: _____

Day 3 continued:

Revealing the Source: When was the first time in your life (possibly childhood) when you recall these emotions and what was the event that triggered them? (pray the Holy Spirit Prayer for guidance)

_____

_____

Name the 3-I emotions that were related: _____

What behavior was engaged in after this event and emotions happened?

_____

_____

Was this an expression of True Intimacy or False Intimacy? _____

__If False Intimacy was chosen:__
(a) Describe where in the process you could have made a different decision and followed True Intimacy. (Event, Thought, Emotions, 3-I's, Needs, etc.)

_____

_____

And:
(b) What True Intimacy steps would you have personally engaged in? Can you do it now?

Self _____

God _____

Others _____

OR

__If True Intimacy was chosen__:
(a) What True Intimacy steps did you engage in?

Self _____

God _____

Others _____

Day 4

1. Did you violate any Primary Boundaries in the last 24hrs?   Yes   No

    If No, go to **#2,** If Yes, then complete the following:

    What Boundary did you violate? _____

    What events led up to the behavior?

    _____

    _____

    What Secondary Boundaries did you violate leading up to the Primary?

    _____

    _____

2. Did you violate any Secondary Boundaries in the last 24hrs?   Yes   No

    If No, go to **#3**, If Yes, then complete the following:

    What Boundaries did you violate?

    _____

    _____

3. What **Gift of Self** did you perform in the last 24hrs?

_____

_____

4. 3-I's Evaluation of a Daily Event *(Remember, big or small event. Find it, pray about it, document it)*

    Describe the event that happened:

    _____

    _____

    Name the emotions that were revealed: _____

Day 4 continued:

    ***Revealing the Source*:** When was the first time in your life (possibly childhood) when you recall these emotions and what was the event that triggered them? (pray the Holy Spirit Prayer for guidance)

_____

_____

Name the 3-I emotions that were related: _____

What behavior was engaged in after this event and emotions happened?

_____

_____

Was this an expression of True Intimacy or False Intimacy? _____

If False Intimacy was chosen:

(a) Describe where in the process you could have made a different decision and followed True Intimacy. (Event, Thought, Emotions, 3-I's, Needs, etc.)

_____

_____

And:

(b) What True Intimacy steps would you have personally engaged in? Can you do it now?

Self _____

God _____

Others _____

OR

If True Intimacy was chosen:

(a) What True Intimacy steps did you engage in?

Self _____

God _____

Others _____

Day 5

1. Did you violate any Primary Boundaries in the last 24hrs?   Yes   No

    If No, go to **#2,** If Yes, then complete the following:

    What Boundary did you violate? _____

    What events led up to the behavior?

    _____

    _____

    What Secondary Boundaries did you violate leading up to the Primary?

    _____

    _____

2. Did you violate any Secondary Boundaries in the last 24hrs?   Yes   No

    If No, go to **#3**, If Yes, then complete the following:

    What Boundaries did you violate?

    _____

    _____

3. What **Gift of Self** did you perform in the last 24hrs?

_____

_____

4. 3-I's Evaluation of a Daily Event *(Remember, big or small event. Find it, pray about it, document it.)*

    Describe the event that happened:

    _____

    _____

    Name the emotions that were revealed: _____

Day 5 continued:

    ***Revealing the Source*:** When was the first time in your life (possibly childhood) when you recall these emotions and what was the event that triggered them? (pray the Holy Spirit Prayer for guidance)

_____

_____

Name the 3-I emotions that were related: _____

What behavior was engaged in after this event and emotions happened?

_____

_____

Was this an expression of True Intimacy or False Intimacy? _____

If False Intimacy was chosen:
(a) Describe where in the process you could have made a different decision and followed True Intimacy. (Event, Thought, Emotions, 3-I's, Needs, etc.)

_____

_____

And:
(b) What True Intimacy steps would you have personally engaged in? Can you do it now?

Self _____

God _____

Others _____

_OR_

If True Intimacy was chosen:
(a) What True Intimacy steps did you engage in?

Self _____

God _____

Others _____

Day 6

1. Did you violate any Primary Boundaries in the last 24hrs?   Yes   No

   If No, go to **#2,** If Yes, then complete the following:

What Boundary did you violate? _____

What events led up to the behavior?

_____

_____

What Secondary Boundaries did you violate leading up to the Primary?

_____

_____

2. Did you violate any Secondary Boundaries in the last 24hrs?   Yes   No

If No, go to **#3**, If Yes, then complete the following:

What Boundaries did you violate?

_____

_____

3. What **Gift of Self** did you perform in the last 24hrs?

_____

_____

4. 3-I's Evaluation of a Daily Event *(Remember, big or small event. Find it, pray about it, document it.)*

Describe the event that happened:

_____

_____

Name the emotions that were revealed: _____

Day 6 continued:

Revealing the Source: When was the first time in your life (possibly childhood) when you recall these emotions and what was the event that triggered them? (pray the Holy Spirit Prayer for guidance)

Name the 3-I emotions that were related: _____

What behavior was engaged in after this event and emotions happened?

Was this an expression of True Intimacy or False Intimacy? _____

If False Intimacy was chosen:
(a) Describe where in the process you could have made a different decision and followed True Intimacy. (Event, Thought, Emotions, 3-I's, Needs, etc.)

And:
(b) What True Intimacy steps would you have personally engaged in? Can you do it now?

Self _____

God _____

Others _____

OR

If True Intimacy was chosen:
(a) What True Intimacy steps did you engage in?

Self _____

God _____

Others _____

Day 7

1. Did you violate any Primary Boundaries in the last 24hrs?   Yes   No

      If No, go to **#2,** If Yes, then complete the following:

      What Boundary did you violate? _____

      What events led up to the behavior?

      _____

      _____

      What Secondary Boundaries did you violate leading up to the Primary?

      _____

      _____

2. Did you violate any Secondary Boundaries in the last 24hrs?   Yes   No

      If No, go to **#3**, If Yes, then complete the following:

      What Boundaries did you violate?

      _____

      _____

3. What **Gift of Self** did you perform in the last 24hrs?

_____

_____

4. 3-I's Evaluation of a Daily Event *(Remember, big or small event. Find it, pray about it, document it.)*

    Describe the event that happened:

    _____

    _____

    Name the emotions that were revealed: _____

Day 7 continued:

    ***Revealing the Source*:** When was the first time in your life (possibly childhood) when you recall these emotions and what was the event that triggered them? (pray the Holy Spirit Prayer for guidance)

_____

_____

Name the 3-I emotions that were related: _____

What behavior was engaged in after this event and emotions happened?

_____

_____

Was this an expression of True Intimacy or False Intimacy? _____

If False Intimacy was chosen:
(a) Describe where in the process you could have made a different decision and followed True Intimacy. (Event, Thought, Emotions, 3-I's, Needs, etc.)

_____

_____

And:
(b) What True Intimacy steps would you have personally engaged in? Can you do it now?

Self _____

God _____

Others _____

OR

If True Intimacy was chosen:
(a) What True Intimacy steps did you engage in?

Self _____

God _____

Others _____

Weekly Action Guide

Appendix G Work

Follow the exercise in **Week 27** of **Appendix G**.

Week 28 Affirmation and Denial

Meeting Protocol

Group Invocation of the Holy Spirit
"Come Holy Spirit, renew me, dwell in me and protect me"

Facilitator Leads the Group in Prayer

Confidentiality Bond – group recites together
"I _____ pledge to honor each person present or not present today in this group. I will do so by keeping all comments and discussions offered here today and at all future meetings confidential. I also pledge to keep the identity of all members confidential. I also pledge to make no statements of judgmental nature about anyone in this group, including myself."

Welcome New Members

Check-in Round 1: Feelings/Mood
Check-in Round 2: Significant event since last meeting (30-60 seconds)
Check-in Round 3: Temptation Rating (On a scale of 1–10; 1 a low temptation, 10 a high temptation)
Check-in Round 4: Primary or Secondary Boundary Violations
   If a Primary Violation occurred, the following questions/factors need to be addressed:
   ✓ **What do you think led to acting out?** – life events 24+ hours before
   ✓ **What were your feelings before acting out?**
   ✓ **Did you call anyone?**
   ✓ **What Secondary Boundaries did you violate this week?** – include those that were prior to your Primary Boundary Violation if you had one.
   ✓ **Group affirmation and acceptance of sharing.**
Check-in Round 5: Victories

Scripture Verse

Psalm 34:18 "The Lord is near to the brokenhearted and saves the crushed in spirit."

Group Discussion Question: How does this verse relate to your life and your battle with sexual sin?

Week 28 Recovery Foundation Lesson

Understanding the Roots of our Pain

Thus far, you have done a tremendous amount of work discovering the sources of your woundedness. You have worked on processes to translate that pain to authentic intimacy, and to avoid old false intimacy paths of behavior. Knowing these truths about your pain and how they impact your life and identity is an important part of your growth and recovery from not only sexual sin but all types of unhealthy behaviors.

The question so many ask, is why do these events in my life cause me to be this way? The answer goes back to what we have stated before: God created mankind to love and to be loved. In the execution of this sole truth, God created us male and female, to be joined as one flesh under God (marriage) – this three-person union is a reflection of the Holy Trinity. Then to exercise the human mechanics of this union, the marital union, or sex, when engaged in, invites God to co-create a third person – a child. Again – a reflection of the Holy Trinity. In this sexual act, the woman (wife) completely empties herself and gives herself to the man (husband). Simultaneously, the man (husband) completely empties himself and gives himself to the woman (wife).

Consider this, when a woman trusts you so much that she can be completely transparent to you, empty herself to you, and offer her body, essentially herself and her very being to you as a free gift – you feel completely accepted, wanted, valued, trusted, desired – you are loved! You feel affirmed. When you experience this, you can't help but to give back in the say way! To love! To return affirmation.

This is the pinnacle experience of love. This is the experience that God intends for us. Unfortunately, for most of us, by the time we find our spouses and enter the married state, we are too wounded to be able to empty and give of ourselves in this way. We cannot be fully transparent and offer the level of trust required for this union in the way God designed.

Affirmation

The authentic experience of God in our lives, to love and be loved, is revealed through affirmation. Complete and unconditional acceptance of you as a person.

You have come far enough in this program that you can see that porn is not affirmation. It is not acceptance of you as a person. It is so far from the love God intends for you that it's not even accurate to call porn counterfeit love. It's simply a selfish act that grossly abuses the intent of God. You can't give yourself to the person on the screen, you can only take. This complete perversion of the gifts of love that God intends for us leaves us empty, guilty, shameful, and literally feeling dirty as if we just ate from the dumpster! It's because we did! – the diabolic spiritual dumpster! Our woundedness, our shame, our false identities, and our false self all have us believing the lies that this is all we deserve. So, we accept it.

In past weeks, we've revealed the sources of the pain and woundedness that trigger this perversion of ourselves. It's now time to reveal where they actually went bad.

For true and authentic healing, we need to recognize the root of our woundedness. Not just the events, but where our experience of the love of God broke down.

The evidence of this love, or lack of evidence of love, is revealed in affirmation or denial.

To be truly affirmed, we must be accepted as worthwhile and loveable precisely as we are. However we so often hear statements from parents, siblings, teachers, and others such as, "I recognize that Johnny is talented – *despite his shortcomings,*" or, "I recognize that Timmy is smart – *he just needs to apply himself more,*" or, "I think it's great that Charles got a B in his math class, *let's try for an A next time,*" or, "Tim gets A's in school, *but I give him an 'F' at cleaning his room.*" These "follow up" statements all negate the affirmation. These statements imply conditional acceptance and love. They tell the child, that he would be good enough IF…. This is in fact, denial.

God loves us in a full and unconditional way. He loves us right where we are. The only "follow up" statement from God is that he desires us to be free of our brokenness so we can more fully receive His love. Since God loves us already, in a full and unconditional way, He desires us to be free of anything that inhibits us receiving His love, namely brokenness and sin. This is why the True Intimacy path of the 3-I's exercise has God in the center. He is the one we need most and He is the one Who can reveal our authentic selves as He created, and He is the one Who can love us as we were created and love us right where we are.

Intimacy

All the building blocks of intimacy that we learned about in Week 13 are the human way to express this love, albeit in our limited human capacity. When spending time with those close to you – spouse, significant others, friends, even co-workers – remember to review the building blocks of intimacy so you can intentionally offer healthy and authentic intimacy to others (Hint: this is another Gift of Self activity).

Denial

Three stories:

Steve, who was a successful businessman, suffered from deep feelings of inferiority, inadequacy and insignificance. Steve was never loved by his mother. She had hated him from the day she failed to abort him with a coat hanger. His mother frequently had rages of anger and frequently neglected Steve.

Jeff suffered from extreme depression and had several unsuccessful suicide attempts. Jeff felt unknown and unaccepted. Jeff's mother was an overbearing woman. His childhood involved his mother always making sure every need was met, making sure he ate everything on his plate and never letting him play with his friends for fear he would get hurt. She even rewarded him when he played in the back yard and kept his clothes clean. Jeff suffered from smothering love and from not being allowed to become his own person.

Maurice was primarily raised by an assortment of babysitters. His mother was an actress and was never home, and his father was a prominent international attorney and was constantly traveling. Maurice suffered from detachment disorder and severe anxiety resulting in depression.

Steve, Jeff, and Maurice's formative years can best be described by denial. While these examples are fairly severe levels of denial, all of us experience denial at some level. This denial simply denies us the basic need of authentic love and affirmation. A love that God designed us for. In the absence of affirmation, we are left empty with no choice but to adopt identities that justify the denial. These are primarily the shame statements identified in Week 19. You can agree that neither Steve, Jeff, nor Maurice deserved the childhood denial that they received. Yet, they adopted significant self-images or identities of inferiority, inadequacy, unworthiness, abandonment and more. A variety of this happens to every single one of us!

Recall **Week 18, "The River Under the River."** You searched for why you behave the way you do. You found the wounds from the past in your lives. Now, look at the "river under the river" of those who denied you. Parents, siblings, pastors, teachers, etc. You can see that you didn't deserve or earn this denial of Godly love and affirmation. They were working from their own brokenness. You weren't affirmed because they weren't affirmed and therefore, they didn't know how to affirm you or what it even means. So, by default, you were denied. This is the crux of generational sin. But since God wired you to be loved, you MUST have it! And if you don't get it from someone else, you will look for it and even create it. And since you likely were never brought up to have a strong and healthy relationship with God, you will accept every counterfeit offer presented to you because you are so desperate and hungry for what God created you for, and what everyone else denied you of. Your woundedness literally blinds you into counterfeit offerings of love.

This denial of love, though mostly unintentional, is at first look, responsible for your shame and brokenness. BUT, now knowing this, you have a choice to take responsibility for your reaction to this denial. You now have the choice to accept ownership of the shame you bear. Hence the "SELF" step in the True Intimacy path of the 3-I's exercise. This ownership gives you the power to give it away, thus surrendering it: surrendering to Christ who paid for all your shame and brokenness with His blood on the cross. In a manner of speaking, He already paid for it, so He owns it! So, give it to Him! The meditation you do in the 3-I's along with the Surrender Prayer you say every day in your homework, is practicing precisely that! But now you have a clearer perspective on the roots of your shame and brokenness, and the actions you can take, or already are taking, to rid yourself of the only thing holding you back from receiving God's full love and Grace.

Being Open to Accept Your Authentic Identity

"In order to be yourself, you must first become yourself. In order to become yourself, you must first receive the gift of yourself. In order to receive this gift, there has to be another who gives, who gives without taking, without demanding anything, who gives you what is not his or her own, but yours, your own goodness." – Conrad Baars – Born Only Once

This perfect one Who can only give completely without taking or demanding, is God. To rest in who you truly are, who you were created to be, without developed ideals, without need to be what you expect others want you to be, is to be authentically you. This is your pure identity. When you are who you were created to be, you accept love in perfect form. And because you can receive perfect love without expectation, you, being created in the image of God, by default, can give back this love to those around you.

Shedding the false identity, the false self that has developed over so many years, allows you to not only finally have internal peace, but to properly love others: Love others as Christ first loved us.

What to Do

In the True Intimacy path of 3-I's meditation is one step: choose to "be" with Christ, let Him sink in, then after you receive Him, step out and "do." Do for others, be a "gift of self," let Christ flow through you.

Become aware of the negative voice. Stop letting it redirect you. When someone says they love you, deny the negative thoughts of, "would they still love me if they really knew me?" This thought pattern is NOT you, it is NOT what God created, therefore treat it as if it is from another outside source – a source whose only interest is to make you self-focused, self-interested, and to turn your back on the Grace that God is embracing you with. Stop it! Let yourself be loved. Give permission to be loved. Accept the love that God and others have for you. Not only have others in your formative years denied you the proper affirmation, but by entertaining these negative thoughts you deny yourself the affirmation that IS being offered by others and, most importantly, by GOD!

Don't Forget the Process

When this negative voice tells you something, remember to:

- **SELF:** Be with it, allow it to speak, see it for what it truly is – as Not from God.

- **GOD:** Recognize this is not who you were created to be and surrender it to God; it's not yours anyway. It is a perversion and contamination of God's creation – you.
  Meditate on this, spend time with God/Christ – use imagery that shows you allowing Christ to love you. Take this time to simply "be" with Him. Accept His Grace and love. Allow God to show you the goodness that he has instilled in you. (It IS there, 100% guaranteed!)

- **OTHERS:** Have a discussion about this experience with a close friend or accountability partner.

The "WOW" Realization

In time, maybe months, maybe years, you will find that you will be having conversations with your accountability partner or close friends about discovering roots of feelings, events you discovered in the past or ones that happened that day, and conversations or experiences with God, rather than continually reaching out to your accountability partner because you are tempted.

Group Questions

✓ Reflecting on your childhood, describe an event where you were denied affirmation. What shame was triggered and what identity statement best describes the result of this event?

✓ What *authentic self* do you see when these lies are shed and surrendered to Jesus?

Meeting Close
Check Out
What do you need? – 5 min
Is there anything the group can offer any member?
– *Prayers*
– *Phone calls/texts*
– *Private meeting*
– *Ride to meetings*
– *Etc.*

Closing Prayers

Week 28 Homework

Journaling Questions

Meditate on each scripture verse below and journal on anything that the Holy Spirit inspires within you.

The Lord will rescue those whose spirits are crushed

Psalm 34:18 "The Lord is near to the brokenhearted, and saves the crushed in spirit."

It is not difficult for Jesus to heal the sick

Matthew 8:16-17 "That evening they brought to him many who were possessed with demons; and he cast out the spirits with a word, and cured all who were sick. This was to fulfill what had been spoken through the prophet Isaiah, "He took our infirmities and bore our diseases.""

By His wounds I am healed

1 Peter 2:24 "He himself bore our sins in his body on the cross, so that, free from sins, we might live for righteousness; by his wounds you have been healed."

Week 28 Recovery Action Guide

Daily Action Guide

Catch Up

For this week, go back to any days of the previous weeks and finish missing work. Also continue with any additional work in any of the **Appendix G** exercises. There are no additional Daily Guide exercises this week.

Week 29 Forgiveness

Meeting Protocol

Group Invocation of the Holy Spirit
"Come Holy Spirit, renew me, dwell in me and protect me"

Facilitator Leads the Group in Prayer

Confidentiality Bond – group recites together
"I _____ pledge to honor each person present or not present today in this group. I will do so by keeping all comments and discussions offered here today and at all future meetings confidential. I also pledge to keep the identity of all members confidential. I also pledge to make no statements of judgmental nature about anyone in this group, including myself."

Welcome New Members

Check-in Round 1: Feelings/Mood
Check-in Round 2: Significant event since last meeting (30-60 seconds)
Check-in Round 3: Temptation Rating (On a scale of 1–10; 1 a low temptation, 10 a high temptation)
Check-in Round 4: Primary or Secondary Boundary Violations
   If a Primary Violation occurred, the following questions/factors need to be addressed:
   ✓ **What do you think led to acting out?** – life events 24+ hours before
   ✓ **What were your feelings before acting out?**
   ✓ **Did you call anyone?**
   ✓ **What Secondary Boundaries did you violate this week?** – include those that were prior to your Primary Boundary Violation if you had one.
   ✓ **Group affirmation and acceptance of sharing.**
Check-in Round 5: Victories

Scripture Verse

Ephesians 4:31-32 "Put away from you all bitterness and wrath and anger and wrangling and slander, together with all malice, and be kind to one another, tenderhearted, forgiving one another, as God in Christ has forgiven you."

Group Discussion Question: How does this verse relate to your life and your battle with sexual sin?

Week 29 Recovery Foundation Lesson

Discovering shame, surrounding false self-images and false identities, resolving denial and affirmation, and the tools you have learned to guide you through this are all powerful steps in your healing and growth. A final step, however, is required to finalize this healing process. This last step is perhaps the most important. It is forgiveness. Without forgiveness, the roots that triggered all your woundedness and related issues will continue to plague you for the rest of your life. Unforgiveness ties you to the original source and will act like a tether to the events that led to your life of misery and addiction.

Forgiveness is not about forgetting what the other person did. Forgiveness does not excuse their behavior. It's not about giving that person permission to do what they did again. Forgiveness also does not mean there are not consequences. For example, if someone sexually abuses you, you can pursue legal action while still forgiving the individual in your heart. Forgiveness is about releasing the person who wronged you from having power over you. It's about freeing you from a heart of bitterness and resentment. A telltale sign that forgiveness is not complete is if the memory of what that person did still brings up deep emotions. This is a sign that you are being held captive by that person or their actions. Memories of events and natural emotions are expected, but when these memories affect your life, your behavior, in other areas, then the experience still has a hold on you. Forgiveness cuts that person loose from having that effect on you. When full and authentic forgiveness happens, you will experience peace. In many instances, people who forgive those who have done something that traumatized them, like sexual abuse or emotional abuse, and they later reflect on these actions, will have compassion and sympathy for the pain and emotional bondage their abuser experienced, which caused them to behave in this manner.

It is important to know that in most cases when serious wrongs have been committed, a "one and done" forgiveness statement isn't enough. Wounds run deep within each of us. When an addictive behavior is present, it commonly signifies that something is painful enough to bring about this behavior – in order to medicate the deep-rooted pain. Forgiveness of such a wound will likely take time. In some cases, years. Repeating the forgiveness statement in your journal will begin the process. If this forgiveness hasn't begun to take place, then it will be very difficult to become completely free of your addiction.

Science of Forgiveness

"Resentment and unforgiveness is like drinking poison and expecting the other person to die."

– Author unknown

Science shows a connection between forgiveness and spiritual, mental, and physical health. When someone holds on to resentment, hostility, and anger against another person for any length of time, it eventually begins to manifest itself in the person's health with elevated stress hormones (cortisol). These hormones are found to increase psychological distress, hostility, restlessness, sadness, and depression. When we fail to offer forgiveness, it's common to experience the physical results of higher blood pressure, increased heart risk, and a poor immune system.

Revealing the painful memories and healing the historical source of the triggering emotions of your behaviors prove to be the path to true freedom.

Forgiveness of Self

All the rules about forgiveness are doubly true when it comes to forgiveness of self. Many addicts experience such guilt about their addictions that forgiving themselves is the last thing they think about. Try saying a forgiveness statement with yourself—that is, forgiving yourself.

Note from author:

After years of recovery, I felt the forgiveness of God as well as of my wife. But I came to realize that I had not yet forgiven myself. Forgiving myself for all the damage I caused to my family and the families of those I had affairs with were only part of the problem. For much of my life, I actually believed that my mother loved me because she was supposed to, not because I was worthy of it. I believed that there was something wrong with me and I didn't deserve her love. By believing this, I created emotional distance from all those in my life—parents, spouse, kids, and especially God, as I believed I wasn't worthy of anyone's love. It wasn't until I realized that I needed to forgive myself for believing this lie (and it was a lie for me, just as it is for you if you believe this about yourself) that I began to get free of the deepest root of all. It was also explained to me by a priest that since God has forgiven me for all I had done that if I didn't' forgive myself, that essentially means I am putting myself above God. This becomes a sin of pride because I believe that my sins are greater than God's mercy. WOW! Was that insight enlightening! We are called to accept God's mercy and to forgive ourselves.

Jesus came so that we may be forgiven of our sins and be redeemed in His blood. Scripture is full of verses about the absolute need of forgiveness.

RESTORING GOD'S FOUNATION • 255

Here are several scripture verses on forgiveness:

- **Colossians 3:13** "Bear with one another and, if anyone has a complaint against another, forgive each other; just as the Lord has forgiven you, so you also must forgive."

- **Matthew 6:14-15** "For if you forgive others their trespasses, your heavenly Father will also forgive you; but if you do not forgive others, neither will your Father forgive your trespasses."

- **Luke 17:3-4** "Be on your guard! If another disciple sins, you must rebuke the offender, and if there is repentance, you must forgive. And if the same person sins against you seven times a day, and turns back to you seven times and says, 'I repent,' you must forgive."

- **Ephesians 4:31-32** "Put away from you all bitterness and wrath and anger and wrangling and slander, together with all malice, and be kind to one another, tenderhearted, forgiving one another, as God in Christ has forgiven you."

- **Hebrews 10:17** "I will remember their sins and their lawless deeds no more."

- **Mark 11:25** "Whenever you stand praying, forgive, if you have anything against anyone; so that your Father in heaven may also forgive you your trespasses."

Practicing Forgiveness

So often we rationalize or justify the behavior of those who hurt us. We look at the events from our adult perspective. Quite frequently, this perspective also prevents us from even recognizing the event that caused a wound.

Here is an example:

Austin had a history of alcohol abuse, regular porn use and multiple affairs. Austin felt a deep need for acceptance and seemed to have an underlying fear of abandonment. He also felt a defeating sense of unworthiness and feeling unwanted. In first speaking to Austin about his childhood and family, he spoke very highly of his father; he always spoke of how well his father took care of the family, always made sure all the kids had everything they needed – enough food, a nice house, good clothes, etc. Austin spoke of how his dad worked two jobs for as long as he could remember, to be a good provider. His father worked as a police officer in the day and a security guard for a second job. Austin, as an adult, justified his father's commitment to providing for the family. In further counseling, it was discovered that the small 5-year-old little boy inside Austin didn't understand why his father was never home, why his father couldn't make his school plays or band concerts, even when he was older. This left him with feelings of abandonment, rejection and general feelings that his father didn't want to be with him – unworthiness.

Austin's father was not malicious, he was not abusive and did an excellent job of taking care of every temporal need of the family. But to a 5-year-old, this didn't matter. This deeply wounded Austin. To break this bond of woundedness, Austin needs to forgive his father. This may seem silly since Austin's father didn't do anything wrong. Although, his actions, while unintentional and responsibly motivated, left Austin wounded, nonetheless. These wounds need healed.

Forgiveness of Austin's wounds would look something like this:

*Lord, I choose to forgive my **FATHER** for the action of **WORKING TWO JOBS AND NOT BEING THERE FOR ME**, which triggered me to feel **REJECTED, ABANDONED, WORTHLESS AND UN-WANTED**. I release this person from any power he or she holds over me in generating my hurt feelings. Lord, I give you permission to take the judgment and the bitterness out of my life. I surrender it to You and ask You to remove it and to heal me where I have been wounded. I surrender my right to be paid back for my loss by the one who sinned against me, and by doing so I declare my trust in God alone as my Righteous Judge.*

*Lord, I ask for your forgiveness in my choosing to react to this person, resulting in my actions of **CHOOSING ALCOHOL TO SOOTHE MY PAIN, CHOOSING IMMORAL SEXUAL BEHAVIORS TO SUBSTITUTE LOVE**, and I choose to **FORGIVE MYSELF** for reacting this way.*

In Jesus' name, Amen.

Whether the wounds are triggered by severe trauma, or abuse by another individual, or something completely passive as with Austin, they are significant to the wounded person. The individuals and events that triggered the emotional wounds need to be forgiven and the tie of damage severed.

Implementation of Forgiveness in the True Intimacy Path

The below text describes what you will now be adding to your homework.

After completing the **Self, God,** and **Others** steps of True Intimacy, add the below exercise and prayer to the process:

Ask yourself, "Which individuals connected to the life events I just explored, either from my current life or from the past, can I forgive for the way they acted or behaved toward me?" If possible, sit in front of the Blessed Sacrament and ask Jesus to reveal to you all those who have hurt you in your life.

After reflecting on this, list those you can forgive by name: _____, _____,

_____, _____, _____.

You will then pray the following forgiveness prayer for each person, one at a time.

Lord, I choose to forgive _____ for the action of _____ that triggered me to feel _____. I release this person from any power he or she holds over me in generating my hurt feelings. Lord, I give you permission to take the judgment and the bitterness out of my life. I surrender it to You and ask You to remove it and to heal me where I have been wounded. I surrender my right to be paid back for my loss by the one who sinned against me, and by doing so I declare my trust in God alone as my Righteous Judge.

Lord, I ask for your forgiveness in my choosing to react to this person, resulting in my actions of _____ _____ and I choose to forgive myself for reacting this way.

In Jesus' name, Amen.

Note: You may find yourself praying for the same people and the same wounds nearly every day. This is perfectly fine and even expected. Many wounds run deep and we have difficulty letting them go, as over time they have become part of our identity (although a false identity). Be patient. Repetition is a good thing.

Group Questions

✓ What individuals easily come to mind that you need to forgive? And for what actions?

✓ What physical conditions or ailments do you have that you think could possibly be caused by unforgiveness?

Meeting Close
Check Out
What do you need? – 5 min
Is there anything the group can offer any member?
- *Prayers*
- *Phone calls/texts*
- *Private meeting*
- *Ride to meetings*
- *Etc.*

Closing Prayers

Week 29 Homework

Appendix G Work

Attempt to start the exercise in **Appendix G** before your Daily Action.

Week 29 Recovery Action Guide

Daily Action Guide

(next page)

Use the chart for reference while doing your homework.

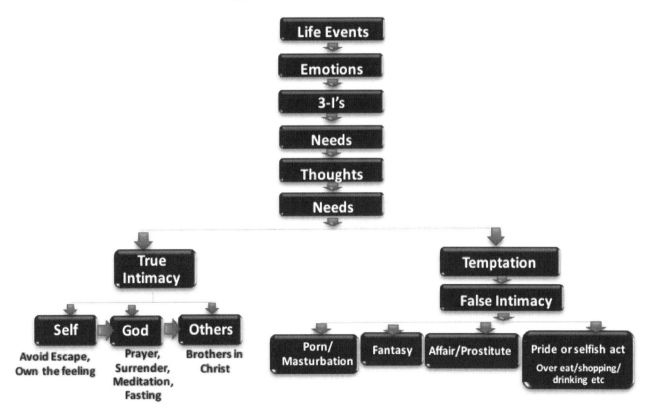

Day 1

1. Did you violate any Primary Boundaries in the last 24hrs? Yes No

If No, go to **#2**, If Yes, then complete the following:

What Boundary did you violate? _____

What events led up to the behavior?

_____

_____

What Secondary Boundaries did you violate leading up to the Primary?

_____

_____

2. Did you violate any Secondary Boundaries in the last 24hrs? Yes No

If No, go to **#3**, If Yes, then complete the following:

What Boundaries did you violate?

_____

_____

3. What **Gift of Self** did you perform in the last 24hrs?

_____

_____

Remember to continue these practices in your daily routine:

- ✓ Prayer/meditation for 30 or more minutes per day.
- ✓ Read Scripture every day.
- ✓ Recite the 7 Cornerstones of Commitment.
- ✓ Recite the Surrender Prayer.
- ✓ Practice some type of intentional fast every day.

Day 1 continued:

4. 3-I's Evaluation of a Daily Event

There will be an event EVERY day. Big or small. Anything from the Starbucks barista who was rude to you, to your car breaking down, to your spouse leaving you. Any level. Any of these events created an emotion that resulted in a reaction on your part. Anything from simple anger or frustration to a sinful behavior. Find it, pray about it, and document it.

Day 1: Describe the event that happened:

_____

_____

Name the emotions that were revealed: _____

Revealing the Source: *When was the first time in your life (possibly childhood) when you recall these emotions and what was the event that triggered them? (pray the Holy Spirit Prayer for guidance)*

_____

_____

Name the 3-I emotions that were related: _____

What behavior was engaged in after this event and emotions happened?

_____

_____

Was this an expression of True Intimacy or False Intimacy? _____

If False Intimacy was chosen:

(a) Describe where in the process you could have made a different decision and followed True Intimacy. (Event, Thought, Emotions, 3-I's, Needs, etc.)

_____

_____

And:

(b) What True Intimacy steps would you have personally engaged in? Can you do it now?

Self _____

God _____

Others _____

Day 1 continued:

OR

If True Intimacy was chosen:
(a) What True Intimacy steps did you engage in?

Self _____

God _____

Others _____

Now if you feel you need to, pray the below forgiveness prayer about the person and event that triggered an emotion in you today, do so now.

Also, pray the forgiveness prayer for each person you discovered in the **Appendix G** exercise. Pray for each, one at a time. If you prayed for this person previously, do it again. Remember, it's not a "check the box, once and done" type of exercise, you need to pray continuously until all negativity, all negative impact on your identity, all animosity, and all other personal impacts have been released.

Lord, I choose to forgive _____ for the action of _____ that triggered me to feel _____. I release this person from any power he or she holds over me in generating my hurt feelings. Lord, I give you permission to take the judgment and the bitterness out of my life. I surrender it to You and ask You to remove it and to heal me where I have been wounded. I surrender my right to be paid back for my loss by the one who sinned against me, and by doing so I declare my trust in God alone as my Righteous Judge.

Lord, I ask for your forgiveness in my choosing to react to this person, resulting in my actions of _____ and I choose to forgive myself for reacting this way.

In Jesus' name, Amen.

Day 2

1. Did you violate any Primary Boundaries in the last 24hrs?   Yes   No

    If No, go to **#2**, If Yes, then complete the following:

    What Boundary did you violate? _____

    What events led up to the behavior?

    _____

    _____

    What Secondary Boundaries did you violate leading up to the Primary?

    _____

    _____

2. Did you violate any Secondary Boundaries in the last 24hrs?   Yes   No

    If No, go to **#3**, If Yes, then complete the following:

    What Boundaries did you violate?

    _____

    _____

3. What **Gift of Self** did you perform in the last 24hrs?

_____

_____

4. 3-I's Evaluation of a Daily Event

    There will be an event EVERY day. Big or small. Anything from the Starbucks barista who was rude to you, to your car breaking down, to your spouse leaving you. Any level. Any of these events created an emotion that resulted in a reaction on your part. Anything from simple anger or frustration to a sinful behavior. Find it, pray about it, and document it.

    Day 1: Describe the event that happened:

    _____

    _____

    Name the emotions that were revealed: _____

Day 2 continued:

Revealing the Source: *When was the first time in your life (possibly childhood) when you recall these emotions and what was the event that triggered them? (pray the Holy Spirit Prayer for guidance)*

_____

_____

Name the 3-I emotions that were related: _____

What behavior was engaged in after this event and emotions happened?

_____

_____

Was this an expression of True Intimacy or False Intimacy? _____

If False Intimacy was chosen:
(a) Describe where in the process you could have made a different decision and followed True Intimacy. (Event, Thought, Emotions, 3-I's, Needs, etc.)

_____

_____

And:
(b) What True Intimacy steps would you have personally engaged in? Can you do it now?

Self _____

God _____

Others _____

Day 2 continued:

OR

If True Intimacy was chosen:
(a) What True Intimacy steps did you engage in?

Self _____

God _____

_____

Others

Now if you feel you need to, pray the below forgiveness prayer about the person and event that triggered an emotion in you today, do so now.

Also, pray the forgiveness prayer for each person you discovered in the **Appendix G** exercise. Pray for each, one at a time. If you prayed for this person previously, do it again. Remember, it's not a "check the box, once and done" type of exercise, you need to pray continuously until all negativity, all negative impact on your identity, all animosity, and all other personal impacts have been released.

Lord, I choose to forgive _____ for the action of _____ that triggered me to feel _____. I release this person from any power he or she holds over me in generating my hurt feelings. Lord, I give you permission to take the judgment and the bitterness out of my life. I surrender it to You and ask You to remove it and to heal me where I have been wounded. I surrender my right to be paid back for my loss by the one who sinned against me, and by doing so I declare my trust in God alone as my Righteous Judge.

Lord, I ask for your forgiveness in my choosing to react to this person, resulting in my actions of _____ _____ and I choose to forgive myself for reacting this way.

In Jesus' name, Amen.

Day 3

1. Did you violate any Primary Boundaries in the last 24hrs?   Yes   No

If No, go to **#2**, If Yes, then complete the following:

What Boundary did you violate? _____

What events led up to the behavior?

_____

_____

What Secondary Boundaries did you violate leading up to the Primary?

_____

_____

2. Did you violate any Secondary Boundaries in the last 24hrs?   Yes   No

If No, go to **#3**, If Yes, then complete the following:

What Boundaries did you violate?

_____

_____

3. What **Gift of Self** did you perform in the last 24hrs?

_____

_____

4. 3-I's Evaluation of a Daily Event

There will be an event EVERY day. Big or small. Anything from the Starbucks barista who was rude to you, to your car breaking down, to your spouse leaving you. Any level. Any of these events created an emotion that resulted in a reaction on your part. Anything from simple anger or frustration to a sinful behavior. Find it, pray about it, and document it.

Day 1: Describe the event that happened:

_____

_____

Name the emotions that were revealed: _____

Day 3 continued:

Revealing the Source: *When was the first time in your life (possibly childhood) when you recall these emotions and what was the event that triggered them? (pray the Holy Spirit Prayer for guidance)*

_____

_____

Name the 3-I emotions that were related: _____

What behavior was engaged in after this event and emotions happened?

_____

_____

Was this an expression of True Intimacy or False Intimacy? _____

If False Intimacy was chosen:
(a) Describe where in the process you could have made a different decision and followed True Intimacy. (Event, Thought, Emotions, 3-I's, Needs, etc.)

_____

_____

And:
(b) What True Intimacy steps would you have personally engaged in? Can you do it now?

Self _____

God _____

Others _____

OR

If True Intimacy was chosen:
(a) What True Intimacy steps did you engage in?

Self _____

God _____

Others _____

Now if you feel you need to, pray the below forgiveness prayer about the person and event that triggered an emotion in you today, do so now.

Also, pray the forgiveness prayer for each person you discovered in the **Appendix G** exercise. Pray for each, one at a time. If you prayed for this person previously, do it again. Remember, it's not a "check the box, once and done" type of exercise, you need to pray continuously until all negativity, all negative impact on your identity, all animosity, and all other personal impacts have been released.

Lord, I choose to forgive _____ for the action of _____ that triggered me to feel _____. I release this person from any power he or she holds over me in generating my hurt feelings. Lord, I give you permission to take the judgment and the bitterness out of my life. I surrender it to You and ask You to remove it and to heal me where I have been wounded. I surrender my right to be paid back for my loss by the one who sinned against me, and by doing so I declare my trust in God alone as my Righteous Judge.

Lord, I ask for your forgiveness in my choosing to react to this person, resulting in my actions of _____ _____ and I choose to forgive myself for reacting this way.

In Jesus' name, Amen.

Day 4

1. Did you violate any Primary Boundaries in the last 24hrs?   Yes   No

If No, go to **#2**, If Yes, then complete the following:

What Boundary did you violate? _____

What events led up to the behavior?

_____

_____

What Secondary Boundaries did you violate leading up to the Primary?

_____

_____

2. Did you violate any Secondary Boundaries in the last 24hrs?   Yes   No

If No, go to **#3**, If Yes, then complete the following:

What Boundaries did you violate?

_____

_____

3. What **Gift of Self** did you perform in the last 24hrs?

_____

_____

4. 3-I's Evaluation of a Daily Event

There will be an event EVERY day. Big or small. Anything from the Starbucks barista who was rude to you, to your car breaking down, to your spouse leaving you. Any level. Any of these events created an emotion that resulted in a reaction on your part. Anything from simple anger or frustration to a sinful behavior. Find it, pray about it, and document it.

Day 1: Describe the event that happened:

_____

_____

Name the emotions that were revealed: _____

Day 4 continued:

Revealing the Source: *When was the first time in your life (possibly childhood) when you recall these emotions and what was the event that triggered them? (pray the Holy Spirit Prayer for guidance)*

_____

_____

Name the 3-I emotions that were related: _____

What behavior was engaged in after this event and emotions happened?

_____

_____

Was this an expression of True Intimacy or False Intimacy? _____

If False Intimacy was chosen:
(a) Describe where in the process you could have made a different decision and followed True Intimacy. (Event, Thought, Emotions, 3-I's, Needs, etc.)

_____

_____

And:
(b) What True Intimacy steps would you have personally engaged in? Can you do it now?

Self
_____

God
_____

Others
_____

OR

If True Intimacy was chosen:
(a) What True Intimacy steps did you engage in?

Self
_____

God
_____

Others
_____

Now if you feel you need to, pray the below forgiveness prayer about the person and event that triggered an emotion in you today, do so now.

Also, pray the forgiveness prayer for each person you discovered in the **Appendix G** exercise. Pray for each, one at a time. If you prayed for this person previously, do it again. Remember, it's not a "check the box, once and done" type of exercise, you need to pray continuously until all negativity, all negative impact on your identity, all animosity, and all other personal impacts have been released.

Lord, I choose to forgive _____ for the action of _____ that triggered me to feel _____. I release this person from any power he or she holds over me in generating my hurt feelings. Lord, I give you permission to take the judgment and the bitterness out of my life. I surrender it to You and ask You to remove it and to heal me where I have been wounded. I surrender my right to be paid back for my loss by the one who sinned against me, and by doing so I declare my trust in God alone as my Righteous Judge.

Lord, I ask for your forgiveness in my choosing to react to this person, resulting in my actions of _____ _____ and I choose to forgive myself for reacting this way.

In Jesus' name, Amen.

Day 5

1. Did you violate any Primary Boundaries in the last 24hrs?   Yes   No

If No, go to **#2**, If Yes, then complete the following:

What Boundary did you violate? _____

What events led up to the behavior?

_____

_____

What Secondary Boundaries did you violate leading up to the Primary?

_____

_____

2. Did you violate any Secondary Boundaries in the last 24hrs?   Yes   No

If No, go to **#3**, If Yes, then complete the following:

What Boundaries did you violate?

_____

_____

3. What **Gift of Self** did you perform in the last 24hrs?

_____

_____

4. 3-I's Evaluation of a Daily Event

There will be an event EVERY day. Big or small. Anything from the Starbucks barista who was rude to you, to your car breaking down, to your spouse leaving you. Any level. Any of these events created an emotion that resulted in a reaction on your part. Anything from simple anger or frustration to a sinful behavior. Find it, pray about it, and document it.

Day 1: Describe the event that happened:

_____

_____

Name the emotions that were revealed: _____

Day 4 continued:

Revealing the Source: *When was the first time in your life (possibly childhood) when you recall these emotions and what was the event that triggered them? (pray the Holy Spirit Prayer for guidance)*

_____

_____

Name the 3-I emotions that were related: _____

What behavior was engaged in after this event and emotions happened?

_____

_____

Was this an expression of True Intimacy or False Intimacy? _____

If False Intimacy was chosen:
(a) Describe where in the process you could have made a different decision and followed True Intimacy. (Event, Thought, Emotions, 3-I's, Needs, etc.)

_____

_____

And:
(b) What True Intimacy steps would you have personally engaged in? Can you do it now?

Self _____

God _____

Others _____

OR

If True Intimacy was chosen:
(a) What True Intimacy steps did you engage in?

Self _____

God _____

Others _____

Now if you feel you need to, pray the below forgiveness prayer about the person and event that triggered an emotion in you today, do so now.

Also, pray the forgiveness prayer for each person you discovered in the **Appendix G** exercise. Pray for each, one at a time. If you prayed for this person previously, do it again. Remember, it's not a "check the box, once and done" type of exercise, you need to pray continuously until all negativity, all negative impact on your identity, all animosity, and all other personal impacts have been released.

Lord, I choose to forgive _____ for the action of _____ that triggered me to feel _____. I release this person from any power he or she holds over me in generating my hurt feelings. Lord, I give you permission to take the judgment and the bitterness out of my life. I surrender it to You and ask You to remove it and to heal me where I have been wounded. I surrender my right to be paid back for my loss by the one who sinned against me, and by doing so I declare my trust in God alone as my Righteous Judge.

Lord, I ask for your forgiveness in my choosing to react to this person, resulting in my actions of _____ _____ and I choose to forgive myself for reacting this way.

In Jesus' name, Amen.

Day 6

1. Did you violate any Primary Boundaries in the last 24hrs?   Yes   No

If No, go to **#2**, If Yes, then complete the following:

What Boundary did you violate? _____

What events led up to the behavior?

_____

_____

What Secondary Boundaries did you violate leading up to the Primary?

_____

_____

2. Did you violate any Secondary Boundaries in the last 24hrs?   Yes   No

If No, go to **#3**, If Yes, then complete the following:

What Boundaries did you violate?

_____

_____

3. What **Gift of Self** did you perform in the last 24hrs?

_____

_____

4. 3-I's Evaluation of a Daily Event

There will be an event EVERY day. Big or small. Anything from the Starbucks barista who was rude to you, to your car breaking down, to your spouse leaving you. Any level. Any of these events created an emotion that resulted in a reaction on your part. Anything from simple anger or frustration to a sinful behavior. Find it, pray about it, and document it.

Day 1: Describe the event that happened:

_____

_____

Name the emotions that were revealed: _____

Day 6 continued:

Revealing the Source: *When was the first time in your life (possibly childhood) when you recall these emotions and what was the event that triggered them? (pray the Holy Spirit Prayer for guidance)*

_____

_____

Name the 3-I emotions that were related: _____

What behavior was engaged in after this event and emotions happened?

_____

_____

Was this an expression of True Intimacy or False Intimacy? _____

<u>If False Intimacy was chosen:</u>
(a) Describe where in the process you could have made a different decision and followed True Intimacy. (Event, Thought, Emotions, 3-I's, Needs, etc.)

_____

_____

And:
(b) What True Intimacy steps would you have personally engaged in? Can you do it now?

Self _____

God _____

Others _____

OR

<u>If True Intimacy was chosen</u>:
(a) What True Intimacy steps did you engage in?

Self _____

God _____

Others _____

Now if you feel you need to, pray the below forgiveness prayer about the person and event that triggered an emotion in you today, do so now.

Also, pray the forgiveness prayer for each person you discovered in the **Appendix G** exercise. Pray for each, one at a time. If you prayed for this person previously, do it again. Remember, it's not a "check the box, once and done" type of exercise, you need to pray continuously until all negativity, all negative impact on your identity, all animosity, and all other personal impacts have been released.

Lord, I choose to forgive _____ for the action of _____ that triggered me to feel _____. I release this person from any power he or she holds over me in generating my hurt feelings. Lord, I give you permission to take the judgment and the bitterness out of my life. I surrender it to You and ask You to remove it and to heal me where I have been wounded. I surrender my right to be paid back for my loss by the one who sinned against me, and by doing so I declare my trust in God alone as my Righteous Judge.

Lord, I ask for your forgiveness in my choosing to react to this person, resulting in my actions of _____ _____ and I choose to forgive myself for reacting this way.

In Jesus' name, Amen.

Day 7

1. Did you violate any Primary Boundaries in the last 24hrs?   Yes   No

If No, go to **#2**, If Yes, then complete the following:

What Boundary did you violate? _____

What events led up to the behavior?

_____

_____

What Secondary Boundaries did you violate leading up to the Primary?

_____

_____

2. Did you violate any Secondary Boundaries in the last 24hrs?   Yes   No

If No, go to **#3**, If Yes, then complete the following:

What Boundaries did you violate?

_____

_____

3. What **Gift of Self** did you perform in the last 24hrs?

_____

_____

4. 3-I's Evaluation of a Daily Event

There will be an event EVERY day. Big or small. Anything from the Starbucks barista who was rude to you, to your car breaking down, to your spouse leaving you. Any level. Any of these events created an emotion that resulted in a reaction on your part. Anything from simple anger or frustration to a sinful behavior. Find it, pray about it, and document it.

Day 1: Describe the event that happened:

_____

_____

Name the emotions that were revealed: _____

Day 7 continued:

Revealing the Source: *When was the first time in your life (possibly childhood) when you recall these emotions and what was the event that triggered them? (pray the Holy Spirit Prayer for guidance)*

_____

_____

Name the 3-I emotions that were related: _____

What behavior was engaged in after this event and emotions happened?

_____

_____

Was this an expression of True Intimacy or False Intimacy? _____

If False Intimacy was chosen:
(a) Describe where in the process you could have made a different decision and followed True Intimacy. (Event, Thought, Emotions, 3-I's, Needs, etc.)

_____

_____

And:
(b) What True Intimacy steps would you have personally engaged in? Can you do it now?

Self _____

God _____

Others _____

OR
If True Intimacy was chosen:
(a) What True Intimacy steps did you engage in?

Self _____

God _____

Others _____

Now if you feel you need to, pray the below forgiveness prayer about the person and event that triggered an emotion in you today, do so now.

Also, pray the forgiveness prayer for each person you discovered in the **Appendix G** exercise. Pray for each, one at a time. If you prayed for this person previously, do it again. Remember, it's not a "check the box, once and done" type of exercise, you need to pray continuously until all negativity, all negative impact on your identity, all animosity, and all other personal impacts have been released.

Lord, I choose to forgive _____ for the action of _____ that triggered me to feel _____. I release this person from any power he or she holds over me in generating my hurt feelings. Lord, I give you permission to take the judgment and the bitterness out of my life. I surrender it to You and ask You to remove it and to heal me where I have been wounded. I surrender my right to be paid back for my loss by the one who sinned against me, and by doing so I declare my trust in God alone as my Righteous Judge.

Lord, I ask for your forgiveness in my choosing to react to this person, resulting in my actions of _____ _____ and I choose to forgive myself for reacting this way.

In Jesus' name, Amen

Weekly Action Guide

Look up these additional scriptures on forgiveness:

2 Cor 5:17, Ephesians 1:7, Hebrews 10:17, Daniel 9:9, Acts 3:19, Isaiah 1:18, Isaiah 43:25-26, 1 John 1:9, Mark 11:25, and Matthew 26:28

Week 30 Resolution of Woundedness / Transforming Pain – Putting it all Together

Meeting Protocol

Group Invocation of the Holy Spirit
"Come Holy Spirit, renew me, dwell in me and protect me"

Facilitator Leads the Group in Prayer

Confidentiality Bond – group recites together
"I _____ pledge to honor each person present or not present today in this group. I will do so by keeping all comments and discussions offered here today and at all future meetings confidential. I also pledge to keep the identity of all members confidential. I also pledge to make no statements of judgmental nature about anyone in this group, including myself."

Welcome New Members

Check-in Round 1: Feelings/Mood
Check-in Round 2: Significant event since last meeting (30-60 seconds)
Check-in Round 3: Temptation Rating (On a scale of 1–10; 1 a low temptation, 10 a high temptation)
Check-in Round 4: Primary or Secondary Boundary Violations
If a Primary Violation occurred, the following questions/factors need to be addressed:
- ✓ **What do you think led to acting out?** – life events 24+ hours before
- ✓ **What were your feelings before acting out?**
- ✓ **Did you call anyone?**
- ✓ **What Secondary Boundaries did you violate this week?** – include those that were prior to your Primary Boundary Violation if you had one.
- ✓ **Group affirmation and acceptance of sharing.**

Check-in Round 5: Victories

Scripture Verse

2 Corinthians 3:18 "And all of us, with unveiled faces, seeing the glory of the Lord as though reflected in a mirror, are being transformed into the same image from one degree of glory to another; for this comes from the Lord, the Spirit."

Group Discussion Question: How does this verse relate to your life and your battle with sexual sin?

Week 30 Recovery Foundation Lesson

The last 12 weeks have likely been overwhelming. You may even be struggling to make sense of it all. Especially in making it all make sense together and how to apply it to your recovery. Here is an example of bringing it all together.

Example: (Using the story from Example #2 from Week 20); Around the 20th of each month, which is bill paying time, I have an intense fear and anxiety of not being able to pay the bills. Yet I have a good job with money in the bank. I know the fear stems from my parents not being able pay the bills when I was six years old. I remember times when there was no food and no heat in the house. I now overcompensate on finances (*Week 18: River Under the River*) because of the irrational fear of not having enough (selfish behavior from beliefs from *Week 17: Beliefs*). The shame that surfaces stems from a fear of not being worthy, along with a fear of my needs (food and heat) not being met (*Week 19: The Shame that Binds Me*). I even feel incompetent because I couldn't help my parents then, and I have a disordered belief today that I am not successful enough to get by (*Week 25/26: Identity*). This is evidenced by the events of, "Every time I get close to the time of the month to pay bills, I am reminded of when my parents couldn't pay the bills and I went without food and heat. When this time comes, I feel incompetent, fearful and unworthy" (*Week 20: Triggers and Warning Signs*). This event causes me to crave the need to medicate so I don't get completely paralyzed with these emotions every month. So, I look at porn (*3-I's, False Intimacy path*). Instead, I've learned that 10 days before it's time to pay bills, I choose to exercise True Intimacy by acknowledging my anticipated feelings and not suppressing them (*Self, in True Intimacy path*), then I pray about my emotions and do short daily meditations about Jesus taking care of me (*God, in True Intimacy path*). I also talk to my wife and a close friend about this anxiety I have (*Others, in True Intimacy path*). Also, since I blame my father *(Week 27: Sources of Wounds)* for not working two jobs or getting a better job so he could take care of us more adequately, I say the following forgiveness prayer (*Week 29: Forgiveness*):

Lord, I choose to forgive my **FATHER** for the action of **NOT MAKING ENOUGH MONEY TO PAY OUR BILLS AND FEED ME,** which triggered me to feel **INSIGNIFI-CANT, INCOMPETENT, WORTHLESS, AND FEARFUL.** I release **MY FATHER** from any power he holds over me in generating my hurt feelings. Lord, I give you permission to take the judgment and the bitterness out of my life. I surrender it to You and ask You to remove it and to heal me where I have been wounded. I surrender my right to be paid back for my loss by the one who sinned against me, and by doing so I declare my trust in God alone as my Righteous Judge.

Lord, I ask for your forgiveness in my choosing to react to this person, resulting in my actions of **CHOOSING PORNOGRAPHY TO SOOTHE MY PAIN AND TO SUBSTITUTE LOVE,** and I choose to **FORGIVE MYSELF** for reacting this way.

In Jesus' name, Amen.

Another way to look at the process is to work backwards. (Note: this can work with nearly any negative behavior).

- **What is the unwanted behavior?** *I looked at pornography.*

- **What emotions led up to expressing this behavior this last time?** *Loneliness.*

- **What event triggered the loneliness?** *I saw two people holding hands and it reminded me that I don't have a girlfriend.*

- **What emotions did this bring up in you?** *Loneliness, feeling unwanted, rejection, insignificance because no one sees me as valuable to have as a boyfriend; incompetence because I'm not good enough to be wanted; and impotence because I can't do anything about it.*

- **When in your past did you feel this way for the first time?** *When my mom left my dad, at age 11.*

- **How did this match these feelings you just experienced?** *I felt like she didn't want me enough, and I wasn't valuable enough to stay with my dad. She abandoned me, and I could do nothing about it.*

- **What do I do now?** *You already looked at pornography so what can you do now, or what could you have done before you medicated with porn?*

  - **Now:** go to Confession to get back in the State of Grace, and also do the following True Intimacy exercise:

    - ✓ **Self:** recognize or even journal the feelings I am experiencing or did experience (Lone-liness, feeling unwanted, rejection, insignificance because no one sees me as valuable to have as a boyfriend, incompetence because I'm not good enough to be wanted, and impotence because I can't do anything about it.)

✓ **God:** Meditate on Jesus showing me He wants to be with me; He accepts me the way I am; I am not lonely when He is with me; He even gives me his Mother (the Virgin Mary) as my new replacement mother; I can choose to give Jesus my pain.

✓ **Others:** Talk to my close friend or accountability partner about my feelings and how I handled them inappropriately.

o **Before:** When the event happened, recognize the beginnings of the loneliness feelings then immediately – even sitting in the car for example, (not while driving, of course), do the 3-I's exercise; even a brief version, then do a more complete version later at home.

✓ **Self:** recognize or even journal the feelings I am experiencing or did experience (loneliness, feeling unwanted, rejection, insignificance because no one sees me as valuable to have as a boyfriend, incompetence because I'm not good enough to be wanted, and impotence because I can't do anything about it).

✓ **God:** Meditate on Jesus showing me He wants to be with me; He accepts me the way I am; I am not lonely when He is with me; He even gives me his Mother (the Virgin Mary) as my new replacement mother; I can choose to give Jesus my pain.

✓ **Others:** Talk to my close friend or accountability partner about my feelings and how I handled them inappropriately.

Forgiveness. The final step is to forgive all involved persons for triggering your feelings and to forgive yourself for responding with your actions.

A Forgiveness Prayer can look like this:

"Lord, I choose to forgive my **MOTHER** for the action of **LEAVING ME AND ABANDONING ME AT 11 YEARS OLD**, which triggered me to feel **REJECTED, LONELY, ABANDONED, UNWANTED, INSIGNIFICANT, INCOMPETENT, AND WORTHLESS.** I release **MY MOTHER** from any power she holds over me in generating my hurt feelings. Lord, I give you permission to take the judgment and the bitterness out of my life. I surrender it to You and ask You to remove it and to heal me where I have been wounded. I surrender my right to be paid back for my loss by the one who sinned against me, and by doing so I declare my trust in God alone as my Righteous Judge.

Lord, I also choose to forgive **THE COUPLE I SAW HOLDING HANDS** because it triggered me to feel **LONELY.** I release **THIS COUPLE** from any power they hold over me in generating my hurt feelings. Lord, I give You permission to take the judgment and the bitterness out of my life. I surrender it to You and ask You to remove it and to heal me where I have been wounded. I surrender my right to be paid back for my loss by the one who sinned against me, and by doing so I declare my trust in God alone as my Righteous Judge.

Lord, I ask for your forgiveness in my choosing to react to this person, resulting in my actions of **CHOOSING PORNOGRAPHY TO SOOTHE MY PAIN AND TO SUBSTITUTE LOVE** and I choose to **FORGIVE MYSELF** for reacting this way.

In Jesus' name, Amen.

While this may seem very intricate and even complicated, it is however the step by step process necessary to:

- Access the source of wounds that trigger unwanted behavior
- Recognize how it affects you
- Name the emotions that are triggered
- Know what to do with them in the 3-I's process, and finally
- Do the forgiveness process to heal and seal the wound

As you have spent several weeks adding information to **Appendix G** from the various lessons, it will be easier to review each section that you have completed and see a pattern or see problem areas that need work.

This process is *transforming pain*: recall earlier we stated that if you don't transform your pain you will transmit it – all sinful and unhealthy behaviors, not just sexual are transmitting pain. In nearly EVERY sinful or negative responsive behavior, there is a wound or pain that needs to be transformed.

Steps *(you will be doing this in your homework)*

- Review the work you did in **Week 17** and in subsequent weeks, resulting from the lesson **Fellowship with God – Beliefs**.
- Next, evaluate the **Week 18, River Under the River** behavioral characteristics you recorded and see if there is a connection.
- Next review the **Week 19, Guilt and Shame Inventory** statements and see if there is a connection there.
- Next, also review **Week 20, Obvious and Subtle Triggers** to determine if any of these triggers are common with the beliefs, emotions, and behavioral characteristics work you recorded.
- Take any of the items in these lists and do a **True Intimacy** exercise.
- Finally do a **Forgiveness Prayer** around these wounds and their resulting behaviors and emotions.

An important fact to recognize is that this process works with everything: not just sexual behaviors, not just addictions, but anything – anger, fear, overeating, compulsive shopping – any unhealthy, unholy or unwanted reactive behavior. These healing steps will change your life.

Counseling

It is not uncommon for individuals who get to this point in the program to feel that some of their emotional history is too difficult to dive into alone. Quite possibly, when you started this program several months ago, you felt that you could get through this more easily. The positive realization is that this program has helped guide you to some areas of woundedness or trauma that need professional help. This program gives you the benefit of meeting with a counselor and having a much clearer idea of what you need to work on, as opposed to spending money on several months of counseling only to get to this point. Most counselors will applaud you for doing this much work already, plus the fact that you already have brothers in Christ to help you with any difficulties you encounter.

Note: make sure you select a Christian or preferably a Catholic counselor.

Here are some recommended sites to help you find a counselor:

- CatholicTherapists.com

- CatholicCounselors.com

- FaithfulCounseling.com

Group Questions

- ✓ How are you feeling about the entire process thus far?

    Helpful? Encouraging? Overwhelmed? Lost?........

- ✓ Have you experienced any freedom thus far from old emotions seeming to control your behaviors?

Meeting Close
Check Out
What do you need? – 5 min
Is there anything the group can offer any member?
- *Prayers*
- *Phone calls/texts*
- *Private meeting*
- *Ride to meetings*
- *Etc.*

Closing Prayers

Week 30 Homework

Using the steps and examples in this week's lesson, review the entries in each week's lesson in Appendix G. Go through the process with each area of brokenness or pain.

Follow as closely as necessary to dig into your emotional pain. If you feel that you need to take small steps at first, and then go deeper with subsequent efforts, that is completely fine. Make sure you ask the Holy Spirit to guide you in the process, so you don't let fear paralyze you in this healing process.

Steps

- Review the work you did in **Week 17,** and in subsequent weeks, resulting from the lesson **Fellowship with God – Beliefs**.
- Next, evaluate Week 18's **River Under the River** behavioral characteristics you recorded and see if there is a connection.
- Next review the **Week 19 Guilt and Shame Inventory** statements and see if there is a connection there.
- Next, also review **Week 20 Obvious and Subtle Triggers** to determine if any of these triggers are common with the beliefs, emotions, and behavioral characteristics' work you recorded.
- Take any of the items in these lists and do a **True Intimacy** exercise.
- Finally, do a **Forgiveness Prayer** around these wounds and their resulting behaviors and emotions.

Review the entries you made in Appendix G: make connections with history, events, behaviors, identities, emotions, etc., and do the above steps for each link you find. It will take multiple attempts, as well as time in prayer and practice, to work through them.

This week's Daily Action Guide only has two days of the tracking and 3-I's work. This will allow you more time to do the above exercises.

Week 30 Recovery Action Guide

Daily Action Guide

(next page)

Day 1

1. Did you violate any Primary Boundaries in the last 24hrs?   Yes   No

    If No, go to **#2**, If Yes, then complete the following:

    What Boundary did you violate? _____

    What events led up to the behavior?

    _____

    _____

    What Secondary Boundaries did you violate leading up to the Primary?

    _____

    _____

2. Did you violate any Secondary Boundaries in the last 24hrs?   Yes   No

    If No, go to **#3**, If Yes, then complete the following:

    What Boundaries did you violate?

    _____

    _____

3. What **Gift of Self** did you perform in the last 24hrs?

_____

_____

Remember to continue these practices in your daily routine:

- ✓ Prayer/meditation for 30 or more minutes per day.
- ✓ Read Scripture every day.
- ✓ Recite the 7 Cornerstones of Commitment.
- ✓ Recite the Surrender Prayer.
- ✓ Practice some type of intentional fast every day.

Day 1 continued:

4. 3-I's Evaluation of a Daily Event

There will be an event EVERY day. Big or small. Anything from the Starbucks barista who was rude to you, to your car breaking down, to your spouse leaving you. At any level. Any of these events created an emotion that resulted in a reaction on your part: anything from simple anger or frustration to a sinful behavior. Find it, pray about it, and document it.

Day 1: Describe the event that happened:

_____

_____

Name the emotions that were revealed: _____

Revealing the Source: *When was the first time in your life (possibly childhood) when you recall these emotions and what was the event that triggered them? (pray the Holy Spirit Prayer for guidance)*

_____

_____

Name the 3-I emotions that were related: _____

What behavior was engaged in after this event and emotions happened?

_____

_____

Was this an expression of True Intimacy or False Intimacy? _____

If False Intimacy was chosen:

(a) Describe where in the process you could have made a different decision and followed True Intimacy. (Event, Thought, Emotions, 3-I's, Needs, etc.)

_____

_____

And:

(b) What True Intimacy steps would you have personally engaged in? Can you do it now?

Self _____

God _____

Others _____

Day 1 continued:

OR

<u>If True Intimacy was chosen</u>:
(a) What True Intimacy steps did you engage in?

Self _____

God _____

Others _____

Now if you feel you need to, pray the below forgiveness prayer about the person and event that triggered an emotion in you today, do so now.

Lord, I choose to forgive _____ for the action of _____ that triggered me to feel _____. I release this person from any power he or she holds over me in generating my hurt feelings. Lord, I give you permission to take the judgment and the bitterness out of my life. I surrender it to You and ask You to remove it and to heal me where I have been wounded. I surrender my right to be paid back for my loss by the one who sinned against me, and by doing so I declare my trust in God alone as my Righteous Judge.

Lord, I ask for your forgiveness in my choosing to react to this person, resulting in my actions of _____ and I choose to forgive myself for reacting this way.

In Jesus' name, Amen.

Day 2

1. Did you violate any Primary Boundaries in the last 24hrs?   Yes   No

    If No, go to **#2**, If Yes, then complete the following:

    What Boundary did you violate? _____

    What events led up to the behavior?

_____

_____

    What Secondary Boundaries did you violate leading up to the Primary?

_____

_____

2. Did you violate any Secondary Boundaries in the last 24hrs?   Yes   No

    If No, go to **#3**, If Yes, then complete the following:

    What Boundaries did you violate?

_____

_____

3. What **Gift of Self** did you perform in the last 24hrs?

_____

_____

4. 3-I's Evaluation of a Daily Event

    There will be an event EVERY day. Big or small. Anything from the Starbucks barista who was rude to you, to your car breaking down, to your spouse leaving you. Any level. Any of these events created an emotion that resulted in a reaction on your part. Anything from simple anger or frustration to a sinful behavior. Find it, pray about it, and document it.

    Day 1: Describe the event that happened:

_____

_____

Name the emotions that were revealed: _____

293

Day 2 continued:

Revealing the Source: *When was the first time in your life (possibly childhood) when you recall these emotions and what was the event that triggered them? (pray the Holy Spirit Prayer for guidance)*

_____

_____

Name the 3-I emotions that were related: _____

What behavior was engaged in after this event and emotions happened?

_____

_____

Was this an expression of True Intimacy or False Intimacy? _____

If False Intimacy was chosen:
(a) Describe where in the process you could have made a different decision and followed True Intimacy. (Event, Thought, Emotions, 3-I's, Needs, etc.)

_____

_____

And:
(b) What True Intimacy steps would you have personally engaged in? Can you do it now?

Self
_____

God
_____

Others
_____

OR

If True Intimacy was chosen:
(a) What True Intimacy steps did you engage in?

Self
_____

God
_____

Others
_____

Day 2 continued:

Now, if you feel you need to, pray the below forgiveness prayer about the person and event that triggered an emotion in you today, do so now.

Lord, I choose to forgive _____ for the action of _____ that triggered me to feel _____. I release this person from any power he or she holds over me in generating my hurt feelings. Lord, I give you permission to take the judgment and the bitterness out of my life. I surrender it to You and ask You to remove it and to heal me where I have been wounded. I surrender my right to be paid back for my loss by the one who sinned against me, and by doing so I declare my trust in God alone as my Righteous Judge.

Lord, I ask for your forgiveness in my choosing to react to this person, resulting in my actions of _____ _____ and I choose to forgive myself for reacting this way.

In Jesus' name, Amen.

Week 31 Transformation in Christ Meditation Audio Exercise

Meeting Protocol

Group Invocation of the Holy Spirit
"Come Holy Spirit, renew me, dwell in me and protect me."

Facilitator Leads the Group in Prayer

Confidentiality Bond – group recites together
"I _____ pledge to honor each person present or not present today in this group. I will do so by keeping all comments and discussions offered here today and at all future meetings confidential. I also pledge to keep the identity of all members confidential. I also pledge to make no statements of judgmental nature about anyone in this group, including myself."

Welcome New Members

Check-in Round 1: Feelings/Mood
Check-in Round 2: Significant event since last meeting (30-60 seconds)
Check-in Round 3: Temptation Rating (On a scale of 1–10; 1 a low temptation, 10 a high temptation)
Check-in Round 4: Primary or Secondary Boundary Violations
If a Primary Violation occurred, the following questions/factors need to be addressed:
  ✓ **What do you think led to acting out?** – life events 24+ hours before
  ✓ **What were your feelings before acting out?**
  ✓ **Did you call anyone?**
  ✓ **What Secondary Boundaries did you violate this week?** – include those that were prior to your Primary Boundary Violation if you had one.
  ✓ **Group affirmation and acceptance of sharing.**
Check-in Round 5: Victories

Scripture Verse

Proverbs 23:26 "My child, give me your heart, and let your eyes observe my ways."

Group Discussion Question: How does this verse relate to your life and your battle with sexual sin?

Week 31 Recovery Foundation Lesson

This week's lesson is a Transformation in Christ meditation exercise. This exercise is designed to help you surrender all pieces of your identity and allow Christ to fill you with the identity that He created you for.

This is a culmination of all that you have worked on over the past few months in an effort to create a fresh start on your self-image, moving forward. In addition to taking part in this meditation in this week's exercise, you can do this anytime you feel like you need clarity and need to empty yourself of unwanted false identity battles or negative thoughts.

Two ways to access the meditation exercise online. If you do not have access to the internet, the script used for this meditation exercise is in Appendix E.

Online Locations:

On YouTube:

https://youtu.be/GKBXisCUdIQ

OR

On the Road to Purity website:

- Go to RoadToPurity.com
- Click on Recovery Resources menu, and in the drop-down menu select Transformation In Christ

The video is 28 minutes in length.

There are no group questions this week.

The facilitator will close with a special prayer.

Week 31 Homework

Use this next week to continue working on the transformation exercises you started last week.

Using the steps and examples in last week's lesson, review the entries in each week's lesson in Appendix G. Go through the process with each area of brokenness or pain.

Follow as closely as necessary to dig into your emotional pain. If you feel that you need to take small steps at first, then go deeper with subsequent efforts that is completely fine. Make sure you ask the Holy Spirit to guide you in the process, so you don't let fear paralyze you in this healing process.

Steps

- Review the work you did in **Week 17** and subsequent weeks, resulting from the lesson **Fellowship with God – Beliefs**.
- Next, evaluate **Week 18 River Under the River** behavioral characteristics you recorded and see if there is a connection.
- Next review the **Week 19 Guilt and Shame Inventory** statements and see if there is a connection there.
- Next, also review **Week 20 Obvious and Subtle Triggers** to determine if any of these triggers are common with the beliefs, emotions and behavioral characteristics work you recorded.
- Take any of the items in these lists and do a **True Intimacy** exercise.
- Finally do a **Forgiveness Prayer** around these wounds and resulting behaviors and emotions.

Review the entries you made in **Appendix G**, make connections with history, events, behaviors, identities, emotions etc. and do the above steps for each link you find. It will take multiple attempts, time in prayer and practice to work through them.

The week's Daily Action Guide only has two days of the tracking and 3-I's work. This will allow you more time to do the above exercises.

Week 31 Recovery Action Guide

Daily Action Guide

(next page)

Day 1

1. Did you violate any Primary Boundaries in the last 24hrs?   Yes   No

    If No, go to **#2**, If Yes, then complete the following:

    What Boundary did you violate? _____

    What events led up to the behavior?

    _____

    _____

    What Secondary Boundaries did you violate leading up to the Primary?

    _____

    _____

2. Did you violate any Secondary Boundaries in the last 24hrs?   Yes   No

    If No, go to **#3**, If Yes, then complete the following:

    What Boundaries did you violate?

    _____

    _____

3. What **Gift of Self** did you perform in the last 24hrs?

_____

_____

Remember to continue these practices in your daily routine:

- ✓ Prayer/meditation for 30 or more minutes per day.
- ✓ Read Scripture every day.
- ✓ Recite the 7 Cornerstones of Commitment.
- ✓ Recite the Surrender Prayer.
- ✓ Practice some type of intentional fast every day.

Day 1 continued:

4. 3-I's Evaluation of a Daily Event

There will be an event EVERY day. Big or small. Anything from the Starbucks barista who was rude to you, to your car breaking down, to your spouse leaving you. Any level. Any of these events created an emotion that resulted in a reaction on your part. Anything from simple anger or frustration to a sinful behavior. Find it, pray about it, and document it.

Day 1: Describe the event that happened:

_____

_____

Name the emotions that were revealed: _____

Revealing the Source: *When was the first time in your life (possibly childhood) when you recall these emotions and what was the event that triggered them? (pray the Holy Spirit Prayer for guidance)*

_____

_____

Name the 3-I emotions that were related: _____

What behavior was engaged in after this event and emotions happened?

_____

_____

Was this an expression of True Intimacy or False Intimacy? _____

If False Intimacy was chosen:

(a) Describe where in the process you could have made a different decision and followed True Intimacy. (Event, Thought, Emotions, 3-I's, Needs, etc.)

_____

_____

And:

(b) What True Intimacy steps would you have personally engaged in? Can you do it now?

Self _____

God _____

Others _____

Day 1 continued:

OR

If True Intimacy was chosen:
(a) What True Intimacy steps did you engage in?

Self _____

God _____

Others _____

Now if you feel you need to, pray the below forgiveness prayer about the person and event that triggered an emotion in you today, do so now.

Lord, I choose to forgive _____ for the action of _____ that triggered me to feel _____. I release this person from any power he or she holds over me in generating my hurt feelings. Lord, I give you permission to take the judgment and the bitterness out of my life. I surrender it to You and ask You to remove it and to heal me where I have been wounded. I surrender my right to be paid back for my loss by the one who sinned against me, and by doing so I declare my trust in God alone as my Righteous Judge.

Lord, I ask for your forgiveness in my choosing to react to this person, resulting in my actions of _____ and I choose to forgive myself for reacting this way.

In Jesus' name, Amen.

Day 2

1. Did you violate any Primary Boundaries in the last 24hrs?   Yes   No

If No, go to **#2**, If Yes, then complete the following:

What Boundary did you violate? _____

What events led up to the behavior?

_____

_____

What Secondary Boundaries did you violate leading up to the Primary?

_____

_____

2. Did you violate any Secondary Boundaries in the last 24hrs?   Yes   No

If No, go to **#3**, If Yes, then complete the following:

What Boundaries did you violate?

_____

_____

3. What **Gift of Self** did you perform in the last 24hrs

4. 3-I's Evaluation of a Daily Event

There will be an event EVERY day. Big or small. Anything from the Starbucks barista who was rude to you, to your car breaking down, to your spouse leaving you. Any level. Any of these events created an emotion that resulted in a reaction on your part. Anything from simple anger or frustration to a sinful behavior. Find it, pray about it, and document it.

Day 1: Describe the event that happened:

_____

_____

Name the emotions that were revealed: _____

Day 2 continued:

Revealing the Source: *When was the first time in your life (possibly childhood) when you recall these emotions and what was the event that triggered them? (pray the Holy Spirit prayer for guidance)*

_____

_____

Name the 3-I emotions that were related: _____

What behavior was engaged in after this event and emotions happened?

_____

_____

Was this an expression of True Intimacy or False Intimacy? _____

<u>If False Intimacy was chosen:</u>
(a) Describe where in the process you could have made a different decision and followed True Intimacy. (Event, Thought, Emotions, 3-I's, Needs, etc.)

_____

_____

And:
(b) What True Intimacy steps would you have personally engaged in? Can you do it now?

Self _____

God _____

Others _____

OR

<u>If True Intimacy was chosen</u>:
(a) What True Intimacy steps did you engage in?

Self _____

God _____

Others _____

Day 2 continued:

Now if you feel you need to, pray the below forgiveness prayer about the person and event that triggered an emotion in you today, do so now.

Lord, I choose to forgive _____ for the action of _____ that triggered me to feel _____. I release this person from any power he or she holds over me in generating my hurt feelings. Lord, I give you permission to take the judgment and the bitterness out of my life. I surrender it to You and ask You to remove it and to heal me where I have been wounded. I surrender my right to be paid back for my loss by the one who sinned against me, and by doing so I declare my trust in God alone as my Righteous Judge.

Lord, I ask for your forgiveness in my choosing to react to this person, resulting in my actions of _____ _____ and I choose to forgive myself for reacting this way.

In Jesus' name, Amen.

Week 32 The Fine Line Between Love and Lust

Meeting Protocol

Group Invocation of the Holy Spirit
 "Come Holy Spirit, renew me, dwell in me and protect me"

Facilitator Leads the Group in Prayer

Confidentiality Bond – group recites together
 "I _____ pledge to honor each person present or not present today in this group. I will do so by keeping all comments and discussions offered here today and at all future meetings confidential. I also pledge to keep the identity of all members confidential. I also pledge to make no statements of judgmental nature about anyone in this group, including myself."

Welcome New Members

Check-in Round 1: Feelings/Mood
Check-in Round 2: Significant event since last meeting (30-60 seconds)
Check-in Round 3: Temptation Rating (On a scale of 1–10; 1 a low temptation, 10 a high temptation)
Check-in Round 4: Primary or Secondary Boundary Violations
 If a Primary Violation occurred, the following questions/factors need to be addressed:
   ✓ **What do you think led to acting out?** – life events 24+ hours before
   ✓ **What were your feelings before acting out?**
   ✓ **Did you call anyone?**
   ✓ **What Secondary Boundaries did you violate this week?** – include those that were prior to your Primary Boundary Violation if you had one.
   ✓ **Group affirmation and acceptance of sharing.**
Check-in Round 5: Victories

Scripture Verses

1 Corinthians 16:14 "Let all that you do be done in love."

1 John 2:16 "For all that is in the world—the desire of the flesh, the desire of the eyes, the pride in riches—comes not from the Father but from the world."

1 Peter 2:11 "Beloved, I urge you as aliens and exiles to abstain from the desires of the flesh that wage war against the soul."

Group Discussion Question: How does this verse relate to your life and your battle with sexual sin?

Week 32 Recovery Foundation Lesson

Lust and love are commonly misunderstood concepts. When Jesus says in **Matthew 5:28,** "But I say to you that everyone who looks at a woman with lust has already committed adultery with her in his heart," what does this actually mean? We need to know what lust really is so we can honor this statement of Christ.

Here are some basic definitions from a Catholic perspective.

Love: "Any strong affection, closeness, or devotion to things or persons." Another common and more direct definition is, "willing the good of another."

Lust: "A disordered desire for, or inordinate enjoyment of, sexual pleasure. Sexual Pleasure is morally disordered when sought for itself, isolated from its procreative and unitive purposes. (CCC 2351)

There can actually be a fine line between love and lust. They can even be compared to two sides of the same coin. From the perspective of the **Restoring God's Foundation** program, using the terms "Gift **OF** Self," and "Gift **TO** Self," are familiar to you and are a good representation.

The Catholic church teaches love as a path of Charity, which is the greatest social commandment. It respects others and their rights. Charity inspires a life of self-giving. This is revealed in Luke 17:33 "Whoever seeks to gain his life will lose it, but whoever loses his life will preserve it."

Here are some characteristics of love and lust.

Love	Lust
Union with God	Disconnect from God
Union with spouse	Disconnect from spouse
Will the good of another	Will the good of self
Sacrifice	Selfish
Fulfilling	To violate and disregard the other
Gift of self	Gift to self
Honor human dignity	Human degradation
Commitment to and adoration of another	To degrade another
Compassion to know	To possess, use, or take
Attracted to a person	Attracted to a body
Desire to connect emotionally	Yearn for sexual gratification

As you see from the list above, lust and love are just like two opposite sides of the same coin. Both involve human interaction, both involve some form of connection, or lack thereof, and both typically (but not always) involve a component of sexuality. Yet both are polar opposites.

Lust is the main objective with pornography. Looking at another with the underlying intent to "take" for your own enjoyment is one characteristic of lust. Pornography degrades the woman (or man) to a mere object used for the other's enjoyment – basically a toy. This fact is further evidenced when you hear testimonies of former porn performers and the radical abusive treatment on the film set. It is not uncommon for an actress to be so physically abused that they need medical attention after a shoot. Countless others will testify that in their opinions, nearly 100 percent of co-actresses are addicted to cocaine, alcohol, Vicodin or other pain killers and a host of other drugs because they need them just to get through a scene. Others take short term amnesiacs in order to chemically cause the brain to have short term memory loss because the performances are so traumatic. Porn actresses also have the highest suicide and drug overdose rate of any profession ever in existence!

We discussed in earlier weeks of the program how pornography use is progressive. In some cases, it can lead to anger and violent sexual tastes. Some psychologists will say that the act of turning a human person into an inanimate object (which lust does) causes a disorder in the brain that triggers anger, as the brain cannot properly process the act of violating the natural order in the way it was wired. The natural way God wired it is to love.

As stated earlier, love is willing the good of another. Not only is lust willing the good of self, it by default of actions, is willing the degradation of another.

The institution of the Holy Eucharist by Jesus was the ultimate form of "*Giving of Self.*" The Holy Eucharist is the sacrament that produces in us, by means of Holy Communion, an increase in habitual or sanctifying grace. It not only preserves the life of our souls but increases it. The Eucharist has always been one of the most important aspects of Christianity. The Catechism of the Catholic Church strongly asserts the 'Real Presence' of Jesus' body in the Eucharist; this is to say that the sacrament is not symbolic of the body and blood of Jesus but rather that *it is His body and blood.*

This ultimate "Gift of Self," the shed blood of Jesus Christ and his payment for your sins, is the purest act of love. Quite the opposite of the description of lust above.

Group Questions

The description of how so many former porn actresses depict the abuse, drug use, and suicide experiences can be very eye opening.

✓ How do these facts impact your perception of watching porn?

✓ Do you have any different feelings of remorse now, than you did before knowing these facts?

You have learned how porn affects you, your body, and your soul. You have likely taken part in many acts of the Sacrament of Reconciliation. Until now, your focus has been on your behavior, the damage to you and your soul.

✓ Now looking not just at yourself, but looking outside yourself, do you see any further ripple effects of your behavior? On your family? Outside your family?

Meeting Close
Check Out
What do you need? – 5 min
Is there anything the group can offer any member?
- *Prayers*
- *Phone calls/texts*
- *Private meeting*
- *Ride to meetings*
- *Etc.*

Closing Prayers

Week 32 Homework

Week 32 Recovery Action Guide

Daily Action Guide

(next page)

Take the standard daily routine of Boundaries, Gift of Self, and the 3-I's. Do them daily, but you do not need to write down the results of your work each day. You need to begin practicing the discipline of doing this work on a regular daily basis without having to actually write down your work every day.

Each day – reflect in prayer on the exercises and questions.

1. Did you violate any Primary Boundaries in the last 24hrs?   Yes   No

     If No, go to **#2,** If Yes, then complete the following:

     What Boundary did you violate?

     What events led up to the behavior?

     What Secondary Boundaries did you violate leading up to the Primary?

2. Did you violate any Secondary Boundaries in the last 24hrs?   Yes   No

     If No, go to **#3**, If Yes, then complete the following:

     What Boundaries did you violate?

3. What **Gift of Self** did you perform in the last 24hrs?

Remember to also do the following:

- ✓ Prayer/meditation for 30 or more minutes per day.
- ✓ Reading Scripture every day.
- ✓ Reciting the 7 Cornerstones of Commitment.
- ✓ Recite the Surrender Prayer.
- ✓ Practice some type of intentional fast every day.

4. 3-I's Evaluation of a Daily Event
    Day 1: Describe the event that happened:

_____

_____

Name the emotions that were revealed: _____

Revealing the Source: *When was the first time in your life (possibly childhood) when you recall these emotions and what was the event that triggered them? (pray the Holy Spirit prayer for guidance)*

_____

_____

Name the 3-I emotions that were related: _____

What behavior was engaged in after this event and emotions happened?

_____

_____

Was this an expression of True Intimacy or False Intimacy? _____

If False Intimacy was chosen:
(a) Describe where in the process you could have made a different decision and followed True Intimacy. (Event, Thought, Emotions, 3-I's, Needs, etc.)

_____

_____

And:
(b) What True Intimacy steps would you have personally engaged in? Can you do it now?

Self _____

God _____

Others _____

OR

If True Intimacy was chosen:
(a) What True Intimacy steps did you engage in?

Self _____

God _____

Others _____

Now if you feel you need to, pray the below forgiveness prayer about the person and event that triggered an emotion in you today, do so now.

Lord, I choose to forgive _____ for the action of _____ that triggered me to feel _____. I release this person from any power he or she holds over me in generating my hurt feelings. Lord, I give you permission to take the judgment and the bitterness out of my life. I surrender it to You and ask You to remove it and to heal me where I have been wounded. I surrender my right to be paid back for my loss by the one who sinned against me, and by doing so I declare my trust in God alone as my Righteous Judge.

Lord, I ask for your forgiveness in my choosing to react to this person, resulting in my actions of _____ _____ and I choose to forgive myself for reacting this way.

In Jesus' name, Amen.

Week 33 What Does it Mean to be a Real Man?

Meeting Protocol

Group Invocation of the Holy Spirit
"Come Holy Spirit, renew me, dwell in me and protect me"

Facilitator Leads the Group in Prayer

Confidentiality Bond – group recites together
"I _____ pledge to honor each person present or not present today in this group. I will do so by keeping all comments and discussions offered here today and at all future meetings confidential. I also pledge to keep the identity of all members confidential. I also pledge to make no statements of judgmental nature about anyone in this group, including myself."

Welcome New Members

Check-in Round 1: Feelings/Mood
Check-in Round 2: Significant event since last meeting (30-60 seconds)
Check-in Round 3: Temptation Rating (On a scale of 1–10; 1 a low temptation, 10 a high temptation)
Check-in Round 4: Primary or Secondary Boundary Violations
   If a Primary Violation occurred, the following questions/factors need to be addressed:
   ✓ **What do you think led to acting out?** – life events 24+ hours before
   ✓ **What were your feelings before acting out?**
   ✓ **Did you call anyone?**
   ✓ **What Secondary Boundaries did you violate this week?** – include those that were prior to your Primary Boundary Violation if you had one.
   ✓ **Group affirmation and acceptance of sharing.**
Check-in Round 5: Victories

Scripture Verse

Ephesians 5:25 "Husbands, love your wives, just as Christ loved the church and gave himself up for her"

Group Discussion Question: How does this verse relate to your life and your battle with sexual sin?

Week 33 Recovery Foundation Lesson

The divorce rate in America is over 50 percent. Why is this? We have men growing up who don't know how to be husbands and fathers. They don't know God, and they don't know their place in the family, much less in society.

God gave us our mission: to serve, to protect, and to defend everything God is entrusting to us. The family is at the top of this mission. This is why Satan's first target is the family. His primary weapon is pride.

We, as men, can choose whether or not to accept this mission of God.

Societal Teaching on Being a Man

Society teaches us that we men can choose our mission, our purpose in life. It also teaches us that we can change our mission any time we choose. If times get too tough, it's ok to drop everything and go find something else, right? If we find something better, like a better woman, we go after it. If the woman we have isn't serving our needs to our expectations, we are perfectly within our "rights" to supplement with others or even use counterfeit means of satisfaction, so long as we get what we want, right? It's about us and what we want. Sound familiar?

With this thinking we become our own god. We worship ourselves and our own needs. We seek gifts TO self, not gifts OF self. Sound familiar? Recall the beginning of this lesson where Satan's primary weapon is pride?

Every time we look at porn, we stab women in the heart. We do this by reducing them to objects. We reduce them from the pinnacle of God's creation to a mere thing, a toy for us to use and throw away. When we do this, we say no to God's mission.

Man uses himself, his free will, to choose himself over God. This was first revealed when Adam ate the fruit of the forbidden tree.

When we don't follow God's plan

Crisis in the family stems from the crisis of manhood and the concept of manhood. So many aspects of society have stemmed from men not being willing to accept the mission that Christ called us to.

- Men pioneered the sexual revolution
- Men pioneered the objectification of women
- Men perfected contraception
- Men pioneered the widespread infiltration of pornography
- Men were the first to push for homosexual unions and marriage
- Men are the ones seeking any biological and social methods to avoid responsibility for families

Men not taking responsibility or being present in the family has produced a multitude of traumatic repercussions.

Both boys and girls without fathers suffer these facts:

- Both engage in sex at a much earlier age
- Girls have radically increased occurrences of single motherhood
- Both have a significantly increased occurrence of sexually transmitted diseases
- Girls have increased relationships with physical and mental abuse
- Girls have increased abortion rates
- Both have a higher dependency on welfare
- Both have increased homelessness
- Boys reflect an increase in violent crimes
- Both experience dramatically higher levels of divorce
- Both show rates of increased suicide
- Boys reflect an increase in drug and alcohol abuse
- Both show a decline in the practice of religion
- Both show increased anxiety disorders
- Both have increased sexual identity issues

And while these facts are higher when the father is not in the picture at all, it is nearly as high when the father is uninvolved in the family. These situations reveal the absence of moral leadership of the father, a lack of influence of faith by the father, and an absence of spiritual and moral protection of the father.

God's Plan for Being a Man

When a man accepts the mission from God to serve, protect and defend, this is how it presents itself:

- The father models masculinity to the boys.
- The father demonstrates to his daughter how a woman should be treated by a man, by modeling it to her mother.
- The father models the Christ-like respect in the house and brings the faith to his family.
- The father protects the family from outside morally questionably influences.
- The father defends against spiritual attacks on his family.

As men, we must stand up for integrity, and for our faith. We are called to be the Military Generals of the family and engage in spiritual warfare for ourselves and the family. The spiritual attack on the family is much greater than any physical attack.

As **1 John 5:19** states, "We know that we are God's children, and that the whole world lies under the power of the evil one."

We, as Christians, must realize that we live in a world that is under the power of the enemy. The enemy seeks to introduce confusion and doubt, thus allowing rationalization and justification of immoral influences and decisions. This is also referred to as moral relativism. To protect the family from the influence of Satan, we must be able to discern what is spiritually clean and unclean. A man who battles his own purity cannot discern the difference to properly protect his family. As the scripture we used to open this week says, *"Husbands, love your wives, just as Christ loved the church and gave himself up for her."* – Jesus died for us, the members of His church. We must be so dedicated in protecting our wives and families that we are willing to die for them.

Make no mistake men, we and our families are under a supernatural attack, and if we are not aligned with Christ and pure of heart, it is impossible to see the war for our souls and those of our families that is taking place all around us.

The father must practice purity and chastity and educate himself on the role of the Father, have a relationship, himself, with God the Father and continually seek to heal his own brokenness, as he constantly increases his depth of surrender to Christ. This will open his eyes to the needs of the family and increase his awareness of attacks on his family, as these attacks are many.

As you see, your history of sexual sin not only impacts you, it has a profound impact on your family.

Single Men

If you are single, then the knowledge of this lesson will prepare you for when you have a family. You will be stronger entering into a new family with this knowledge and the understanding and progress from your work on purity, than a man who is asked to change directions in the middle of his family. Satan will defend his stronghold of an existing family with more vengeance than preventing a family from ever being in his hold to begin with.

If a family is in your past or not in God's plan for you at all, then these truths will assist you in engaging others and helping them be better educated. Not to mention saving your own soul.

This entire program is not only to get you free, but to guide you in becoming a real man, a faithful man, and a healed man.

As you continue to grow, heal and increase your relationship with Christ, know that real men look for the good in others and the good to do. Revenge, eye for eye type justice, negativity of yourself and others is not from our Father in heaven; don't let it be part of your identity.

Knowing God

In any capacity that God puts before you, whether it be single, married, father, priest or single missionary, the foremost action you absolutely <u>must</u> take is to have a dedicated prayer life. You must know God and His will. You must be a man after God's own heart. After all He is after yours! Prayer will make a man strong in faith and strong in resisting the devil. Prayer will make a man knowledgeable of the enemy and his tactics. Our mission as men will flow from our interior life.

As Jesus made clear in every Gospel, "put your sword in its sheath." Our true battle is not of this world. Your true identity must be that of a "just" man before God. Not the identities that we discovered in our shame and identity lessons several weeks ago.

The following is so important, that we will repeat it here, taken from Lesson 17.

First and foremost, we are ALL called to be saints. We are also ALL given the grace to achieve this but must accept the invitation of God to make it happen.

> **1 Corinthians 1:2** "To the church of God that is in Corinth, to those who are sanctified in Christ Jesus, called to be saints, together with all those who in every place call on the name of our Lord Jesus Christ, both their Lord and ours:"

> "None of us can make ourselves saints. None of us can even say the name of Jesus in faith without his grace. It is God who reaches out to us, not we who first choose God. God reaches out to us every day in a million ways, so grace is always there. It all starts with God and it ends

with God, and in between there are nothing but God-laden moments, although we may not always recognize them as such." - Lucy Fuchs PhD – Franciscan Spirit

"It is by living with love and offering Christian witness in our daily tasks that we are called to become saints… Always and everywhere you can become a saint, that is, by being receptive to the grace that is working in us and leads us to holiness." – Pope Francis

Prayer is so very critical. Do NOT say, "I will <u>try</u> to pray every day" but say, "I <u>will</u> pray <u>every day</u> as if my life and soul depended on it" – because it does!

To be a good leader, a good husband, a good father, and an example to all those God entrusts to us, we must first be a good son. We are all adopted sons of the Father. We must be a son who is obedient to his Father in heaven, a son who seeks to know Him and His will for us.

Love

Love is to "will the good of another." So, *will* the good of those that God entrusts to us – again, our mission from God. The main purpose of a husband and father is to get your wife and children to heaven, It is your responsibility to educate, catechize and lead them in matters of purity, chastity and obedience to God. If you are not a natural leader and you tell yourself, "I'm not good at that," then ask for help from your spouse. Tell her you have discovered this mission from God. Be transparent with her and ask for help. She will respect your being vulnerable, sharing your fear and discomfort, and most of all your desire to be the man that God is calling you to be.

(Statistical data is a combination of reports from UNICEF, Focus on the Family, Daniel Passini of Asystematic Theology and Psychology Today)

Group Questions

✓ What changes do I need to make in my family to answer God's call to *serve, to protect and to defend?*

✓ Who in my family will be the most resistant to this change? How will I address this resistance?

✓ What are you willing to sacrifice to be the man you now know God is calling you to be?

Meeting Close
Check Out

What do you need? – 5 min

Is there anything the group can offer any member?

- *Prayers*
- *Phone calls/texts*
- *Private meeting*
- *Ride to meetings*
- *Etc.*

Closing Prayers

Week 33 Homework

In **Appendix H,** read and follow the action plan for implementation of change in your family and yourself.

Week 33 Recovery Action Guide

Daily Action Guide

(next page)

Take the standard daily routine of Boundaries, Gift of Self, and the 3-I's. Do them daily, but you do not need to write down the results of your work each day. You need to begin practicing the discipline of doing this work on a regular daily basis without having to actually write down your work every day.

Each day – reflect in prayer on the exercises and questions.

1. Did you violate any Primary Boundaries in the last 24hrs?   Yes   No

If No, go to **#2,** If Yes, then complete the following:

What Boundary did you violate?

What events led up to the behavior?

What Secondary Boundaries did you violate leading up to the Primary?

2. Did you violate any Secondary Boundaries in the last 24hrs?   Yes   No

If No, go to **#3**, If Yes, then complete the following:

What Boundaries did you violate?

3. What **Gift of Self** did you perform in the last 24hrs?

Remember to also do the following:

- ✓ Prayer/meditation for 30 or more minutes per day.
- ✓ Reading Scripture every day.
- ✓ Reciting the 7 Cornerstones of Commitment.
- ✓ Recite the Surrender Prayer.
- ✓ Practice some type of intentional fast every day.

4. 3-I's Evaluation of a Daily Event
Recall an event that happened today.

Name the emotions that were revealed: _____

Revealing the Source: When was the first time in your life (possibly childhood) when you recall these emotions and what was the event that triggered them? (pray the Holy Spirit prayer for guidance)

Name the 3-I emotions that were related: _____

What behavior was engaged in after this event and emotions happened?

Was this an expression of True Intimacy or False Intimacy? _____

If False Intimacy was chosen:
 (a) Reflect on where in the process you could have made a different decision and followed True Intimacy. (Event, Thought, Emotions, 3-I's, Needs, etc.)

And:

(b) What True Intimacy steps would you have personally engaged in? Can you do it now?

Self

God

Others

OR

<u>If True Intimacy was chosen</u>:

(a) What True Intimacy steps did you engage in?

Self

God

Others

Now if you feel you need to, pray the below forgiveness prayer about the person and event that triggered an emotion in you today, do so now.

Lord, I choose to forgive _____ for the action of _____ that triggered me to feel _____. I release this person from any power he or she holds over me in generating my hurt feelings. Lord, I give you permission to take the judgment and the bitterness out of my life. I surrender it to You and ask You to remove it and to heal me where I have been wounded. I surrender my right to be paid back for my loss by the one who sinned against me, and by doing so I declare my trust in God alone as my Righteous Judge.

Lord, I ask for your forgiveness in my choosing to react to this person, resulting in my actions of _____ _____ and I choose to forgive myself for reacting this way.

In Jesus' name, Amen.

No additional Weekly Action Guide exercise this week.

Week 34 Making Amends

Meeting Protocol

Group Invocation of the Holy Spirit
"Come Holy Spirit, renew me, dwell in me and protect me."

Facilitator Leads the Group in Prayer

Confidentiality Bond – group recites together
"I _____ pledge to honor each person present or not present today in this group. I will do so by keeping all comments and discussions offered here today and at all future meetings confidential. I also pledge to keep the identity of all members confidential. I also pledge to make no statements of judgmental nature about anyone in this group, including myself."

Welcome New Members

Check-in Round 1: Feelings/Mood
Check-in Round 2: Significant event since last meeting (30-60 seconds)
Check-in Round 3: Temptation Rating (On a scale of 1–10; 1 a low temptation, 10 a high temptation)
Check-in Round 4: Primary or Secondary Boundary Violations
   If a Primary Violation occurred, the following questions/factors need to be addressed:
   ✓ **What do you think led to acting out?** – life events 24+ hours before
   ✓ **What were your feelings before acting out?**
   ✓ **Did you call anyone?**
   ✓ **What Secondary Boundaries did you violate this week?** – include those that were prior to your Primary Boundary Violation if you had one.
   ✓ **Group affirmation and acceptance of sharing.**
Check-in Round 5: Victories

Scripture Verse

Matthew 5:23-24 "So when you are offering your gift at the altar, if you remember that your brother or sister has something against you, leave your gift there before the altar and go; first be reconciled to your brother or sister, and then come and offer your gift."

Group Discussion Question: How does this verse relate to your life and your battle with sexual sin?

Week 34 Recovery Foundation Lesson

Why Make Amends?

Making amends involves apologizing for hurting someone else as well as making restitution for the damage caused by your behavior. The Catholic Church refers to this restitution as reparation.

Every offense committed against justice and truth entails the duty of reparation, even if its author has been forgiven. When it is impossible publicly to make reparation for a wrong, it must be made secretly. If someone who has suffered harm cannot be directly compensated, he must be given moral satisfaction in the name of charity. This duty of reparation also concerns offenses against another's reputation. This reparation, moral and sometimes material, must be evaluated in terms of the extent of the damage inflicted. It obliges in conscience. CCC 2487

The act of apologizing to others helps to heal both parties by bringing sin to light, *"what is in darkness is under the power of the enemy."*

Here are some practical reasons for making reparation:

- Exercising the virtue of Humility
- Making restitution
- Healing broken relationships
- Helping alleviate guilt and shame
- Starting to live a new life of integrity
- Solidifying your new identity of honesty and taking responsibility
- Helping with self-forgiveness, whether or not others forgive you as we are called to accept God's mercy and to forgive ourselves. It is not conditional on whether or not we have been forgiven by another.

Who Do I Make Amends To?

First and foremost, to God. This is done through the Sacrament of Reconciliation. (You should be doing this already. Review **Week 9 "Sacraments are the Cornerstone of Grace"** if necessary). The other obvious person is your spouse or significant other in your life. There can be many not-so-obvious persons you need to make amends to, as well. Looking back at your addictive behavior, you may realize you hurt more people than just by your sexual behavior.

You may need to make amends for behaviors such as:

- Ignoring your spouse.
- Isolating yourself from family.
- Being distant to children.
- Stealing money for prostitutes or other activities.
- Hiding credit card activity used for behaviors.
- Being dishonest with job resources such as time on computer or travel expenses.

A general rule in making amends is to consider whether by publicly confessing your behavior, you will do more damage than good. This comes primarily when telling someone who doesn't already know and doesn't necessarily need to know. (We're not talking about your spouse here.) When making amends, you must take into account that you want to tell children so as to not hurt them in a different way than you already have. Maybe just apologize for not being there – you could say you, "were going through some personal emotional troubles and have gotten help – or are getting help."

If you can't make amends with a person directly (i.e., not available, passed on, won't return phone calls, not appropriate to tell, etc.) then in much the same way a priest sometimes says in confession, you can do an act of charity in the name of the offense. One good example: You can have a Mass offered in their name. If your ex-wife moved away and you are unable to reach her, you can do some volunteer work as a self-penance, or even offer to work with your church in helping others get through the same battles that you have *(CCC 2487 quoted above, speaks to this)*.

With respect to a job, admitting use of computer time to a company may cost a father his livelihood and that of his family. A possible answer may be to work through lunch or after hours without pay for a certain number of hours until the estimated extra amount of time is made up.

Work with your accountably partner on this process. At times, addicts are so zealous to make amends that they leap without thinking; sometimes causing more damage than necessary by opening old wounds, bringing pain to a situation that has been previously resolved, or to persons who are not aware of what you did. Therefore, disclosure could cause damage where there was none (telling your children is a prime example). Your accountability partner can be a reasonable sounding board for your mission.

If your mission of confession to others has an undertone of arrogance, then think twice before acting (Yes, this happens!)

Surrender.... Again!

Up to now, you have practiced surrendering your own desires and negative self-images in order to be proactive in changing your behavior. Using the surrender prayer, you have even practiced surrendering yourself so Christ can work in you. You will find that the act of reaching out to others and confronting your fears and confessing your behavior, or being accountable to others that you have hurt, will require a different level of surrender. This time you will need to surrender your pride and step out in humility by allowing yourself to be vulnerable when bearing your soul to those whom you hurt. You don't really know how others will react. Those who already know, and to whom you are trying to make amends to, will be a different than telling those who don't have any idea about your addictive behavior. While it is important to reveal your behavior to all those you have hurt, this is the time to discern whether revealing your behavior will do more damage than good to the individuals you tell. A serious consideration here, is the awareness of how you need to make restitution for your behavior.

Making Amends with your Spouse

In most cases, your spouse already knows your sexually inappropriate behaviors. Many times, this was the catalyst for your starting the Restoring God's Foundation program, initially! Making amends with your spouse is a lengthy process. Many times, men are completely unaware of how deeply they have hurt their spouses. Consider this statistic: 90% of spouses of porn addicts suffer from PTSD (Post Traumatic Stress Disorder). As the author of this program, I can tell you that that was the case with me and with literally 100% of every married man that I have encountered in counseling. In the situation of making amends with your spouse (if not divorced), and depending on what your transgressions or offenses were, this can take many years. Understand that you made a serious violation of trust and you simply obliterated your marriage vows. You have sinned against the one that you are joined with as one flesh under God! Depending on her own past brokenness, your actions may run even more deeply. But, how wounded she was to start with is not a consideration of your current need for amends and the actions you must take. You are one flesh under God, and you inherited her brokenness and must make restitution, no matter the cost. This may seem harsh, but your job as a man is to protect her heart and get her to heaven. (Week 33).

In regaining her trust and making amends, I strongly suggest the book, **"Worthy of Her Trust" by Jason Martinkus**. Speaking as the author, I will share personally that one of many things I did was to install on my iPhone the, "Find My Friends" app and my wife can always look to see where I am. Even 15 years later! I never question why she desires to know where I am. This is one way I rebuild trust. Honestly, 15 years later, she rarely even looks, but she always knows she can if she wants.

Things to Consider:

- By making amends you are committing to a continuous process of change.
- It doesn't matter how your efforts to make amends are received, it's the act of genuinely attempting to make them that impacts your growth and commitment to your integrity and new life.
- Know that while your actions have serious consequences, your choice to make amends may also. This is simply taking responsibility for your actions. Be a man and step up to what you have done and those you have hurt.
- Remember, the act of making amends increases the virtue of Humility.
- Be aware that while you are asking others to forgive you for your actions, you may need to forgive others who refuse to forgive you for yours.

Group Questions

✓ Do I have fears about making amends?

✓ Am I worried that someone may reject me?

✓ What have I done before today to make amends? And to Whom?

Meeting Close
Check Out
What do you need? – 5 min
Is there anything the group can offer any member?
– *Prayers*
– *Phone calls/texts*
– *Private meeting*
– *Ride to meetings*
– *Etc.*

Closing Prayers

Week 34 Homework

Journaling Questions

Other than sexual behaviors, what behaviors do I need to amend?

_____

_____

_____

Make a list of who I need to make amends to, and for what.

_____   _____

_____   _____

_____   _____

Make a list of goals, to complete my first step of making amends.

_____

_____

_____

If you are married, set a date of when you will have a conversation with your spouse, to find out what she would like you to do to start making amends. Write these below on the list.

Date:_____

List of amends to make:

_____   _____

_____   _____

_____   _____

_____   _____

_____   _____

Week 34 Recovery Action Guide

Daily Action Guide

(next page)

Take the standard daily routine of Boundaries, Gift of Self, and the 3-I's. Do them daily, but you do not need to write down the results of your work each day. You need to begin practicing the discipline of doing this work on a regular daily basis without having to actually write down your work every day.

Each day – reflect in prayer on the exercises and questions.

1. Did you violate any Primary Boundaries in the last 24hrs?   Yes   No

    If No, go to **#2,** If Yes, then complete the following:

    What Boundary did you violate?

    What events led up to the behavior?

    What Secondary Boundaries did you violate leading up to the Primary?

2. Did you violate any Secondary Boundaries in the last 24hrs?   Yes   No

    If No, go to **#3**, If Yes, then complete the following:

    What Boundaries did you violate?

3. What **Gift of Self** did you perform in the last 24hrs?

Remember to also do the following:

- ✓ Prayer/meditation for 30 or more minutes per day.
- ✓ Reading Scripture every day.
- ✓ Reciting the 7 Cornerstones of Commitment.
- ✓ Recite the Surrender Prayer.
- ✓ Practice some type of intentional fast every day.

4. 3-I's Evaluation of a Daily Event
   Recall an event that happened today.

Name the emotions that were revealed: _____

Revealing the Source: When was the first time in your life (possibly childhood) when you recall these emotions and what was the event that triggered them? (pray the Holy Spirit prayer for guidance)

Name the 3-I emotions that were related: _____

What behavior was engaged in after this event and emotions happened?

Was this an expression of True Intimacy or False Intimacy? _____

If False Intimacy was chosen:
(a) Reflect on where in the process you could have made a different decision and followed True Intimacy. (Event, Thought, Emotions, 3-I's, Needs, etc.)

And:

(b) What True Intimacy steps would you have personally engaged in? Can you do it now?

Self _____

God _____

Others _____

OR

If True Intimacy was chosen:

(a) What True Intimacy steps did you engage in?

Self _____

God _____

Others _____

Now if you feel you need to, pray the below forgiveness prayer about the person and event that triggered an emotion in you today, do so now.

Lord, I choose to forgive _____ for the action of _____ that triggered me to feel _____. I release this person from any power he or she holds over me in generating my hurt feelings. Lord, I give you permission to take the judgment and the bitterness out of my life. I surrender it to You and ask You to remove it and to heal me where I have been wounded. I surrender my right to be paid back for my loss by the one who sinned against me, and by doing so I declare my trust in God alone as my Righteous Judge.

Lord, I ask for your forgiveness in my choosing to react to this person, resulting in my actions of _____ _____ and I choose to forgive myself for reacting this way.

In Jesus' name, Amen.

Week 35 When Will I be Normal? Where do I go From Here?

Meeting Protocol

Group Invocation of the Holy Spirit
"Come Holy Spirit, renew me, dwell in me and protect me."

Facilitator Leads the Group in Prayer

Confidentiality Bond – group recites together
"I _____ pledge to honor each person present or not present today in this group. I will do so by keeping all comments and discussions offered here today and at all future meetings confidential. I also pledge to keep the identity of all members confidential. I also pledge to make no statements of judgmental nature about anyone in this group, including myself."

Welcome New Members

Check-in Round 1: Feelings/Mood
Check-in Round 2: Significant event since last meeting (30-60 seconds)
Check-in Round 3: Temptation Rating (On a scale of 1–10; 1 a low temptation, 10 a high temptation)
Check-in Round 4: Primary or Secondary Boundary Violations
   If a Primary Violation occurred, the following questions/factors need to be addressed:
   ✓ **What do you think led to acting out?** – life events 24+ hours before
   ✓ **What were your feelings before acting out?**
   ✓ **Did you call anyone?**
   ✓ **What Secondary Boundaries did you violate this week?** – include those that were prior to your Primary Boundary Violation if you had one.
   ✓ **Group affirmation and acceptance of sharing.**
Check-in Round 5: Victories

Scripture Verses

Isaiah 41:10 "Do not fear, for I am with you, do not be afraid, for I am your God;
I will strengthen you, I will help you, I will uphold you with my victorious right hand."

John 10:27 "My sheep hear my voice. I know them, and they follow me."

Group Discussion Question: How do these verses relate to your life and your FUTURE AS WE COMPLETE THIS PROGRAM?

Week 35 Recovery Foundation Lesson

Are we done? Really?

CONGRATULATIONS!

Yes, it has been nearly a year and you have persevered through the entire Restoring God's Foundation Program. But now you are left with two remaining questions. First, you are, and probably have been asking:

When Will I Be Normal?

As the author of this program, and a counselor, I get asked this question all the time. My question back is – What is Normal? For most, they want to be able to watch what they want on TV and in movies without being triggered, they want to see provocatively dressed women and not be attracted to them, etc.

Let me ask you this: Does it seem normal to take the sexually explicit ways of our culture – the ideas, the images, the belief system that conditioned you to believe that non-Godly exhibited sexual ideals were the "normal" way of life – to take these ideas that created selfish ways and ways of ignoring human dignity, all for the sake of your enjoyment, to take this way of life, and consume it for entertainment and not be affected? It's equivalent to saying, "I want to drink poison and not get sick or die." If that is what you mean by normal, I hope you can agree that you will never be "normal." Hopefully, you see that not following the ways of the world, to choose to "buck" the system as some say, and to follow God IS "normal."

Recall once again these Scripture Verses:

> **1 John 5:19** "We know that we are God's children, and that the whole world lies under the power of the evil one."

> **1 Peter 2:11** "Beloved, I urge you as aliens and exiles to abstain from the desires of the flesh that wage war against the soul."

> **Ephesians 2:19** "So then you are no longer strangers and aliens, but you are citizens with the saints and also members of the household of God."

This IS normal! Denial of the ways of the enemy. Denial of the lies of the evil one. Rejection of sin. And surrendering your very self to Christ IS normal.

Where Do I Go from Here?

This is the end of the Restoring God's Foundation structured program. But hopefully it isn't the end of your recovery. From here you continue to live life doing many of the weekly action steps you have been doing for months. Prayer, Meditation, Scripture, Fasting, Self-awareness, using the 3-I's every time a strong emotion or event presents itself, and continuing in life with a goal to always be a gift OF self.

In practice, many groups continue meeting, doing the check-ins and making their own studies. These are your brothers in Christ, they have walked with you a long way. They know you and may be life supporters. In a way, you can look at it as maintenance. Many groups even move to a coffee shop to meet weekly or twice a month.

Maintenance

The **Road to Purity** website, (www.roadtopurity.com) under the **Restoring God's Foundation** heading, has ideas for continued work for groups to engage in for maintenance. Take a look and see if anything is of interest to your group.

Group Questions

✓ Discuss which members would like to continue meeting, and the potential schedule.

✓ If you have internet access, review the potential topics for maintenance groups and discuss.

Meeting Close
Check Out
What do you need? – 5 min

Is there anything the group can offer any member?

- *Prayers*
- *Phone calls/texts*
- *Private meeting*
- *Ride to meetings*
- *Etc.*

Closing Prayers

Appendices

Appendix A: Feelings Wheel and Chart

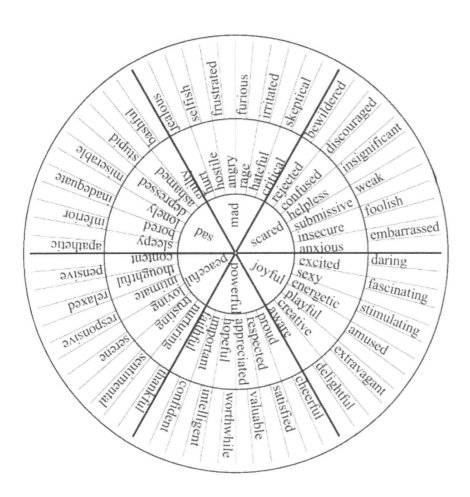

Intensity of Feelings	HAPPY	SAD	ANGRY	AFRAID	ASHAMED
HIGH	Elated Excited Overjoyed Thrilled Exuberant Ecstatic Fired up Passionate	Depressed Agonized Alone Hurt Dejected Hopeless Sorrowful Miserable	Furious Enraged Outraged Boiling Irate Seething Loathsome Betrayed	Terrified Horrified Scared stiff Petrified Fearful Panicky Frantic Shocked	Sorrowful Remorseful Defamed Worthless Disgraced Dishonored Mortified Admonished
MEDIUM	Cheerful Gratified Good Relieved Satisfied Glowing	Heartbroken Somber Lost Distressed Let down Melancholy	Upset Mad Defended Frustrated Agitated Disgusted	Apprehensive Frightened Threatened Insecure Uneasy Intimidated	Apologetic Unworthy Sneaky Guilty Embarrassed Secretive
LOW	Glad Contented Pleasant Tender Pleased Mellow	Unhappy Moody Blue Upset Disappointed Dissatisfied	Perturbed Annoyed Uptight Resistant Irritated Touchy	Cautious Nervous Worried Timid Unsure Anxious	Bashful Ridiculous Regretful Uncomfortable Pitied Silly

The five core emotions run left to right across the top of the table. Manifestations of each emotion based upon the intensity felt are described down each of the columns in the table.

Appendix B: The 7 Cornerstones of Commitment

Seven Cornerstones of Commitment
To be read out loud each morning and night

Cornerstone 1: I pledge that I will stop looking at pornography, masturbating, flirting, having affairs, committing fornication, or communicating with any person in any way that can incite lust or potentially lead to ungodly relations.

Cornerstone 2: I pledge to pray or meditate for at least 10 minutes every day.

Cornerstone 3: I pledge to read at least one scripture verse every day.

Cornerstone 4: I pledge to say the following Surrender Prayer every day: "Dear Lord Jesus Christ, I desire the desire to surrender my heart and my entire being to you but I cannot do it, I fear the abandonment of losing control of who I am. I ask that you take what little space I can open to you, use it and invade my heart, take it captive and protect it from all evil. I beg for your help in my complete surrender to you."

Cornerstone 5: I pledge to honestly look within myself and take responsibility for my actions and not blame anyone else for my behaviors.

Cornerstone 6: I pledge to give of myself selflessly in some way to someone every day.

Cornerstone 7: I pledge that if I am struggling with temptation that I will call someone to help me through the battle.

Appendix C: Sponsor Guidelines

Your sponsor Contact: (and other people in your group you choose to connect with. These people can also be an emergency contact if you cannot reach your sponsor.)

Name: _____ Phone#: _____

Name: _____ Phone#: _____

Name: _____ Phone#: _____

Name: _____ Phone#: _____

Name: _____ Phone#: _____

Guidelines of Being a Good Sponsor

- Be compassionate. As you already know, this addiction is hard. Being compassionate and empathetic to someone is powerful. And being accepted and affirmed for the person they are is critical to the healing process. Remember, though, that compassion and affirmation are NOT the same as permissiveness.

- Be tough. Don't let them get away with comments like, "I just wanted to" or "I just couldn't stop myself." Ask what triggered them. What feelings were they experiencing in the hours or days prior to acting out? And if they didn't have a fall, talk about what's going on in their life. It's entirely possible that their current stresses, if not discussed, may be a catalyst for a fall tomorrow.

- Share victories. This is very important. No matter how small they seem, share your successes and encourage your partner to share his as well. If you only talk about battles and difficulties, you'll likely feel depressed and defeated. By developing this practice, you will notice that over time your discussion of victories outweighs the discussions of falls and battles. Remember to praise your partner for achieving victories.

- Daily connection. Make a commitment to contact each other daily. Maybe even set a regular time. The more structured and consistent your communication, the more likelihood of success.

- Connect in person or by phone. Do not contact each other by text or email whenever possible. It's too passive and too easy. Talking directly to your partner will provide more interaction, and the very act of the discussion empowers healing.

Possible Questions in a Sponsor Conversation

These are some basic guidelines. Before making contact, make a quick prayer and invite the Holy Spirit to guide the conversation.

- What has your general mood been since we last connected?

- On a scale of 1-10, what has been your temptation level since we last connected?

- Have you engaged in any sexual or romantic fantasies?

- Have you violated any boundaries, primary or secondary since we last connected?
    - If yes, what happened the hours or days prior to the violation, and how do you think it contributed to the behavior?
    - If yes, what attempts did you make (if any) to fight the battle? What did or didn't work?

- Have you had any victories since we last connected?
    - If yes, what were they? Can you identify what led to temptation and what you did that successfully overcame it?

- Are you doing anything to enjoy life? Hobbies, etc. (other than TV, computer games or internet time) – something that avoids isolation.

- Have you been able to spend any time with Jesus in adoration?

- Is there anything in your life that is causing stress? And if so, what are you doing to deal with it?

- What are you looking forward to in the next few days or weeks?

- How has your prayer time been?

- Is there anything that you want to share? – remember this is a safe conversation.

- Finish by praying for the needs of the other.

Appendix D: Additional Prayers

Surrender Prayer

Dear Lord Jesus Christ, I desire the desire to surrender my heart and my entire being to You, but I cannot do it. I fear the abandonment of losing control of who I am. I ask that You take what little space I can open to You, use it, and invade my heart, take it captive, and protect it from all evil. I beg for Your help in my complete surrender to You.

Battle Prayer

Lord Jesus Christ, I cannot fight this battle anymore. I'm done, I hand You the dragon to slay, I hand You the lizard of lust to slay, I hand You the battle and walk away; it's Yours. I'm done. I can't do this anymore. It's not my battle anymore.

Prayer to Reveal Emotions

"Come Holy Spirit, bring peace to my heart. Please reveal to me events and emotions that were recently present in my life." Be with this thought for a few minutes and observe what comes to you.

Litany of Purity

Pause for at least two to three seconds and meditate on each line of each of the three segments of this litany. Ask the Holy Spirit to reveal any emotions present in you.

O Holy Spirit, I call to Thee to reveal the recent events that trigger emotions deep inside of me.

Any feelings of hurt or pain… *Reveal to me, Holy Spirit*

Feelings of anger… *Reveal to me, Holy Spirit*

Feelings of disrespect… *Reveal to me, Holy Spirit*

Feelings of rejection… *Reveal to me, Holy Spirit*

Feelings of incompetence… *Reveal to me, Holy Spirit*

Feelings of insignificance… *Reveal to me, Holy Spirit.*

Feelings of impotence… *Reveal to me, Holy Spirit*

Feelings of belittlement… *Reveal to me, Holy Spirit*

Feelings of worthlessness… *Reveal to me, Holy Spirit*

O Holy Spirit, reveal to me how I attach these feelings to beliefs of my identity.

The shame from hurt or pain… *Holy Spirit, reveal how it distorts my identity.*

The shame from anger… *Holy Spirit, reveal how it distorts my identity.*

The shame from disrespect… *Holy Spirit, reveal how it distorts my identity.*

The shame of rejection… *Holy Spirit, reveal how it distorts my identity.*

The shame of incompetence… *Holy Spirit, reveal how it distorts my identity.*

The shame of insignificance… *Holy Spirit, reveal how it distorts my identity.*

The shame of impotence… *Holy Spirit, reveal how it distorts my identity.*

The shame of belittlement… *Holy Spirit, reveal how it distorts my identity.*

The shame of worthlessness… *Holy Spirit, reveal how it distorts my identity.*

O Jesus, all powerful, loving, and merciful, I ask Your forgiveness for allowing myself to believe these lies about my identity, as they are not who You created me to be.

All feelings of hurt or pain... *I surrender to you, O Jesus.*

All feelings of anger... *I surrender to you, O Jesus.*

All feelings of disrespect... *I surrender to you, O Jesus.*

All feelings of rejection... *I surrender to you, O Jesus.*

All feelings of incompetence... *I surrender to you, O Jesus.*

All feelings of insignificance... *I surrender to you, O Jesus.*

All feelings of impotence... *I surrender to you, O Jesus.*

All feelings of belittlement... *I surrender to you, O Jesus.*

All feelings of worthlessness... *I surrender to you, O Jesus.*

Jesus, I beg You to fill my heart with all that which is of You.

Jesus, please grant me the peace that is from Your endless love and the ability to see myself as You see me.

Litany of Humility

O Jesus, meek and humble of heart,
Hear me.
From the desire of being esteemed,
Deliver me, O Jesus.
From the desire of being loved,
Deliver me, O Jesus.
From the desire of being extolled,
Deliver me, O Jesus.
From the desire of being honored,
Deliver me, O Jesus.
From the desire of being praised,
Deliver me, O Jesus.
From the desire of being preferred to others,
Deliver me, O Jesus.
From the desire of being consulted,
Deliver me, O Jesus.
From the desire of being approved,
Deliver me, O Jesus.
From the fear of being humiliated,
Deliver me, O Jesus.
From the fear of being despised,
Deliver me, O Jesus.
From the fear of suffering rebukes,
Deliver me, O Jesus.
From the fear of being calumniated,
Deliver me, O Jesus.
From the fear of being forgotten,
Deliver me, O Jesus.
From the fear of being ridiculed,
Deliver me, O Jesus.
From the fear of being wronged,
Deliver me, O Jesus.
From the fear of being suspected,
Deliver me, O Jesus.
That others may be loved more than I,
Jesus, grant me the grace to desire it.
That others may be esteemed more than I,
Jesus, grant me the grace to desire it.
That, in the opinion of the world, others may increase and I may decrease,
Jesus, grant me the grace to desire it.
That others may be chosen and I set aside,
Jesus, grant me the grace to desire it.
That others may be praised and I go unnoticed,
Jesus, grant me the grace to desire it.
That others may be preferred to me in everything,
Jesus, grant me the grace to desire it.
That others may become holier than I, provided that I may become as holy as I should,
Jesus, grant me the grace to desire it.

Soul Tie Prayer

(To be prayed for every event of fornication or adultery)

In the name of Jesus Christ and by the power of His Cross and Blood, I take the sword of the Holy Spirit and cut myself free from all previous sexual partners. I especially cut myself free from: (list partners)

_____, _____, _____etc.

I cut myself free from these people physically, spiritually, emotionally, and mentally. I not only cut myself free from these people, Lord, but I cut myself free from anyone and everyone else they have ever had sex with. I now place the Cross and the Blood of Jesus between myself and each of these people. I pray for a total cleansing and purification of my mind, body, and spirit, so that I may walk in wholeness, purification, and redemption.

Lord, please fill me with the power of Your Holy Spirit, that I may walk in Your abundant grace and mercy. Fill me with Your incredible love, that it may permeate all the dark and lonely places. Most of all, Lord, help me to know how much You love me and how special I am to You. Amen!

Litany of Trust

-Written by Sr. Faustina Maria Pia, Sister of Life

From the belief that
I have to earn Your love
Deliver me, Jesus.
From the fear that I am unlovable
Deliver me, Jesus.
From the false security
that I have what it takes
Deliver me, Jesus.
From the fear that trusting You
will leave me more destitute
Deliver me, Jesus.
From all suspicion of
Your words and promises
Deliver me, Jesus.
From the rebellion against
childlike dependency on You
Deliver me, Jesus.
From refusals and reluctances
in accepting Your will
Deliver me, Jesus.
From anxiety about the future
Deliver me, Jesus.
From resentment or excessive preoccupation
with the past
Deliver me, Jesus.
From restless self-seeking
in the present moment
Deliver me, Jesus.
From disbelief in Your love
and presence
Deliver me, Jesus.
From the fear of being asked
to give more than I have
Deliver me, Jesus.
From the belief that my life
has no meaning or worth
Deliver me, Jesus.
From the fear of what love demands
Deliver me, Jesus.
From discouragement
Deliver me, Jesus.
That You are continually holding me
sustaining me, loving me

Jesus, I trust in you.
That Your love goes deeper than my sins and
failings, and transforms me
Jesus, I trust in you.
That not knowing what tomorrow brings is an
invitation to lean on You
Jesus, I trust in you.
That You are with me in my suffering
Jesus, I trust in you.
That my suffering, united to Your own, will
bear fruit in this life and the next
Jesus, I trust in you.
That You will not leave me an orphan, that
You are present in Your Church
Jesus, I trust in you.
That Your plan is better
than anything else
Jesus, I trust in you.
That You always hear me and in
Your goodness always respond to me
Jesus, I trust in you.
That You give me the grace to accept
forgiveness and to forgive others
Jesus, I trust in you.
That You give me all the strength
I need for what is asked
Jesus, I trust in you.
That my life is a gift
Jesus, I trust in you.
That You will teach me to trust You
Jesus, I trust in you.
That You are my Lord and my God
Jesus, I trust in you.
That I am Your beloved one
Jesus, I trust in you

Appendix E: Transformation in Christ Meditation

This is the Transformation in Christ exercise

This can be a powerful meditation experience.

This is the culmination of identifying your inner wounds, your identity and surrendering to Christ and allowing Him to revive the person He created you to be.

Read slowly.

START

Make the sign of the Cross.

Close your eyes.

Put both feet flat on the floor.

Put your hands on your legs palms up.

Take several slow deep breaths, feeling your lungs fill with air and then feeling the air leave your lungs.

Feel the air around you on your skin.

Feel your feet inside your shoes.

Feel your shoes on the floor.

Relax, clear your mind.

Every thought that comes – let it pass by.

Visualize yourself in an empty room.

All the walls, floor and ceiling are white

It's clean and almost sterile.

You notice you are holding a large silver platter.

Look at the details of the platter, how ornate it is; see if it has gold trim, engraved flowers, etc.

Is it simple or very extravagant?

Notice how heavy the platter is.

You see yourself placing the platter on a small table in front of you.

Slowly become aware of any emotions you may be feeling right now.

Are you feeling anxious?

Are you feeling tired or bored?

Feelings of anticipation, or maybe peace or joy.

Pick one of those emotions, hold it out in front of you, notice its color, its weight, shape and smell.

See yourself placing the emotion on the silver platter.

Now take the next emotion, notice the same details about it, size, shape, color, smell, weight.

Put it on the platter, too.

And the next.

Now dig a little deeper and be aware of some underlying emotions, maybe loneliness.

Maybe you feel anger or have feelings of rejection.

Take one of those feelings and think about what event in your life may have caused you to feel that way.

Maybe it was something that happened today or even in the last hour.

Experience the emotion – don't suppress it.

Did you have a fight with your wife or girlfriend, leaving you hurt and feeling uncared for?

Did your boss reprimand you, making you feel incompetent or insignificant?

Did you break down on the side of the road leaving you feeling embarrassed or frustrated?

Take that emotion and see yourself putting it on the platter.

Take the associated event and put that on the platter too.

Now dig even deeper.

Remember an event from childhood, something that someone did to you.

Someone that you still hold anger towards, maybe animosity.

Maybe a teacher embarrassed you in front of the class, or a classmate teased you on the playground.

Let the memories come forward.

Maybe there is something that you've buried for a long time.

Maybe your father abandoned you as a child.

Maybe your wife left you for someone else, or your girlfriend broke up with you.

See your feelings, whether it be anger, resentment, abandonment, rejection or fear; see yourself putting the pain you felt, and continue to feel, as well as all associated emotions, one by one, on the platter.

And see yourself putting the related event on the platter, as well.

Do this for each emotion, one by one, as well as the related event in your life.

Slowly take each one, identify it, see it, and place it on the platter.

Think of the last small (venial) sin you committed,

Maybe you judged another person based on how they were dressed,

Maybe the last time you cursed or used the Lords name in vain.

Maybe you were rude to the cashier at the grocery store.

Whatever it is, recall all that you can think of and bring them forward into your mind.

Then slowly one by one, place each of them on the platter.

Now think of something a little bigger, a little more serious.

Did you steal a candy bar when you were a kid or even last week?

Maybe you lusted after a girl that you saw at work or at the McDonald's you just came from.

Maybe you haven't forgiven someone for something they did to you.

Maybe you looked at pornography three times this week and masturbated.

Maybe you had an affair or visited a prostitute or maybe several.

Maybe you embezzled money from the company you work for or even your church.

Maybe you paid for someone to get an abortion or just took them to the clinic where they could get one.

Maybe you even murdered someone.

Again, bring all of the events forward in your mind becoming aware of each one, and then, one by one, place them on the platter.

Take a look at yourself as a person. Your identity, who you see yourself to be.
Maybe one of your parents abandoned you when you were a child, so now you see yourself as unlovable or unwanted or unworthy. Put that part of you on the platter.

If you aided in an abortion, maybe you see yourself as the killer, and as a person who doesn't deserve God's love; you see yourself as unforgivable.
Put that part of you on the platter.

Maybe you are a porn addict or sex addict, you are not worthy of truly being loved.
You loathe yourself. You see yourself as a weak person because you can't beat this on your own.
Take that chunk of who you are, that part of your identity, and put it on the platter.

Keep looking at who you see yourself to be. Maybe as a person you are prideful, boastful, self-centered, egotistical, greedy or aggressive.
Put each of these personal characteristics and parts of your identity on the platter.

If you are needy, if you are unattractive, inadequate or shameful, put that part of who you are on the platter.

If you're a good athlete, intelligent, or good looking, take that characteristic of your identity and put it on the platter.
If you're a compassionate person, see yourself as humble or empathetic, put that part of your identity on the platter.

Look at everything else you see yourself as, anything else that defines you as a person,
Find your identity.
Put each and every single one of those parts of you on the platter. One by one.

Look at the events in your life that shaped you; as early as you can remember: family vacations, holidays, elementary school, junior high, and high school.

Friends, your different jobs, different bosses, girlfriends, your spouse or spouses.

Recall every life shaping event and, one by one, put them on the platter.

Maybe your dad was too busy to play catch with you, and you live with the rejection of your father.

Maybe you project that rejection to God.

You live with underlying anger over the pain and resentment of how your father treated you.

Maybe you have un-forgiveness in your heart toward your father or God.

Take those feelings and the events that caused them and put them on the platter.

Maybe your teacher scolded you in front of the class and you're carrying that embarrassment to this day, and now you have a fear of stepping forward with ideas or contributing answers at work or with friends, for fear of being ridiculed or humiliated. Put those feelings and the events on the platter.

Maybe a scout leader, teacher or neighbor molested you and warned you not to tell.

Now sharing your emotions or any emotional pain is too risky, so you keep them all inside, and you feel like you can never truly get your needs met. You can never be free.

Go back as early as you can remember, bring each event – big or small, positive or negative – forward in your mind.

Put each memory on the platter and then, one by one, move forward through time, continuing to do this by putting each memory on the platter.

As these memories flash through your mind, continue, one by one, from the earliest to the present time.

Maybe you even see yourself as a strong person because of these events.

Maybe these events shaped you making you able to deal with adversity.

Take that strength and adversity and put it on the platter.

As you move through your memories, slowly take these memories and events and feelings, one by one, and put each of them on the silver platter.

Now as you've put each of these emotions, events, and memories and parts of your identity on the platter, be aware that they are no longer a part of you.

They are not present within you.

Look at yourself and see what's left. If there is happiness and joy, take those feelings and put it on the platter.

If there's loneliness put on the platter, if there is emptiness, put it on a platter.

If there are feelings or memories that you can't quite get a handle on or really identify, take those undefined pieces and put each of them on the platter.

Maybe there is a dark place that you can't see what it is, or it's too painful to look into,

It might be ugly and unpleasant to even look at – it may be very heavy.

Take that dark lump of undefined emotions, of undefined woundedness, and put it on the platter.

If one of the feelings is fear or abandonment, put it on the platter.

Keep going until you have nothing left.

What remains is a mere shell of a man, a naked soul, no memories, no personality and no identity that were created previously by choices and environment.

You see it all in a mound on the platter in front of you. All that remains is the mere infant soul of the human that God created. The pure and innocent soul.

You have completely and totally surrendered your entire being. Your identity.

Notice how high the mound of your existence is on the platter. It's huge, there is a lot there.

Now you see Jesus entering the room. He is pure and bright. You take notice of what He is wearing, how light His clothes are. You see the color of His skin, light, dark, brown, pale….

How long His hair is, its color; does He have any facial hair?

You see every detail of your Savior.

He walks over to your side. You can see the color of His eyes. He is so close you can see your reflection in His loving eyes.

You are kneeling before Him and saying "Jesus hold me" He kneels next to you and wraps His arms around you, You can feel His heart beating – just be still and rest in Him.

Jesus says to you, "I want you to know my Father, He is your Father. Pray with Me like I taught you.

You pray silently with Jesus: (VERY slowly)

"Our Father, who art in heaven, Hallowed be Thy name.

Thy kingdom come, Thy will be done,

On earth as it is in heaven.

Give us this day our daily bread,

Forgive us our trespasses as we forgive those who have trespassed against us.

Lead us not into temptation but deliver us from evil.

For Thine is the kingdom, the power and the glory, now and forever. Amen

You feel the endless unconditional love of Jesus AND His father flowing through you.

Jesus now asks if you have something for Him, you pick up the platter, noticing how incredibly heavy it is,

And you hand it to Him.

He smiles, Jesus is pleased beyond anything you could've imagined. He is so pleased that you have offered yourself, your complete self, as a gift to Him.

You have never seen joy like this.

As you again kneel before Him, He puts His hand on your head and you feel the radiant warmth of heaven flow into your shell. A shell that only contains the naked soul. A shell that is void of all previously perceived identity. A shell that is now the bare soul placed by God when you were created.

You look up and the platter has vanished, it's gone forever.

All your memories, all of your pain, your identity as you knew it, the history of what made you who you are, all gone. Everything you put on the platter is gone.

You have surrendered your very existence to Christ.

But, you suddenly realize that a few seconds ago, when Jesus put His hand on your head, He revived the person that he originally created. You feel this now to the very core of your being, every fiber of who you are! Every extremity, every part of who you are, from your toes to your hair, all perceives the beloved son that God created you to be, His love, and what He intends for you to become.

You are free from lust, free from the desire to be needed, free from the desire to be accepted, free from pride, anger, hurt or pain, free from any emotional distress.

You are encased in what feels like a warm blanket with the radiant and immense power of His Spirit within you, unblemished and boundless. The love of God the Father and the Holy Spirit pour over you without limits. It flows though you with ease.

As you sit here, basking in the radiant love of the Trinity, you begin to recognize some of what Jesus revived in you, some of what is actually the man He created you to be. It's suddenly all so clear.

You are a man of many virtues.

You feel a sense of sacrifice for your family and all those around you, your own needs are second to everyone else's.

You now feel compassion for those around you. You no longer feel anger at the person who cuts you off on the freeway, instead you feel empathy for the anxiety, the stress, and the lack of peace of the other driver, and you forgive him as he goes on his way.

You feel empathy for other people's struggles, and you have an overwhelming instinct to pray for those in need or those who have difficult trials in their lives.

Any prejudice, resentment, or judgment you once had simply doesn't exist.

You have flowing forgiveness for anyone who has ever wronged you or caused you pain.

You need nothing else in this world to make you happy, nothing to make you feel accepted, nothing to make you feel loved and admired, because you are completely filled with the Spirit of God and His Son, Jesus Christ.

You begin to silently pray, asking Jesus to reveal to you other characteristics of the man He created you to be. And in that prayer, you begin to realize that you are completely secure and can still feel the boundless love of Jesus, the Holy Spirit, and God the Father.

Nothing can prevent this love from running strong within you. There <u>is nothing</u> to prevent it.
It is boundless and endless. Your very existence has been transformed.
Rest in this revived and seemingly new identity.

Slowly become aware of the air touching your new skin. Your shoes on the floor and you're feet in them.
Sense yourself breathing, breathing the air that God provided, filling your new lungs.

Take deep breath, open your eyes. Now go and be the man God created you to be.

Appendix F: Scriptures

Scripture verses are from the New Revised Version Catholic Edition.

Lust Adultery and the Flesh

Matthew 5:27-28 "You have heard that it was said, 'You shall not commit adultery.' But I say to you that everyone who looks at a woman with lust has already committed adultery with her in his heart.

Attempting to dabble with temptation without acting out:
Proverbs 6:27 "Can fire be carried in the bosom without burning one's clothes?"

Revelation 21:8 "But as for the cowardly, the faithless, the polluted, the murderers, the fornicators, the sorcerers, the idolaters, and all liars, their place will be in the lake that burns with fire and sulfur, which is the second death."

Exodus 20:17 "You shall not covet your neighbor's house; you shall not covet your neighbor's wife, or male or female slave, or ox, or donkey, or anything that belongs to your neighbor."

1 Corinthians 6:13-15 ".... The body is meant not for fornication but for the Lord, and the Lord for the body. And God raised the Lord and will also raise us by his power. Do you not know that your bodies are members of Christ? Should I therefore take the members of Christ and make them members of a prostitute? Never!"

1 Corinthians 6:16 "Do you not know that whoever is united to a prostitute becomes one body with her? For it is said, "The two shall be one flesh.""

Hebrews 13:4 "Let marriage be held in honor by all, and let the marriage bed be kept undefiled; for God will judge fornicators and adulterers."

Romans 8:13 "for if you live according to the flesh, you will die; but if by the Spirit you put to death the deeds of the body, you will live."

1 Peter 4:3 "You have already spent enough time in doing what the Gentiles like to do, living in licentiousness, passions, drunkenness, revels, carousing, and lawless idolatry."

Romans 7:5 "While we were living in the flesh, our sinful passions, aroused by the law, were at work in our members to bear fruit for death."

Romans 13:14 "Instead, put on the Lord Jesus Christ, and make no provision for the flesh, to gratify its desires."

Proverbs 6:32-33 "But he who commits adultery has no sense; he who does it destroys himself. He will get wounds and dishonor, and his disgrace will not be wiped away."

Proverbs 6:25-29 "Do not desire her beauty in your heart, and do not let her capture you with her eyelashes; for a prostitute's fee is only a loaf of bread but the wife of another stalks a man's very life. Can fire be carried in the bosom without burning one's clothes? Or can one walk on hot coals without scorching the feet? So is he who sleeps with his neighbor's wife; no one who touches her will go un-punished."

1 John 2:16 "for all that is in the world—the desire of the flesh, the desire of the eyes, the pride in riches—comes not from the Father but from the world."

1 Corinthians 6:9-10 "Do you not know that wrongdoers will not inherit the kingdom of God? Do not be deceived! Fornicators, idolaters, adulterers, male prostitutes, sodomites, thieves, the greedy, drunk-ards, revilers, robbers—none of these will inherit the kingdom of God."

Mark 7:20-23 "And he said, "It is what comes out of a person that defiles. For it is from within, from the human heart, that evil intentions come: fornication, theft, murder, adultery, avarice, wickedness, deceit, licentiousness, envy, slander, pride, folly. All these evil things come from within, and they defile a person."

2 Peter 2:14-18 "They have eyes full of adultery, insatiable for sin. They entice unsteady souls. They have hearts trained in greed. Accursed children! They have left the straight road and have gone astray, following the road of Balaam son of Bosor, who loved the wages of doing wrong, but was rebuked for his own transgression; a speechless donkey spoke with a human voice and restrained the prophet's mad-ness. These are waterless springs and mists driven by a storm; for them the deepest darkness has been reserved. For they speak bombastic nonsense, and with licentious desires of the flesh they entice people who have just escaped from those who live in error."

Romans 8:6 "To set the mind on the flesh is death, but to set the mind on the Spirit is life and peace."

Galatians 5:16-21 "Live by the Spirit, I say, and do not gratify the desires of the flesh. For what the flesh desires is opposed to the Spirit, and what the Spirit desires is opposed to the flesh; for these are opposed to each other, to prevent you from doing what you want. But if you are led by the Spirit, you are not subject to the law. Now the works of the flesh are obvious: fornication, impurity, licentiousness, idolatry, sorcery, enmities, strife, jealousy, anger, quarrels, dissensions, factions, envy, drunkenness, carousing, and things like these. I am warning you, as I warned you before: those who do such things will not inherit the kingdom of God."

Ephesians 5:5-6 "Be sure of this, that no fornicator or impure person, or one who is greedy (that is, an idolater), has any inheritance in the kingdom of Christ and of God. Let no one deceive you with empty words, for because of these things the wrath of God comes on those who are disobedient."

Matthew 5:29-30 "If your right eye causes you to sin, tear it out and throw it away; it is better for you to lose one of your members than for your whole body to be thrown into hell. And if your right hand causes you to sin, cut it off and throw it away; it is better for you to lose one of your members than for your whole body to go into hell."

Romans 1:21-27 "for though they knew God, they did not honor him as God or give thanks to him, but they became futile in their thinking, and their senseless minds were darkened. Claiming to be wise, they became fools; and they exchanged the glory of the immortal God for images resembling a mortal human being or birds or four-footed animals or reptiles. Therefore God gave them up in the lusts of their hearts to impurity, to the degrading of their bodies among themselves, because they exchanged the truth about God for a lie and worshiped and served the creature rather than the Creator, who is blessed forever! Amen. For this reason, God gave them up to degrading passions. Their women exchanged natural intercourse for unnatural, and in the same way also the men, giving up natural intercourse with women, were consumed with passion for one another. Men committed shameless acts with men and received in their own persons the due penalty for their error."

Empowerment and Action

Romans 12:2 "Do not be conformed to this world, but be transformed by the renewing of your minds, so that you may discern what is the will of God—what is good and acceptable and perfect."

Romans 6:13-14 "No longer present your members to sin as instruments of wickedness, but present yourselves to God as those who have been brought from death to life, and present your members to God as instruments of righteousness. For sin will have no dominion over you, since you are not under law but under grace."

Romans 12:1-2 The New Life in Christ "I appeal to you therefore, brothers and sisters, by the mercies of God, to present your bodies as a living sacrifice, holy and acceptable to God, which is your spiritual worship. Do not be conformed to this world, but be transformed by the renewing of your minds, so that you may discern what is the will of God—what is good and acceptable and perfect."

1 Corinthians 6:19-20 "Or do you not know that your body is a temple of the Holy Spirit within you, which you have from God, and that you are not your own? For you were bought with a price; therefore glorify God in your body."

Psalm 51:10 "Create in me a clean heart, O God, and put a new and steadfast spirit within me."

1 Timothy 5:2 "…to older women as mothers, younger women as sisters, with absolute purity."

Job 31:1 "I have made a covenant with my eyes; how then could I look upon a virgin?"

Proverbs 31:3 "Do not give your strength to women, your ways to those who destroy kings."

Proverbs 5:8 "Keep your way far from her, and do not go near the door of her house;"

Colossians 3:5 "Put to death, therefore, whatever in you is earthly: fornication, impurity, passion, evil desire, and greed (which is idolatry)."

James 1:13-15 "No one, when tempted, should say, "I am being tempted by God"; for God cannot be tempted by evil and he himself tempts no one. But one is tempted by one's own desire, being lured and enticed by it; then, when that desire has conceived, it gives birth to sin, and that sin, when it is fully grown, gives birth to death."

1 Corinthians 9:27 "but I punish my body and enslave it, so that after proclaiming to others I myself should not be disqualified."

Galatians 5:24 "And those who belong to Christ Jesus have crucified the flesh with its passions and desires."

Ephesians 4:22 "You were taught to put away your former way of life, your old self, corrupt and deluded by its lusts…"

1 Thessalonians 4:4-5 "that each one of you know how to control your own body in holiness and honor, not with lustful passion, like the Gentiles who do not know God;"

1 John 1:8-9 "If we say that we have no sin, we deceive ourselves, and the truth is not in us. If we confess our sins, he who is faithful and just will forgive us our sins and cleanse us from all unrighteousness."

2 Timothy 2:22 "Shun youthful passions and pursue righteousness, faith, love, and peace, along with those who call on the Lord from a pure heart."

Titus 2:11-12 "For the grace of God has appeared, bringing salvation to all, training us to renounce impiety and worldly passions, and in the present age to live lives that are self-controlled, upright, and godly."

1 Peter 2:11 "Beloved, I urge you as aliens and exiles to abstain from the desires of the flesh that wage war against the soul."

Ephesians 5:3 "But fornication and impurity of any kind, or greed, must not even be mentioned among you, as is proper among saints."

James 5:16 "Therefore confess your sins to one another, and pray for one another, so that you may be healed. The prayer of the righteous is powerful and effective."

Galatians 2:20 "…and it is no longer I who live, but it is Christ who lives in me. And the life I now live in the flesh I live by faith in the Son of God, who loved me and gave himself for me."

Colossians 3:1-10 "So if you have been raised with Christ, seek the things that are above, where Christ is, seated at the right hand of God. Set your minds on things that are above, not on things that are on earth, for you have died, and your life is hidden with Christ in God. When Christ who is your life is revealed, then you also will be revealed with him in glory. Put to death, therefore, whatever in you is earthly: fornication, impurity, passion, evil desire, and greed (which is idolatry). On account of these the wrath of God is coming on those who are disobedient. These are the ways you also once followed, when you were living that life. But now you must get rid of all such things—anger, wrath, malice, slander, and abusive language from your mouth. Do not lie to one another, seeing that you have stripped off the old self with its practices and have clothed yourselves with the new self, which is being renewed in knowledge according to the image of its creator."

Job 31:1 "I have made a covenant with my eyes; how then should I look upon a virgin?"

Proverbs 31:3 "Do not give your strength to women, your ways to those who destroy kings."

Sirach 21:2 "Flee from sin as from a snake; for if you approach sin, it will bite you. Its teeth are lion's teeth, and can destroy human lives."

1 Timothy 6:11-12 "But as for you, man of God, shun all this; pursue righteousness, godliness, faith, love, endurance, gentleness. Fight the good fight of the faith; take hold of the eternal life, to which you were called and for which you made the good confession in the presence of many witnesses."

Hebrews 4:15-16 "For we do not have a high priest who is unable to sympathize with our weaknesses, but we have one who in every respect has been tested as we are, yet without sin. Let us therefore approach the throne of grace with boldness, so that we may receive mercy and find grace to help in time of need."

1 Corinthians 6:15-20 "Do you not know that your bodies are members of Christ? Should I therefore take the members of Christ and make them members of a prostitute? Never! Do you not know that whoever is united to a prostitute becomes one body with her? For it is said, "The two shall be one flesh." But anyone united to the Lord becomes one spirit with him. Shun fornication! Every sin that a person commits is outside the body; but the fornicator sins against the body itself. Or do you not know that your body is a temple of the Holy Spirit within you, which you have from God, and that you are not your own? For you were bought with a price; therefore, glorify God in your body."

Ephesians 4:22-24 "You were taught to put away your former way of life, your old self, corrupt and deluded by its lusts, and to be renewed in the spirit of your minds, and to clothe yourselves with the new self, created according to the likeness of God in true righteousness and holiness."

Quote: "The struggle is the sign of holiness. A Saint is a sinner that keeps trying." – St Josemaria Escriva

Quote: "When tempted, think, 'I will not give my power to that woman.'"

Surrender and Self-Denial

Romans 12:1 "I appeal to you therefore, brothers and sisters, by the mercies of God, to present your bodies as a living sacrifice, holy and acceptable to God, which is your spiritual worship."

Job 11:13 "If you direct your heart rightly, you will stretch out your hands toward him."

Romans 6:13 "No longer present your members to sin as instruments of wickedness, but present yourselves to God as those who have been brought from death to life, and present your members to God as instruments of righteousness."

Matthew 16:24-25 "Then Jesus told his disciples, "If any want to become my followers, let them deny themselves and take up their cross and follow me. For those who want to save their life will lose it, and those who lose their life for my sake will find it."

Mark 8:35 "For those who want to save their life will lose it, and those who lose their life for my sake, and for the sake of the gospel, will save it."

Luke 5:27-28 "After this he went out and saw a tax collector named Levi, sitting at the tax booth; and he said to him, "Follow me." And he got up, left everything, and followed him."

Mark 9:43 "If your hand causes you to stumble, cut it off; it is better for you to enter life maimed than to have two hands and to go to hell, to the unquenchable fire."

Galatians 5:16 "Live by the Spirit, I say, and do not gratify the desires of the flesh."

Matthew 19:21 "Jesus said to him, "If you wish to be perfect, go, sell your possessions, and give the money to the poor, and you will have treasure in heaven; then come, follow me."

Matthew 19:29 "And everyone who has left houses or brothers or sisters or father or mother or children or fields, for my name's sake, will receive a hundredfold, and will inherit eternal life."

2 Timothy 2:21 "All who cleanse themselves of the things I have mentioned will become special utensils, dedicated and useful to the owner of the house, ready for every good work."

James 4:7 "Submit yourselves therefore to God. Resist the devil, and he will flee from you."

1 Peter 4:2 "…so as to live for the rest of your earthly life no longer by human desires but by the will of God."

Genesis 39:7-10 "And after a time his master's wife cast her eyes on Joseph and said, 'Lie with me.' But he refused and said to his master's wife, 'Look, with me here, my master has no concern about anything in the house, and he has put everything that he has in my hand. He is not greater in this house than I am, nor has he kept back anything from me except yourself, because you are his wife. How then could I do this great wickedness, and sin against God?' And although she spoke to Joseph day after day, he would not consent to lie beside her or to be with her."

Philippians 2:4 "Let each of you look not to your own interests, but to the interests of others."

Proverbs 5:20 "Why should you be intoxicated, my son, by another woman and embrace the bosom of an adulteress?"

Mark 10:28 "Peter began to say to him, 'Look, we have left everything and followed you.'"

Self-Awareness

James 1:14 "But one is tempted by one's own desire, being lured and enticed by it;"

John 10:10 "The thief comes only to steal and kill and destroy. I came that they may have life, and have it abundantly."

Mark 7:21-23 "For it is from within, from the human heart, that evil intentions come: fornication, theft, murder, adultery, avarice, wickedness, deceit, licentiousness, envy, slander, pride, folly. All these evil things come from within, and they defile a person."

Sirach 23:19 "His fear is confined to human eyes and he does not realize that the eyes of the Lord are ten thousand times brighter than the sun; they look upon every aspect of human behavior and see into hidden corners."

Ephesians 4:17-19 "Now this I affirm and insist on in the Lord: you must no longer live as the Gentiles live, in the futility of their minds. They are darkened in their understanding, alienated from the life of God because of their ignorance and hardness of heart. They have lost all sensitivity and have abandoned themselves to licentiousness, greedy to practice every kind of impurity."

Encouragement and Strength

Romans 7:15-24 "I do not understand my own actions. For I do not do what I want, but I do the very thing I hate. Now if I do what I do not want, I agree that the law is good. But in fact, it is no longer I that do it, but sin that dwells within me. For I know that nothing good dwells within me, that is, in my flesh. I can will what is right, but I cannot do it. For I do not do the good I want, but the evil I do not want is what I do. Now if I do what I do not want, it is no longer I that do it, but sin that dwells within me."

1 Corinthians 6:18-20 "Shun fornication! Every sin that a person commits is outside the body; but the fornicator sins against the body itself. Or do you not know that your body is a temple of the Holy Spirit within you, which you have from God, and that you are not your own? For you were bought with a price; therefore, glorify God in your body."

Ephesians 6:11 "Put on the whole armor of God, so that you may be able to stand against the wiles of the devil."

Romans 8:13 "…for if you live according to the flesh, you will die; but if by the Spirit you put to death the deeds of the body, you will live."

1 Peter 1:13-16 "Therefore prepare your minds for action; discipline yourselves; set all your hope on the grace that Jesus Christ will bring you when he is revealed. Like obedient children, do not be conformed to the desires that you formerly had in ignorance. Instead, as he who called you is holy, be holy yourselves in all your conduct; for it is written, "You shall be holy, for I am holy.""

Philippians 4:8 "Finally, beloved, whatever is true, whatever is honorable, whatever is just, whatever is pure, whatever is pleasing, whatever is commendable, if there is any excellence and if there is anything worthy of praise, think about these things."

Romans 6:14 "For sin will have no dominion over you, since you are not under law but under grace."

Proverbs 7:25-27 "Do not let your hearts turn aside to her ways; do not stray into her paths. For many are those she has laid low, and numerous are her victims. Her house is the way to Sheol, going down to the chambers of death."

Romans 6:6-11 "We know that our old self was crucified with him so that the body of sin might be destroyed, and we might no longer be enslaved to sin. For whoever has died is freed from sin. But if we have died with Christ, we believe that we will also live with him. We know that Christ, being raised from the dead, will never die again; death no longer has dominion over him. The death he died, he died to sin, once for all; but the life he lives, he lives to God. So, you also must consider yourselves dead to sin and alive to God in Christ Jesus."

The Whole Armor of God

Ephesians 6:10-15 "Finally, be strong in the Lord and in the strength of his power. Put on the whole armor of God, so that you may be able to stand against the wiles of the devil. For our struggle is not against enemies of blood and flesh, but against the rulers, against the authorities, against the cosmic powers of this present darkness, against the spiritual forces of evil in the heavenly places. Therefore take up the whole armor of God, so that you may be able to withstand on that evil day, and having done everything, to stand firm. Stand therefore, and fasten the belt of truth around your waist, and put on the breastplate of righteousness. As shoes for your feet put on whatever will make you ready to proclaim the gospel of peace."

The Fruit of the Spirit

Galatians 5:18-23 "But if you are led by the Spirit, you are not subject to the law. Now the works of the flesh are obvious: fornication, impurity, licentiousness, idolatry, sorcery, enmities, strife, jealousy, anger, quarrels, dissensions, factions, envy, drunkenness, carousing, and things like these. I am warning you, as I warned you before: those who do such things will not inherit the kingdom of God. By contrast, the fruit of the Spirit is love, joy, peace, patience, kindness, generosity, faithfulness, gentleness, and self-control. There is no law against such things.

Freedom in Christ!

Romans 13:12-14 "...the night is far gone; the day is near. Let us then lay aside the works of darkness and put on the armor of light; let us live honorably as in the day, not in reveling and drunkenness, not in debauchery and licentiousness, not in quarreling and jealousy. Instead, put on the Lord Jesus Christ, and make no provision for the flesh, to gratify its desires."

Romans 12:1-2 "I appeal to you therefore, brothers and sisters, by the mercies of God, to present your bodies as a living sacrifice, holy and acceptable to God, which is your spiritual worship. Do not be conformed to this world, but be transformed by the renewing of your minds, so that you may discern what is the will of God—what is good and acceptable and perfect."

Ephesians 2:8-9 "For by grace you have been saved through faith, and this is not your own doing; it is the gift of God – not the result of works, so that no one may boast."

1 Corinthians 10:12-13 "So if you think you are standing, watch out that you do not fall. No testing has overtaken you that is not common to everyone. God is faithful, and he will not let you be tested beyond your strength, but with the testing he will also provide the way out so that you may be able to endure it."

Galatians 5:13 "For you were called to freedom, brothers and sisters; only do not use your freedom as an opportunity for self-indulgence, but through love become slaves to one another."

Philippians 4:8 "Finally, beloved, whatever is true, whatever is honorable, whatever is just, whatever is pure, whatever is pleasing, whatever is commendable, if there is any excellence and if there is anything worthy of praise, think about these things."

1 Thessalonians 4:3-5 "For this is the will of God, your sanctification: that you should abstain from sexual immorality; that each of you should know how to possess his own vessel in sanctification and honor, not in passion of lust, like the Gentiles who do not know God."

2 Corinthians 5:9-10 "So whether we are at home or away, we make it our aim to please him. For all of us must appear before the judgment seat of Christ, so that each may receive recompense for what has been done in the body, whether good or evil."

John 14:15 "If you love me, you will keep my commandments."

Matthew 26:41 "Stay awake and pray that you may not come into the time of trial; the spirit indeed is willing, but the flesh is weak."

Matthew 5:8 "Blessed are the pure in heart, for they will see God."

1 Peter 5:8 "Discipline yourselves, keep alert. Like a roaring lion your adversary the devil prowls around, looking for someone to devour."

Quote "A man first collapses in the prayer closet." To go days without prayer is spiritual suicide. The problem is that many of us have a weak and inconsistent prayer life. We allow busyness, friends and worldly entertainments to eat into our time. Never compromise on prayer life. – Leonard Ravenhill

Quote "Sinful pleasure at its very best and in the most promising state is still an inferior pleasure."

Quote "God asks us to rest in Him, and Him alone. And when we do not do that, meaning in our lives is lacking. And when this happens, we try to replace it with feelings and sensations, namely addictions. Pornography is the premier replacement for meaning in our lives. Chasing feelings and sensations is a meaningless proposition resulting in frustration, commonly leading to self-destruction, or even violence. An infinite amount of worldly pleasures giving satisfaction will not equal the peace and happiness of connection and relationship with God. "

Psalms and Proverbs

Psalm 62:1 "For God alone my soul waits in silence;"

Psalm 51:10 "Create in me a clean heart, O God, and put a new and right spirit within me."

Psalm 97:10 "The Lord loves those who hate evil; he guards the lives of his faithful; he rescues them from the hand of the wicked."

Psalm 25:20-21 "O guard my life, and deliver me; do not let me be put to shame, for I take refuge in you. May integrity and uprightness preserve me, for I wait for you."

Psalm 119:9 "How can young people keep their way pure? By guarding it according to your word."

Psalm 51:1-17

1. Have mercy on me, O God, according to your
   steadfast love; according to your abundant mercy
   blot out my transgressions.
2 Wash me thoroughly from my iniquity, and cleanse
   me from my sin.
3 For I know my transgressions, and my sin is ever
   before me.
4 Against you, you alone, have I sinned, and done
   what is evil in your sight, so that you are justified
   in your sentence and blameless when you pass

judgment.

5 Indeed, I was born guilty, a sinner when my mother
conceived me.

6 You desire truth in the inward being; therefore
teach me wisdom in my secret heart.

7 Purge me with hyssop, and I shall be clean; wash
me, and I shall be whiter than snow.

8 Let me hear joy and gladness; let the bones that
you have crushed rejoice.

9 Hide your face from my sins, and blot out all my
iniquities.

10 Create in me a clean heart, O God, and put a
new and right spirit within me.

11 Do not cast me away from your presence, and do
not take your holy spirit from me.

12 Restore to me the joy of your salvation, and
sustain in me a willing spirit.

13 Then I will teach transgressors your ways, and
sinners will return to you.

14 Deliver me from bloodshed, O God, O God of
my salvation, and my tongue will sing aloud of
your deliverance.

15 O Lord, open my lips, and my mouth will
declare your praise.

16 For you have no delight in sacrifice; if I were to
give a burnt offering, you would not be pleased.

17 The sacrifice acceptable to God is a broken
spirit; a broken and contrite heart, O God, you
will not despise.

Psalm 51:1-2 "Have mercy on me, O God, according to your steadfast love; according to your abundant mercy blot out my transgressions. Wash me thoroughly from my iniquity, and cleanse me from my sin."

Proverbs 6:25 "Do not desire her beauty in your heart, and do not let her capture you with her eyelashes."

Proverbs 31:3 "Do not give your strength to women, your ways to those who destroy kings."

Proverbs 7:1-5
"My child, keep my words

and store up my commandments with you;
keep my commandments and live,
   keep my teachings as the apple of your eye;
bind them on your fingers,
   write them on the tablet of your heart.
Say to wisdom, "You are my sister,"
   and call insight your intimate friend,
that they may keep you from the loose woman,
   from the adulteress with her smooth words."

Proverbs 6:32-33 "But he who commits adultery has no sense; he who does it destroys himself. He will get wounds and dishonor, and his disgrace will not be wiped away."

Proverbs 7:21-22 "With much seductive speech she persuades him; with her smooth talk she compels him. Right away he follows her, and goes like an ox to the slaughter, or bounds like a stag toward the trap."

Proverbs 7:25-27 "Do not let your hearts turn aside to her ways; do not stray into her paths. For many are those she has laid low, and numerous are her victims. Her house is the way to Sheol, going down to the chambers of death."

Proverbs 6:25-29

"Do not desire her beauty in your heart,
   and do not let her capture you with her eyelashes;
for a prostitute's fee is only a loaf of bread
   but the wife of another stalks a man's very life.
Can fire be carried in the bosom
   without burning one's clothes?
Or can one walk on hot coals
   without scorching the feet?
So is he who sleeps with his neighbor's wife;
   no one who touches her will go unpunished."

Proverbs 2:10-16

"for wisdom will come into your heart, and knowledge will be pleasant to your soul;
  prudence will watch over you;
    and understanding will guard you.
It will save you from the way of evil,
    from those who speak perversely,
who forsake the paths of uprightness
    to walk in the ways of darkness,
who rejoice in doing evil
    and delight in the perverseness of evil;
those whose paths are crooked,
    and who are devious in their ways.
You will be saved from the loose woman,
    from the adulteress with her smooth words,"

Proverbs 5:1-4

"My child, be attentive to my wisdom;
    incline your ear to my understanding,
so that you may hold on to prudence,
    and your lips may guard knowledge.
For the lips of a loose woman drip honey,
    and her speech is smoother than oil;
but in the end she is bitter as wormwood,
    sharp as a two-edged sword."

Proverbs 3:5-8 "Trust in the Lord with all your heart, and do not rely on your own insight. In all your ways acknowledge him, and he will make straight your paths. Do not be wise in your own eyes; fear the Lord, and turn away from evil. It will be a healing for your flesh and a refreshment for your body."

Proverbs 23:26-28 "My child, give me your heart, and let your eyes observe my ways. For a prostitute is a deep pit; an adulteress is a narrow well, she lies in wait like a robber and increases the number of the faithless."

Proverbs 5:20 "Why should you be intoxicated, my son, by another woman and embrace the bosom of an adulteress?"

Appendix G: Self Discovery Activities

Appendix G contains multiple sections. The work you do in each section will carry forward to later lessons and work that you do.

G: Week 17 Fellowship with God – Beliefs

Week 17
What beliefs do I have about myself that cause me to be selfish?

_____

_____

_____

Subsequent Weeks *(Add to the list each week as you discover more beliefs.)*
What *NEW* beliefs, in addition to those previously discovered, do I have about myself that cause me to be selfish?

_____

_____

_____

_____

_____

_____

_____

_____

G: Week 18 The River Under the River

Name at least 5 behavioral characteristics you have that are a result of, or are fueled by, your untransformed pain.

_____

_____

_____

_____

_____

Humility Triggers

Pray the **_Litany of Humility Prayer_** in Appendix D. Take special note when one of the lines creates some internal discomfort. Write this below in the first column. In the second column, write how it makes you feel. As the weeks and lessons progress, you will address these as triggers of emotions.

<u>Line in Prayer</u>	<u>Feeling it triggers</u>
Example: From the desire of being approved	I need approval from others, so I don't feel rejected.

G: Week 19 Guilt and Shame Inventory

From Lesson 19 - Record below the shame statements that you marked and/or added.

_____   _____

_____   _____

_____   _____

_____   _____

_____   _____

_____   _____

_____   _____

Recognizing the shame that you carry, write a short statement or words that describe how you secretly see yourself.

_____

_____

_____

Describe how you think God sees you.

_____

_____

_____

...continued Week 19

Humility Triggers

Pray the *Litany of Humility Prayer* in Appendix D. Take special note when one of the lines creates some internal discomfort. Write this below in the first column. In the second column, write how it makes you feel. As the weeks and lessons progress, you will address these as triggers of emotions.

<u>Line in Prayer</u>	<u>Feeling it triggers</u>
Example: From the desire of being approved	I need approval from others, so I don't feel rejected.

G: Week 20 Triggers and Warning Signs

From Lesson 20 - Record below some **OBVIOUS TRIGGERS** you experience (you will add to this list as time progresses, and you become more aware of them).

_____   _____

_____   _____

_____   _____

_____   _____

_____   _____

From Lesson 20 - Record below some **SUBTLE TRIGGERS** you experience (you will add to this list as time progresses, and you become more aware of them).

_____   _____

_____   _____

_____   _____

_____   _____

_____   _____

...continued Week 20

Humility Triggers

Pray the ***Litany of Humility Prayer*** in Appendix D. Take special note when one of the lines creates some internal discomfort. Write this below in the first column. In the second column, write how it makes you feel. As the weeks and lessons progress, you will address these as triggers of emotions.

<table>
<thead>
<tr><th>Line in Prayer</th><th>Feeling it triggers</th></tr>
</thead>
<tbody>
<tr><td>**Example:** From the desire of being approved</td><td>I need approval from others, so I don't feel rejected.</td></tr>
<tr><td></td><td></td></tr>
<tr><td></td><td></td></tr>
<tr><td></td><td></td></tr>
<tr><td></td><td></td></tr>
<tr><td></td><td></td></tr>
</tbody>
</table>

From Week 20 Lesson, record below at least **two** events that brought on feelings of loneliness or created a desire for connection or intimacy.

Start now and continue to add, each week, as you discover more.

_____

_____

_____

_____

_____

_____

_____

_____

_____

_____

_____

_____

G: Week 24 Rewiring Neural Pathways and True Intimacy

From Lesson 24, Record below some ideas of **TRUE INTIMACY** choices that you can engage in.

Use the below descriptions from the lesson for ideas in using these and/or creating your own.

Action
- Choose an exit strategy you already have in place to break the current cycle.
- Next, begin the Self, God, and Others actions.

Self
- Name the negative or unpleasant emotions or feelings you are experiencing, or even any temptations.
- Identify any shame feelings that are present.
- Focus on recognizing them and not denying them.
- Ask the Holy Spirit to reveal to you why they are there.
- Meditate on these feelings and separate them from yourself – maybe even imagine them in a trash can in front of you.

God
- Meditate on taking the emotions and giving them to Christ (see Lesson 22 for full example).
- Engage specific prayers you like.
- Choose scripture verses that help you refocus or motivate you.
- Make a decisive statement to deny negative identity thoughts or feelings.
- Create your own surrender imagery (see lesson 22 for full example).
- Go to an adoration chapel and silently pray to and talk with Jesus.
- Choose whatever actions, imagery or even fantasy that brings God or Jesus to you, and potentially brings euphoria.

Others
- Make a list of people you can contact to discuss the event that is triggering your negative experience.
- Accountability partner, friend, priest, counselor, spouse, significant other, etc.

...continued Week 24 True Intimacy exercise

Action (like exit strategies)

_____ _____

_____ _____

_____ _____

Self

_____ _____

_____ _____

_____ _____

God

_____ _____

_____ _____

_____ _____

Others

_____ _____

_____ _____

_____ _____

G: Week 27 Sources of Wounds

"Holy Spirit I ask You to come into my heart. I ask You to reveal to me the sources of my turmoil, my emotional and spiritual pain. I am experiencing feelings of_____ resulting from the event of _____. I ask You to bring forward memories of when in the past these same feelings were present. I ask You, Holy Spirit, to reveal to me the first time these emotions and feelings were present and who was present at that time, as well as the event that triggered these feelings and emotions. I surrender to You any fear and anxiety that arises from these past events and persons, as well as all current anxiety and fears that I am experiencing."

Describe an event that surrounds a wound from your **father**.

_____

_____

_____

Name the emotional wound that needs to be healed.

_____

_____

What false identity image do you hold as a result of this wound?

_____

_____

What behaviors do you exhibit that result from this wound?

_____

_____

Describe an event that surrounds a wound from your **mother**.

_____

_____

_____

Name the emotional wound that needs to be healed.

_____

_____

What false identity image do you hold as a result of this wound?

_____

_____

What behaviors do you exhibit that result from this wound?

_____

_____

Name of another person the Holy Spirit revealed that wounded you: _____

Describe the wound and the event that surrounds this wound.

_____

_____

_____

Name the emotional wound that needs to be healed.

_____

_____

What false identity image do you hold as a result of this wound?

_____

_____

What behaviors do you exhibit that result from this wound?

_____

_____

Repeat this as the Holy Spirit reveals more persons who have triggered wounds in you.

G: Week 29 Forgiveness

Start this exercise on Day 1 of the week. Then also at some point in the week, spend time in front of the Blessed Sacrament and ask the Holy Spirit to reveal persons whom you need to forgive.

Name of a person that you need to forgive: _____

What did this person do to you that needs forgiveness?

_____

_____

_____

What wounds, emotions, or false identities surround this event?

_____

_____

_____

Name of a person who you need to forgive: _____

What did this person do to you that needs forgiveness?

_____

_____

_____

What wounds, emotions or false identities surround this event?

_____

_____

_____

Name of a person who you need to forgive: _____

What did this person do to you that needs forgiveness?

_____

_____

_____

What wounds, emotions, or false identities surround this event?

_____

_____

_____

_____

Name of a person who you need to forgive: _____

What did this person do to you that needs forgiveness?

_____

_____

_____

What wounds, emotions, or false identities surround this event?

_____

_____

_____

Appendix H: Implementation of Change in the Family

As the Father, the Spiritual leader, and Protector of the family, what changes do you need to implement?

Don't be a tyrant and just make changes. Educate your spouse first, get her on board, then together educate and implement with the family. Reveal to them that your mission as a man is to get them to heaven and protect them from the world. Realize though, that you must still live in the world. Protection doesn't necessarily mean to completely cut off oneself from the outside. Education, preceded by prayer, is the best weapon.

Suggestions

Check off each item you like:

Prayer

Yourself

____ Pray at least 15 minutes every day.
____ Attend daily Mass if possible.
____ Do a Holy Hour at least once per week.
____ Educate yourself on the Virtues taught by the Catholic Church.
____ Read scripture every day – even listen to an electronic version of the bible in the car.

Spouse

____ Pray together with our spouse every day – even just 5 minutes.
____ Pray for each other in one another's presence.
____ Pray for a good day.
____ Pray for anxieties at work to be resolved.
____ Read scripture together – even one paragraph a day.
____ Pray the rosary together.
____ Read the daily Church readings together.

Note: Praying the family rosary grants each member a plenary indulgence (all time out of purgatory) when fulfilled with all the normal conditions. (confession within 8 days, Holy Communion received on that same day, prayers offered for the Holy Father – Our Father, Hail Mary, and the Apostles' Creed – and being free of all attachment to sin at the time the indulgence is received.)

Family

____ Prayer together as a family – even just 5 minutes.
____ Pray for each other in one another's presence.
____ Pray for a good day.
____ Pray for anxieties at school to be resolved.
____ Read scripture together – even one paragraph a day.
____ Pray the rosary together.
____ Read the daily church readings together.
____ Attend Mass together.
____ Dinner together.
____ Pray before meals.
____ Put away all electronic devices at meals.

TV/Movies

Choice of content (violence, suggestive or sexually explicit, adult content – even rated R or TV 14 often contains suspect content).

____ Discuss TV rating changes with each child.
____ Discuss going to movies with friends.

Electronic Devices

No one ever needs to have their phone or tablet in bed with them. Have chargers in an area central to the house and at a certain time (8:00 for example) put the devices "to bed." If they use it for an alarm, buy a $10 alarm clock for their room.

Electronic devices are a dangerous item that easily allows entry to impure content. Viewing this in isolation is never a wise choice. It also stimulates thought patterns and fantasy brain patterns while sleeping. Science has also proven that the stimulation of an electronic device immediately before bed impairs sleep.

Implement apps that measure screen time. Choose a limit for devices, maybe different limits for different ages. You can also set most apps to stop internet access after certain times of day, limits of time per day, and limits of time per week.

Put filters on electronic devices. It is not a question of "IF" but "WHEN" they are exposed to porn or sexually suggestive content. This IS NOT a final solution, but a start. Review the Road to Purity website for more complete information on how to handle pornography with your children.

Know what your kids are looking at. They are under 18. They are living in your house. There is no such thing as privacy that forbids you from looking at their history to keep their souls safe. Yes, their souls are at stake, what's it worth to you? If you don't protect them, you will be judged in the end. That may seem harsh but check with God on it if you are unsure. If they are hiding something, this is a red flag. If this is a bigger battle than you are prepared to handle, you can install an internet router that tracks history of device use. This cannot be blocked or bypassed with private settings on devices. Install it, and you don't have to let your kids know you can still see their internet history – otherwise they will bypass and just use a cell signal. They can even use their phone as a hotspot to bypass their laptop from the home internet WiFi.

Whatever you do, don't just turn your back and say to yourself, "Oh, they'll be fine." Re-read the part of the lesson on Fathers that are not present in the family. This also means not engaging with the family.

Social Media

Limit social media time and sites. Social media has been shown to limit quality personal communication and impairs God-created communion with others. Think about the Restoring God's Foundation program. The small group experience is foundational to its success. Consider this: Do you think this program would be as successful if you merely read the book and texted a friend your check-in answers? Social media impairs personal bonding and community.

Educate

Educate yourself and your family on the topic of Theology of the Body. Search for YouTube videos from Christopher West and Jason Evert on this topic.

As a family, watch some of the Jason Evert YouTube videos on dating, sexuality, etc.
Start early. There are multiple age appropriate books on Theology of the Body starting at age 2!
(The Road to Purity website has multiple links with references for materials if you need. Also, email us for suggestions or help if you need).

Have your children (possibly 12 and older) read this Restoring God's Foundation lesson on being a man (daughters can read it too!). This way, they know where you are coming from and why you want to make changes.

Consider these Scripture Verses:

> **1 John 5:19** "We know that we are God's children, and that the whole world lies under the power of the evil one."

> **1 Peter 2:11** "Beloved, I urge you as aliens and exiles to abstain from the desires of the flesh that wage war against the soul."

> **Ephesians 2:19** "So then you are no longer strangers and aliens, but you are citizens with the saints and also members of the household of God."

This clearly shows that, as children of God, this world is not ours. We are strangers in a foreign (non-Godly) land. We must constantly resist the temptations of this world that pull us away from God, from His Holy desires for us, His desire to be close to us, and His desire to have us with Him in His kingdom.

Your Additional Changes

List additional changes that you and your spouse have prayed about and desire to make in your family.

_____

_____

_____

_____

_____

_____

_____

_____

Pushback from Children

It is very likely that you will have pushback from your kids on these changes; especially if they seem to come "out of the blue" for no apparent reason. You may want to consider bringing in the changes slowly, starting with prayer. A common resistance is the phone at the dinner table or at family time. Ask your child, "Is the person you are NOT with, more important than the person you ARE with?"

Made in the USA
Middletown, DE
19 November 2021